Dictionary

OF SPECIAL
EDUCATION AND
REHABILITATION

Third Edition

Glenn A. Vergason, *Georgia State University*

LOVE PUBLISHING COMPANY®
Denver, Colorado 80222

Preface to Third Edition

This reference work is offered in response to a need I have observed during years of work in special education and rehabilitation. That need is still there, as testified to by the many people who are continuing to use this resource. One of the first problems encountered by new recruits in college is the vocabulary specific to the field. Anyone, in fact, who is not experienced in or directly involved in special education and rehabilitation is likely to be confused by the terminology and jargon. Through this resource, I hope to give more meaning to the language of special education and rehabilitation.

I have sought to provide an understandable explanation of the terminology most commonly used by educators and by rehabilitation workers. This work is not categorical but tries to cover the specialties with equal attention to all. The terms were selected after perusing the pages and indexes of close to 100 currently used texts and professional books, and some are from the 1971 publication entitled *A Dictionary of Exceptional Children.*

An attempt was made to compose the definitions in the clearest, most practical manner possible; and key terms defined within the *Dictionary* are cross-referenced by use of italics. Pronunciations, where needed, are included in a phonetic style. The word-by-word method is used for alphabetization. In this style, acoustic neuroma precedes acoustically handicapped, for example.

I am indebted to Stan Love for his belief in and support of this project. The current edition represents the fourth form in which this dictionary has appeared since its publication as the first *Dictionary of Exceptional Children* by Dr. Leo Kelly in 1971. Subsequent editions were authored by Dr. Kelly and Dr. Vergason. I am indebted to Dr. Kelly for the inspiration and groundwork he laid for such a dictionary. Dr. Kelly had the vision to know that people new to the fields of special education and rehabilitation needed such a resource.

The present edition represents a major expansion, improvement, and updating. The listings of resources at the back the book have undergone extensive revisions. Associations and journals that have changed names or ceased to exist are noted. New associations and journals have been added. The current list represents the best that can be obtained at a point in time. Every effort was made to verify accuracy. Canadian entries are included. Alphabetizing is done by major words within the name. Thus, "or" and "of" are ignored in alphabetization.

I ask the more experienced professionals in the field to recognize the value of this work not so much for themselves as for those they are helping to learn about it, and those with whom they are interacting to further the knowledge of special education and rehabilitation—students, parents, paraprofessionals, aides, laypersons, general educators, and other professionals. It is for them that this source was primarily compiled.

Previous editions contained acknowledgments to numerous individuals. By the time of this edition, the teachers, colleagues, typists, and graduate assistants have become too numerous to list all of them. My thanks to all of you who have assisted in any way.

a– A prefix meaning without, or absent, as in *agenesis* (absence of organ or tissue).

ABA design The most common form of behavior treatment design, in which *baseline* data are collected, then the treatment is conducted, followed by a return to no treatment and derivation of a second baseline.

ABAB design A behavioral treatment design in which *baseline* data are collected, then the *intervention* is introduced, followed by a reinstatement of baseline, then a reinstatement of the intervention followed by a return to baseline. Sometimes referred to as repeated baseline procedures.

abacus (ab′-uh-kus) A device used in counting and performing calculations by sliding counters along rods or in grooves; often useful as an aid in teaching basic arithmetic, especially to students with *mental retardation* and *visual impairment.*

abbreviated speech The use of incomplete *language* units; may be the result of shyness, failure to develop sufficient command of language, underlying speech problems, or a style of communication that the speaker's environment has forced him/her to adopt. (see also *holophrastic speech*)

abduction (ab-duck′-shun) Movement of a limb outward and away from the center of the body, as in raising an arm laterally. May also refer to abduction of the vocal folds during *phonation* for speech. Opposite of *adduction.*

aberration Deviation from normal, either physical or mental. "Abnormality" or "deviation" could be used synonymously.

ability grouping The gathering of pupils into separate sections according to their basic competence or achievement in a specific area of study; often determined on the basis of academic achievement or results of *standardized tests.*

ability profile A graphic representation of *grade level* or age level equivalents for an individual child, showing strengths and weaknesses on various ability dimensions.

abiotrophy (ab-ee-ot′-roe-fee) *Degeneration* or failure of tissues, resulting in a loss of vitality and resistance to infection.

ablation Removal of a body part by surgery.

ablutomania (ab-loo-toe-may′-nee-ah) A psychologically abnormal *compulsion* to clean or wash one's body.

1

abrachia (ah-brak′-ee-ah) A *congenital* absence of the arms.

absence seizures See *petit mal.*

absolute threshold See *threshold.*

absolutely profoundly handicapped A term coming into use in the late 1980s to describe persons who are so *severely retarded* or *multiply handicapped* that no program or training methodology is likely to produce change. (see also *relatively profoundly handicapped*)

abstract concept 1. An idea or an image of a situation, symbol, or object that can be selected from any specific attributes in our environment; e.g., shape (squareness) is an abstraction (abstract concept) from a physical object, which has many aspects in addition to shape. 2. Sometimes used to refer to complex ideas, generally of symbolic origin, that tend to be difficult to understand.

abstract intelligence An *intellectual* capacity to comprehend from symbolic, intangible situations and *language.*

abstract reasoning The ability to understand relationships and to deal with ideas, images, and symbols that are more intangible than objects. The inability to reason abstractly generally is associated with *mental retardation* or *neurological impairment.*

abulia (ah-byew′-lee-ah) Loss of willpower and ability to make a decision. An individual affected by this condition has little initiative.

academic achievement The level of performance in one or more of the basic school subjects; generally measured by *standardized* (achievement) *tests* or in the classroom by teachers on less formal instruments. An *achievement level* of 2.2 in math would indicate that in most math skills the person is like beginning second graders.

academic aptitude The combination of abilities and potential necessary to achieve in schoolwork. Also called "scholastic aptitude" and "academic potential."

academic inventory A series of test items, arranged in order of difficulty, which is administered to a pupil to determine level of academic functioning. Results of the inventory become a basis for planning future learning activities.

academic learning time (ALT) The amount of time in which students are engaged in academic activities in which they have high success rates. ALT has the added advantage over *engaged time* and *allocated time* of specifying a high success rate.

acalculia (ay-kal-kyew′-lee-ah) A condition in which an individual has severe problems with, or total inability to do, simple arithmetic calculations. (see also *dyscalculia*)

acampsia (ah-kamp′-see-ah) The inflexibility or *rigidity* of a limb or joint; limits *mobility.*

acataphasia (ah-kat-ah-fay′-zee-ah) The inability to phrase words into connected, meaningful sentences.

acceleration 1. The process by which a student with academic ability *(gifted)* completes the work of school grades at a rate of more than one grade each year, thus reducing the time to complete a course of study. Practices such as early admission, grade-skipping, *advanced placement, telescoping* of grade levels in upgraded situations, and credit by examination are some of the approaches used in acceleration. 2. In *behavior modification,* acceleration refers to an increase in the rate of occurrence of behavior.

accent The syllable(s) in a word that receive(s) more force than the other syllables when spoken. If a child does not learn the correct accent in a word, the resulting *vocalization* may be distorted.

access-time The time span required to move to and from a point. This may be an important aspect in planning building evacuation procedures with disabled individuals.

accessible A term often used to denote building facilities that are *barrier-free,* which enhances use by persons with *physical handicaps.*

accommodation (v., **accommodate**)   1. Adjustment of the eye by changing the shape of the *lens* to allow a person to see clearly at different *focal lengths.* 2. Adjusting teaching methods and modes of responding to student's handicap.

acculturation (ah-kult-sure-ray'-shun)   The process whereby one group absorbs certain features of the culture of a second group.

acedia (ah-see'-dee-ah)   A mental disorder in which the individual is *depressed, apathetic,* and generally in a state of *melancholy.*

acetone (ass'-eh-tone)   A liquid *ketone* found in abnormally large quantities in the urine of a person with *diabetes.*

achievement level   The degree of success a student has in an academic subject area as determined by *formal* or *informal testing* methods. Thus, a child with an achievement level of 3.2 in math would be achieving like beginning third grade students.

achievement test   An instrument designed to measure a person's knowledge, skills, and understanding in a subject matter area. Typically, an achievement test may consist of measures of more than one type; e.g., reading, math, spelling.

achilles (ah-kill'-eez) **tendon**   The strong, fibrous tissue that joins the muscle in the calf of the leg to the heel bone; often affected by physical conditions involving the feet, such as *clubfoot* and *cerebral palsy.*

achondrogenesis (ah-kahn-droe-jen'-eh-sis)   A *hereditary* form of *dwarfism* characterized by markedly shortened limbs, with normal head and trunk size.

achondroplasia (ah-kahn-droe-play'-zee-ah)   A rare defect in the formation of *cartilage* and the skeleton that results in *dwarfism.* In this form of dwarfism, the limbs are short, with normal trunk and a small face.

achromatopsia (ah-crow-mat-op'-see-ah)   A *congenital* eye condition resulting from absence or abnormality of the *retinal* cones used for color differentiation. Vision is generally improved in reduced illumination. In the more severe disorder, color vision is completely lacking.

acid (vernacular)   A term widely used for the *hallucinogen* LSD-25.

acoria (ah-core'-ee-ah)   A condition in which a person cannot satisfy his/her hunger and as a result feels he/she has never had enough to eat.

acoustic (uh-koo'-stik)   Related to the sense of hearing or to the science of sound.

3

acoustic method 1. A way of teaching persons who are *deaf* to speak properly and to understand speech through stimulation and training of the *auditory* and *tactile* sense organs with sound vibrations produced by the voice or by sonorous instruments; utilizing *residual hearing* to the fullest possible extent. 2. An approach to teaching a new sound or altering the improper production of an old one during speech training or *speech correction* lessons; this method was developed by Max Goldstein.

acoustic neuroma A tumor of the eighth cranial *(auditory)* nerve.

acoustically handicapped Describes hearing impairment to an extent that the person requires special services. (see also *hearing loss*)

acquisition The initial learning of information or skills.

acrocephaly See *oxycephaly.*

acromegaly (ak-roe-meg'-ah-lee) A condition wherein a *mature* person develops enlarged nose, jaw, fingers, toes, or other skeletal *extremities.* This enlargement is caused by the hypersecretion of *pituitary gland* growth *hormones.*

acronym (ak'-roe-nim) A word or nickname formed by the initial letters of the principal components of a compound name or term (e.g., CEC for Council for Exceptional Children).

acroparesthesia (ak-roe-pare-es-thee'-zee-ah) A condition characterized by a tingling, numbness, or stiffness in the fingers, hands, forearms, or other body *extremities.*

acting-out behavior Inappropriate actions that involve more than usual activity; may be destructive or *aggressive* in nature.

active assisted motion A technique in which physical therapy assists an individual in carrying out *physical therapy* in which the *therapist* helps a child in carrying out prescribed motions in an attempt to strengthen muscles that are too weak to carry out the motion unaided.

active listening A technique in counseling whereby the counselor is able to convey to the client, through appearance, reflective statements, and gestures, an understanding of and interest in what the client is saying. This is an important technique in teaching *exceptional children.*

activity program services A group of professionally recognized *disciplines* (art, dance, music, *occupational therapy, therapeutic recreation*) that have time-proven their roles in *special education* and *rehabilitation* treatment programs.

activity time-out The removal of a disruptive student from a specified activity for a specified period of time. (see also *time-out*)

actometer (ack-tah'-meh-turr) A self-winding calendar wristwatch that has been modified so that movement of the *extremity* to which it is attached produces a quantitative reading by changes in hours, seconds, or days; used to determine how active individuals are.

acuity (ah-kyew'-ih-tee) Ability to note the occurrence of a *sensory stimulus.* Commonly used to refer to how well a person can see, hear, or feel, as in *visual acuity.*

acute   Manifesting rapid development of *symptoms* in an illness.

acute otitis media   A severe but usually brief case of *otitis media* (*inflammation* of the middle ear), usually accompanied by pain.

adapted physical education   See *adaptive physical education.*

adaptive behavior   The effectiveness and degree to which an individual meets standards of self-sufficiency and social responsibility for his/her age-related cultural group. Included in all definitions of *mental retardation,* it involves noncognitive skills, or "street sense" or ability to cope with the environment. Usually measured on *adaptive behavior scales.*

adaptive behavior scales   Measures developed to *assess* an individual's functioning in non-academic, nonintellectual skill areas such as social living and *maturation.*

adaptive physical education   A specially designed program of physical activities that meets the limitations of a person with some disability.

addict(ion)   One who becomes habituated to the use of or has a *compulsive* need for something, such as alcohol or drugs. The condition is termed an addiction.

additions   1. An *articulatory* disorder in which the individual adds sounds to words, as in "buhrown" for brown. 2. A reading error in which sounds are added to words as they are read.

adduction   The movement of a limb inward toward the center of the body, as in lowering an arm from a lateral position. Opposite of *abduction.*

adenoid   A mass of *lymph*-like tissue located between the mouth and the *esophagus* which, when infected, may become enlarged and obstruct breathing.

adenomia subaceum (add-eh-no´-mee-uh suh-bay´-shum)   A butterfly-shaped collection of fibrous tumors on the face around the nose; found in certain forms of *mental retardation* (e.g., *tuberous sclerosis*).

ADHD   see *attention deficit disorder.*

adiadochokinesis (ah-dee-ah-doe-koe-kin-ee´-sis)   A *"soft"* sign of *minimal brain dysfunction* in which the child being tested has difficulty executing rapid alternating movements such as synchronizing quick turns of the hands over and over. Children with minimal brain dysfunction display uncoordinated movements.

adipose (add´-ih-poce)   Pertaining to fat or the state of being fat. Adipose tissue stores fat.

adjunctive services   Special programs that support the child in regular education.

ADL (Activities of Daily Living)   A term referring to practical skills needed to function in society—e.g., dressing, eating, using money. Also termed *independent living skills.*

Adlerian disciplinary approach   One of several conceptional approaches, based on the work of Adler and proponents such as Dreikers and Dinkmeyer, emphasizing commonsense responses using logical behavior consequences to deal with the four most common behaviors of attention seeking, power struggling, revenge seeking, and assumed disability.

administrative remedies   An internal set of procedures in an agency or school system that does not involve judicial action. The system provides a non-legal series of appeals that a parent can pursue regarding a child's placement, diagnosis, etc.

adrenalin (ah-dren'-ah-lin)   1. Secretion of the **adrenal** glands of the body. 2. Trademark for a crystalline compound prepared as an extract from the adrenal glands; used as a heart *stimulant* and for arresting *hemorrhages.*

adult education   An important societal movement aimed at teaching knowledge and skills required to meet needs throughout life; offers opportunities for training and retraining persons with *disabilities* after they have left public school.

adult training center   A facility for adults with *disabilities* that offers work experiences and recreation under community supervision.

advanced placement (AP)   Refers to *acceleration* of courses offered to *gifted* students, which yields grades toward graduation and also college credit if exam grades exceed a certain *criterion* level.

adventitious (add-ven-tish'-us)   Acquired after birth through accident or illness. (compare with *congenital*)

adventitious deafness   A condition in which a person born with normal hearing sensitivity loses hearing as a result of accident or disease. The loss may be in varying degrees and may be classified according to the nature of the disorder, such as *perception* deafness, *toxic* deafness, or *conductive hearing loss.*

adverse reaction   An unwanted reaction or side effect caused by medication.

advisory committee   A group of knowledgeable individuals including parents and consumers, chosen from outside the staff of the program involved, who counsel in the development of services offered by the program. The use of advisory committees has grown in recent years, as a result of the nature and extent of legislation and program guidelines.

advocacy (add'-voe-kah-see)   Full support for and representation of interests of another individual or group as if these were self-interests, in a manner free from conflict of interest. A person or group involved in this activity is called an **advocate.**

adynamia (ah-die-nah'-mee-ah)   The absence of normal vitality and strength; some forms of this condition culminate in *paralysis.*

afebrile (ah-feb'-ril) **convulsion**   Involuntary muscle contractions that occur without fever, usually in young children.

affective   Pertaining to emotions, feelings, or attitudes of an organism. Affective education refers to school objectives that deal with *motivation* and development of self-image.

afferent (af'-er-ent) **nerves**   The nerves of the body that convey impulses inward from the *sensory* endings toward the nerve centers or the *central nervous system.*

affirmative action   Denotes a plan for greater involvement of minorities in employment, enrollment, etc., which may in some instances amount to quotas even though this intent may not be clear. Under *Section 504* of the *Rehabilitation Act of 1973,* the term "voluntary action" has been used; this is sometimes viewed as a weaker term.

6

Affirmative Industries   A nonprofit business that employs those with and without *disabilities.* The nondisabled workers set the production standards, *modeling* for the disabled workers. Affirmative Industries differs from *sheltered workshops* and training centers by the former's emphasis on private enterprise.

aftercare   Provision of medical, educational, or treatment services following an individual's release from a hospital or *institution.*

age equivalent   A *raw score* or *standard score* expressed in years and months, corresponding with the average score for that age group. For example, a score of 52 on a *standardized test* might be the score achieved by average seventh grade students, and expressed as 7.2. (see also *grade equivalent*)

age norms   Numerical values indicative of the average performance on a given instrument or in an activity for individuals of stated age groups.

age of onset   The age at which an individual's *disability* or disease occurs or becomes apparent; e.g., the age at which an individual became *blind.*

agenesis (ah-jen'-eh-sis)   Absence of organ or tissue.

ageusia (ahg-yew'-zee-ah)   Absence or *impairment* of the sense of taste.

aggression (adj., **aggressive**)   *Hostile* and attacking behaviors often displayed by individuals with *behavior disorders*; may be destructive or injurious.

agitation   Restlessness as a result of *anxiety* and tension.

agitographia (aj-ih-toe-graf'-ee-ah)   Poor writing ability that may show the qualities of rapid writing movements, distortion of words, or omission of letters or entire words.

agitolalia (aj-ih-toe-lay'-lee-ah)   Speech produced with such great rapidity that it is incoherent or nearly incoherent. Sometimes called **agitophasia** or *cluttering.*

agnosia (ag-noe'-zee-ah)   The inability to recognize familiar objects through *sensory stimuli,* especially with a particular sense organ. Examples are *auditory* agnosia, color agnosia, *tactile* agnosia.

agoraphobia (ag-oh-rah-foe'-bee-ah)   A fear of becoming panic-stricken in public places. Persons who are severely afflicted may fear leaving their homes.

agrammatism (ah-gram'-uh-tizm)   A secondary condition evoked by *hearing loss,* in which the child is impaired in the ability to sequence words, omits prefixes and suffixes, and has difficulty mastering quality speech.

agraphia (ah-graf'-ee-ah)   A form of *aphasia* characterized by the loss of ability or the inability of a person to write, because of a *lesion* in the *central nervous system.* Individuals with agraphia do not seem to be able to relate the mental images of words to the *motor* movements in order to write them.

aide   A person who assists another as in a classroom aide to a teacher; may be paid or unpaid. (see also *teacher aide*)

AIDS   The acronym for the disease complex called acquired immune deficiency, which affects the body's disease-fighting capacity so that the person is susceptible to a number of diseases that the body otherwise is able to fight off.

7

AIDS dementia   A mental condition associated with AIDS in which rational thought and purpose remain but the individual uses fear of contagion to intimidate other individuals.

air conduction   In normal hearing and measurement of hearing, sound waves (vibrations in air) entering the external canal of the ear, strike the *ear drum* and cause it to vibrate, which starts the chain reaction resulting in hearing.

akathisia (ack-ah-thee'-zee-ah)   *Motor* restlessness that may be manifested in inability to sit, lie quietly, or sleep. Often seen in *toxic* reactions to drugs for treatment of *psychotic* conditions.

akinesia (ay-kih-nee'-zee-ah)**(akinesis)**   Loss of movement in a body part without permanent physical or neurological *impairment,* as in the temporary *paralysis* of a muscle when injected with certain drugs.

akinetic (ay-kih-net'-ik) **seizure**   An *epileptic* activity characterized by temporary loss of consciousness and falling in a passive manner.

alalia (ah-lay'-lee ah)   Loss or absence of the ability to talk.

alaryngeal (ay-lare-en'-jee-ahl) **speech**   Speech produced without the use of one's *larynx.*

albinism (al'-bih-niz-um) **(albino)**   An inherited condition that results in a deficiency of pigment in the skin, hair, and *iris* of the eye. The condition causes the eyes to appear pinkish and in most cases is accompanied by defective vision and *photophobia* (sensitivity to light).

alcohol embryopathy   See *fetal alcohol syndrome.*

alexia (ah-lek'-see-ah)   A *cerebral* disorder that results in the inability to associate meaning with printed or written words. (see also *dyslexia*)

alkalosis (al-kah-loe'-siss)   A condition of blood or tissue characterized by above average alkalinity.

allergen   Any substance that causes an **allergic** reaction when it comes in contact with the body. An **allergy** is an exaggerated reaction to a substance that does not cause a similar reaction in the average person.

allesthesia (al-ess-thee'-zee-ah)   A condition in which one senses being touched at a point other than that where he/she is actually touched.

allocated time   A term used in effective instruction to describe the time period scheduled for an activity but doesn't necessarily imply the time the child is on task or paying attention.

alpha-fetoprotein (alpha-fetal protein) screening A test used for identifying *neutral tube defects* in children while the *fetus* is still in the womb. When combined with *ultrasonography,* this test offers 90% correct *diagnosis* of these defects.

alternative living   Community-based living arrangement as a substitute for *institutionalization.* Individuals with various mental and physical *disabilities* live in apartments or *group homes* under some level of supervision.

Alzheimer's (all'-sie-murz) **disease** A *degenerative* condition affecting older individuals (usually over age 60); involves *neural* transmitters and results in memory loss, *depression*, and in the latter stages, violent personality outbursts. Much of the present treatment consists of reducing *stress* for the person and family members.

amaurosis (am-aw-roe'-sis) *Blindness* occurring as a result of disease of the *optic nerve*, spine, or brain without changing the structure of the eye.

amaurotic (am-uh-rot'-ik) **family (familial) idiocy (AFI)** A *hereditary* disease producing *retardation*, marked changes in the *macula* of the *retina*, increasing failure of vision, *seizures*, and death. AFI is a *degenerative* disease resulting from faulty *lipid* (fat) *metabolism*. The early *infantile* variety is also known as *Tay Sachs disease*.

ambidextrous (am-bih-dek'-strus) The ability to use both hands with equal ease and skill.

ambivalence A simultaneous conflict of attitude (e.g., love-hate) toward a person, object, activity, idea, etc; may create frustration that interferes with activity.

amblyopia (am-blee-oh'-pea-ah) A *visual* condition in which the two eyes do not see on the same plane, thus causing one eye to *mask* the other eye to prevent double vision.

ambulatory Commonly used to refer to an individual who is able to walk or move about independently; not bedridden.

amelia (ah-mee'-lee-ah) A condition in which an individual has no limbs.

ameliorate (ah-mee'-lee-oh-rate) To improve, as in the condition of a sick person or for a specific skill.

amenorhea (ah-men-oh-ree'-ah) The absence of a female's menstrual cycle.

amentia (ah-men'-chuh) Nondevelopment of the mind, as contrasted with *dementia*, the loss or *deterioration* of the mind; used with reference to *severe* or *profound mental retardation*.

American Sign Language (ASL) A system of communication among *deaf* persons, employing the arms, hands, and parts of the body to represent thought units. The structure of this language tends to be *concept*-based rather than word-based. Also called *Ameslan*.

Ameslan Same as *American Sign Language*.

ametropia (am-eh-troe'-pea-ah) A condition of the eye in which images are not properly focused on the *retina*, which may produce *myopia, astigmatism*, or *hypermetropia*.

amimia (ah-mih'-mee-ah) Inability to express oneself through use of gestures or signs.

aminia (ah-mih'-nee-ah) A behavioral characteristic in which an individual does not show expression or change in facial expression, appearing indifferent.

amino acids A group of complex *organic* nitrogen compounds that combine in a variety of ways to form proteins. Abnormalities of the amino acid *metabolism* can cause a number of *anomalies*, such as *phenylketonuria* and *albinism*.

amnesia (am-nee'-zee-ah) Loss of the ability to remember or identify past experiences. Amnesia may be either *organic* or *functional*, with fatigue, shock, fever, injury to the brain, or extreme *depression* being the causal factors.

amniocentesis (am-nee-oh-sen-tee´-sis)   A procedure for analyzing factors in the *amniotic fluid* of the *uterus* to determine certain aspects of *fetus* development. Tests of amniotic fluid can aid in identifying *Down syndrome, spina bifida,* and other *congenital* defects.

amniotic fluid   The liquid in which the developing *fetus* is immersed during pregnancy. Chemical components of this fluid can be analyzed in a procedure called *amniocentesis* to determine if the developing fetus has certain handicapping disorders.

amorphous (ah-more´-fuss)   Having no definite form (in pharmacy, not crystallized).

amphetamine (am-fet´-uh-meen)   A drug with *stimulant* properties, used legally in diet pills but also may be used for other reasons as a body stimulant. In slang, called "uppers" or "speed."

amplification device   See *hearing aid.*

amputee   One who has had a limb surgically removed from the body. The process is called **amputation.** The term *congenital amputee* is used when a limb is missing or mostly missing at birth as a result of developmental problems.

amusia (ah-mew´-zee-ah)   The inability to recognize or produce musical tones. (see also *tone deafness*)

amyotonia congenita (ah-my-oh-toe´-nee-uh kon-jen´ -ih-tuh)   Muscular weakness as is usually experienced in neuromuscular diseases such as *muscular dystrophy.*

anaclitic (an-ah-klit´-ik)   Describes a *dependence* on someone or something, as in a newborn baby's developing relationship with the mother. In anaclitic *depression,* a young child's physical, social, or *intellectual* development is slowed by a sudden separation from the mother figure. This may become more serious as the period of separation lengthens.

anakusis (anacusis) (an-ah-kyew´-sis)   A complete loss of hearing resulting in total *deafness.*

analgesic (an-uhl-jee´-zik)   Any drug used to relieve pain without loss of consciousness.

analytic touch   A concept pertaining to *blind* people; experiencing *tactile* impressions of something, such as a building, that must be integrated to get a total concept. Because they do not see the entire object but experience only parts of it, the perception that is pieced together is based on analytic touch. (see also *synthetic touch*)

anaphia (an-ah´-fee-ah)   The absence of or loss of the sense of touch.

anaplasty (an´-ah-plas-tee)   Restorative (plastic) surgery. **Anaplastic** (an-ah-plas´-tik) describes the restoration of a lost or absent part of the body. A specialist who constructs artificial portions of the body to replace areas that have been destroyed, removed, or were absent is called an **anaplastologist.**

anarthria (an-ar´-three-ah)   A severe defect in the *central nervous system* that causes inability to articulate words, resulting in speechlessness.

ancillary   Refers to supplementary support or assistance, as in "ancillary personnel" or "ancillary services." *Speech therapy* and *physical therapy* are two examples.

anecdotal (an'-ek-dote-ul) **method**   A means of recording and analyzing child behavior by observing and reporting, in narrative form, separate occurrences of the child's activities.

anechoic (an-ek-oh'-ik) **chamber**   A specially built room designed with soft surfaces to provide maximum sound absorption, which helps keep sound reverberation (echoes) to a minimum. Optimum measurement of *hearing acuity* can be obtained in such facilities, which usually are found in research settings, and also may be referred to as "dead rooms."

anemia (ah-nee'-mee-ah)   A condition of the blood in which the red corpuscles are reduced in number or a deficiency in *hemoglobin* exists. Anemia may result in skin pallor, loss of vitality, shortness of breath, and palpitation of the heart.

anencephalus (an-en-cef'-ah-lus)   A condition in which the brain of a *fetus* fails to develop and may be almost totally absent. At birth, *severe mental retardation* is present, and life expectancy is limited.

anenesis (ah-nen'-eh-siss)   Failure of a body to develop.

anesthesiologist (an-es-thee-zee-ahl'-oh-gist)   A physician who is certified by the American Board of Anesthesiology or who has the equivalent education and experience; administers the *anesthetic* during surgery.

anesthetic (an-es-thet'-ik)   A drug used to cause the loss of sensation or consciousness; usually administered in conjunction with surgery.

anesthetist (an-es'-thu-tist)   A *generic* term used to identify *anesthesiologists,* other physicians or dentists in that role, or qualified nurses who administer *anesthetics.*

aneurysm (an'-you-rizm)   An abnormal bulge or sac in the wall of an artery, vein, or heart.

angiocardiography (an-jee-oh-kar-dee-ah'-gruh-fee)   Radiographic use of X-ray technology for examination of the heart and its vessels.

aniridia (an-ih-rid'-ee-ah)   A *visual* condition resulting from failure of the *iris* to develop fully; produces hypersensitivity to light.

aniseikonia (an-ih-sih-koe'-nee-ah)   A *visual* disorder in which images produced by the two eyes are of unequal size. If the discrepancy in size is large, *fusion* of the image into *binocular vision* is not accomplished and two images may be seen or one eye "masks" the image of the other.

anisopetropia (an-ih-so-meh-troe'-pea-ah)   A *visual impairment* of inequality in refractive power of the two eyes to a considerable degree.

ankylosis (ang-kill-oh'-sis)   Stiffening or fixation of a joint, often caused by fibrous or bony tissues growing into joint spaces.

annual goals   One of the stipulations of *PL 94-142;* written statements of what a child is targeted to accomplish within a year's time.

annual review   Just as the *PL 94-142* requirement of written *annual goals*, a requirement of at least once-a-year *evaluation* of how the instructional program has worked for the child.

anomaly (ah-nom′-ah-lee) Deviation from the standard, or an irregularity in development. The term is often used to refer to handicapping conditions without naming specific conditions.

anomia (ah-no′-mee-ah) A condition of not recalling or remembering words or the names of objects well.

anopia (an-oh′-pea-ah) Absence or imperfect development of the eye, resulting in *visual impairment.*

anorectic (an-oh-rek′-tik) Describes a substance that reduces the appetite.

anorexia (an-oh-rek′-see-uh) Partial or complete loss or lack of appetite; self-imposed deprivation of food.

anorexia nervosa (an-oh-rek′-see-ah ner-voe′-sah) A serious condition in which an individual refuses to eat, which results in a loss of weight, vitality, and, if untreated, death. This occurs most often in teenage girls who have emotional problems related to their physical image. A similar condition is *bulimia.*

Anorexia Nervosa (307.10) One of the classifications of the *DSM* III System; refers to those who have intense fears of becoming obese.

anosmics (an-oz′-mix) Lack of the sense of smell, thus negating the use of *olfactory stimuli* to aid in learning and reacting to danger. The condition, although rare, is observed most often in individuals who have *albinism.*

ANOVA The parametric statistical treatment known as analysis of variance.

anoxemia (an-ok-see′-mee-ah) A condition in which the oxygen content of the blood is lowered to a level below that needed to sustain the life of cells.

anoxia (ah-nock′-see-ah) An inadequate supply of oxygen in the body system which, if severe, may result in *brain injury* or other *organic* damage.

antagonistic Struggling against, as in a muscle acting in opposition to another muscle. In *spastic cerebral palsy* antagonistic muscles that should be relaxed remain contracted.

antecedent (an-teh-see′-dent) A condition or event that precedes a response and is observed to be associated with its occurrence.

anterior Toward the front or face side, as the anterior of the body. Opposite of *posterior.*

anti– A prefix meaning against or opposed to, as in *anticonvulsant* (an agent that works against convulsions).

antibody A substance in the blood system that serves to combat germs or nullify the disease-causing effects of germs.

anticonvulsant A group of medications administered to help control *seizures.* With these medications, about 50% of *epileptic* individuals achieve complete control and about another 30%, partial control.

antidepressant Any drug taken for the purpose of relieving *depression* or elevating the mood of an individual.

antidote   Any drug or substance used to combat or remedy the harmful effects of poisons.

antigen   An agent which, when introduced into the body, promotes the formation of *antibodies.*

antimetropia (an-tie-meh-troe'-pea-ah)   A *visual* condition in which one eye is *nearsighted* and the other is *farsighted;* suppression of vision in one eye frequently occurs.

antipyresis (an-tie-pie-ree'-sis)   The administration of remedies to combat fever.

anxiety   Emotional tension or confusion coupled with a feeling of generalized threat based upon unknown conditions or sources. (If the source were known, the condition would be called fear.) Children who are helped to understand or deal with their anxiety may show remarkable improvement in school adjustment or achievement.

apathy (ap'-ah-thee) (adj. **apathetic**)   Indifference or a lack of feeling and emotion.

Apert's syndrome   An inherited disorder manifested by a high, narrow *cranial* cavity and often early closure of the skull sutures; associated *mental retardation* may be reduced through early surgical *intervention.*

Apgar test   The most used *screening* instrument for determining a newborn child's health status. Babies are rated on a 0-2 scale for five vital signs: *a*ppearance or coloring, *p*ulse, *g*rimace, *a*ctivity, and *r*espiration. (The first letter in each word combines to make the *acronym* APGAR).

aphakia (ah-fay'-kee-ah)   Absence of the *lens* of the eye.

aphasia (ah-fay'-zee-ah) (adj., **aphasic**)   A disorder caused by disease or injury to brain centers resulting in the loss or *impairment* of ability to produce or to comprehend *language.* It may affect either written or spoken language. (see also *sensory aphasia*)

aphonia (ah-foe'-nee-ah)   A loss of voice or absence of voice resulting from *paralysis* of the vocal cords; may have either *organic* or psychological causes.

aplasia (ah-play'-zee-ah)   Lack of development, as in a body organ.

apoplexy (ap'-uh-pleck-see)   A sudden loss of consciousness, sensation, and/or voluntary motion, caused by rupture or obstruction of a *cerebral* artery, as in a *stroke.*

apperception (ap-er-sep'-shun)   The process of assimilating new events and their relation to previously acquired knowledge, and of evaluating these current experiences in the light of past experiences.

applied behavioral analysis   See *behavioral analysis.*

appropriate education   See *free appropriate public education.*

apraxia (ah-prak'-see-ah)   Inability to carry out purposeful speech in the absence of *paralysis* or other *motor impairment.* May result in the loss of ability to perform elementary units in the expression of *language.* Results in an *expressive language* disorder associated with interneurosensory processing that seems to be related to memory of the *motor act of speech.* (see also *learning disability*)

13

aptitude test   A device or measure administered for the purpose of indicating an individual's potential ability to perform a certain type of activity or readiness to learn in a specific area, such as a musical aptitude test or a mechanical aptitude test.

aqueous (ah'-kwee-us) **humor**   The fluid that fills the front chamber of the eye in front of the crystalline *lens*.

ARC (AIDS related complex.)   A precursor stage to AIDS, which may or may not develop into AIDS itself.

architectural barrier   Any part of the physical, manmade environment or arrangement of structures within an environment or building that can inhibit or prevent *persons with disabilities* from using facilities or moving about. When such barriers are removed, the resulting environment may be described as *barrier-free*. The Architectural Barriers Act of 1968, as amended, required that all public buildings receiving federal financing must be barrier-free and *accessible* to those with *physical handicaps*.

arithmetic (air-ith-met'-ik) **processes**   A term referring to the basic computations of addition, subtraction, multiplication, and division.

arithmetic reasoning   The use of basic mathematical processes in problem-solving situations of the everyday environment.

arrested development   Incomplete growth of an individual or a part of an individual that takes place some time in the life cycle prior to total *maturation*.

arrhythmia (arhythmia) (ah-rith'-mee-ah)   Any change from the normal rhythm of the heart beat.

art therapy   Designates widely varying practices in education, *rehabilitation,* and *psychotherapy* in which the materials and activities of visual arts are used for *therapeutic* purposes, particularly with children who have an *emotional disturbance*. It allows *nonverbal* self-expression through manipulation of art media.

arteriosclerosis (ar-teer-ee-oh-skler-oh'-sis)   Hardening or thickening of the walls of the arteries.

arthritis   A disease condition of skeletal joints that causes *inflammation* and *motor impairment*. Arthritis has several forms, usually associated with severe pain and medication needs.

arthrodosis (ar-throw-doe'-sis)   The surgical fixation or *immobilization* of a joint by removing *cartilaginous* substances so the bones grow solidly together.

arthrogryposis (ar-throw-gri-poh'-sis)   A severe crippling disease of children in which the joints become fixed or bend only partially.

arthroplasty (ar'-throw-plas-tee)   The surgical rebuilding or formation of new joints.

articulation (adj., **articulatory**)   Speech sound production by modification of the stream of voiced and unvoiced breath, usually through movements of the jaws, lips, tongue, and soft *palate;* can also refer to speech sound *discrimination*.

articulators   The parts of the body's speech mechanism responsible for formation of speech sounds, including lips, teeth, gum ridge, *hard palate* and *soft palate,* tongue.

articulatory defect   Poor or indistinct speech resulting from failure or inability to properly *vocalize* essential speech sounds. These defects usually are characterized as *omissions, substitutions,* or *distortions.* Preferred term is now *phonological disorder.*

asphyxia (az-fix´-ee-ah)   Deprivation of oxygen, as in smoke suffocation or drowning. If the deprivation is prolonged, the person may go into a *coma,* with accompanying *brain injury* or death.

aspiration   1. A desire to succeed in what is above one's current level of functioning. The level of aspiration is the maximum goal that an individual or a group desires to reach at any given moment in a specific activity. 2. Expulsion of breath during speech.

assault   An intentional *tort* in which the aggressor creates a circumstance in which the party being accosted feels a fear of imminent peril without actually being touched—e.g., shaking a threatening fist or threatening to strike with an object. (see also the related term *battery*)

assessment (v., **assess**)   Special *diagnosis* that may include mental, social, psychological, and educational *evaluations,* used to determine assignment to programs or services; a process employing observation, testing, and *task analysis* to determine an individual's strengths and weaknesses for educational and social purposes.

assimilation (v., **assimilate**)   1. The incorporation of newly learned knowledge, or that to be learned, into one's thought patterns for use in solving problems. 2. The process by which the body absorbs food for constructive *metabolism.*

assistive device (AD)   Any tool that can aid a person with a *disability* in becoming more independent.

associated method   A *multisensory* training approach developed by Margaret McGinnis at the Central Institute for the Deaf, St. Louis, to teach speech and a total *language* program to the *deaf, aphasics,* and other language-deficient children.

astereognosis (as-tare-ee-ahg-no´-sis)   Inability to identify objects by touch. A type of *agnosia.*

asthenia (az-thee´-nee-ah)   Weakness or loss of strength.

asthenopia (az-thee-no´-pea-ah)   A term describing weakness or fatigue of the *visual* organs, usually accompanied by headaches, eye pain, and poor vision.

asthma (adj., **asthmatic**)   A *chronic respiratory* condition in which the individual has episodes of difficulty in breathing. Emotional factors can contribute to asthmatic conditions.

astigmatism (ah-stig´-muh-tizm)   An eye condition involving a refractive error in which rays from one point of an object are not brought to a single *focus* because of a difference in the degree of refraction in the different meridians of the eye; causes blurred *visual* images.

asymbolia (ay-sim-boe´-lee-ah)   The inability or loss of ability to comprehend symbols such as words, figures, signs, and gestures. (see also *strephosymbolia*)

asymmetrical (ay-sih-meh´-trih-kal)   Describes a condition in which two sides of the body (that normally are alike) are different, or lack symmetry. This imbalance may cause poor body functioning.

at-risk   A term applied to children or adolescents who appear to have a higher than usual probability of expressing some social, psychological, or physical deviation in the future. In *special education* the term has been used most often to designate *preschool* children who are potentially *handicapped* but for whom we wish to avoid a *categorical* label. (see also *high risk*).

ataxia (ah-tack´-see-ah) (adj., **ataxic**)   A type of *cerebral palsy* in which lack of muscle coordination results in loss of precision movement and, sometimes, balance. Ataxia is attributed to injury to the *cerebellum;* the high *incidence* of *visual* problems relates to proximity to the visual centers.

athetosis (ath-eh-toe´-sis) (adj., **athetoid**)   A form of *cerebral palsy* in which involuntary motions cause purposeless, repetitive movements of the *extremities,* head, and tongue. Speech becomes difficult to master, and all willed movements must be superimposed on the involuntary motions.

atonia (atony)   Loss of normal muscle tone; *flaccid.*

atresia (ah-tree´-zee-ah)   A *congenital* closure of a natural body opening; e.g., the ear.

atrophy (at´-roe-fee)   The *degeneration* or wasting away of an organ or muscular portion of the body because of disease, disuse, or lack of nourishment.

attendant   A title given one who aids in the care of *handicapped* persons within an *institution* or *residential* facility.

attention (v., **attend**)   Selectivity in *perception;* the direction of perception to certain *stimuli* rather than others.

Attention Deficit Disorder with Hyperactivity (314.01)   One of the classifications of the *DSM* III System; inattention, *impulsivity,* and *hyperactivity* are present before age 7. Attention Deficit Hyperactivity Disorder is the same as *attention deficit disorder* except emphasis is placed on the hyperactivity. Either ADD or ADHD is acceptable language.

attention span   The length of time an individual can concentrate on a specific subject or activity without thinking of or attending to something else.

attenuate (ah-ten´-you-ate)   To reduce in *intensity.*

attribution theory   A *concept* in which a child's perseverance in the face of failure is viewed as being related to whether he/she perceives success and/or failure to occur as a result of his/her own efforts and ability, the whims of fate, or the influence of powerful others.

atypical   Having characteristics that differ to some degree from those of the normal population; describes a person who in some way differs to a marked degree from others of a specific type, class, or category.

auding   Hearing, recognizing, and interpreting a spoken *language.*

audiogram   A graph of hearing *threshold* levels as measured by an *audiometer* and plotted for different pure tone *frequencies* for each ear.

audiologist   A professional person trained in the use of an *audiometer,* who studies *auditory* function based on behavioral observations. The audiologist serves in *diagnosis* of *hearing losses* and in selecting and fitting *hearing aids.*

audiology The science of hearing. In *special education* and *rehabilitation*, refers to the *discipline* that researches hearing, *assesses* and trains individuals with hearing disorders.

audiometer (au-dee-om'-eh-ter) An instrument that measures hearing sensitivity and *acuity.* The measurement of *hearing loss* is recorded in terms of *decibels,* units of hearing loss, or as a percentage of normal hearing sensitivity. Sometimes called *pure-tone audiometer.*

audiometric zero The level of sound just perceivable by the average hearing human; the level of zero *decibels* on an *audiometer.*

audiometry The measurement of hearing through use of an *audiometer.*

audiovisual Describes any mode of presentation directed to both sight and hearing. TV, for example, is audiovisual.

audition The process of hearing.

auditory Pertaining to the sense of hearing.

auditory acuity One's ability to hear sounds; sensitivity of the auditory mechanism; i.e., how well one hears.

auditory agnosia (ag-noe'-zee-ah) The inability to relate sounds to their meanings.

auditory association The ability to understand the meaning and relationship of words as they are being spoken.

auditory blending The ability to combine *vocally* the *phonemes* of a word that has been pronounced with separations between phonemes in a way that the word is accurately recognized as a whole.

auditory canal The passageway from the outer ear to the middle ear.

auditory closure The ability of an individual to complete a whole word, phrase, or sound, based upon presentation of only a part (e.g., hearing several musical notes and being able to recognize the song they represent). Auditory closure is a normal skill among most children and, if lacking or impaired, causes *language* processing problems.

auditory decoding One's ability to understand the meaning of spoken words and environmental sounds.

auditory discrimination The ability to hear differences and similarities among and between sounds. Poor discrimination can lead to problems in the use of spoken *language.*

auditory feedback See *feedback.*

auditory learner A term applied to an individual whose optimal learning vehicle is through sound; a child with *learning disorders* who has the ability to learn auditorially while other *modalities* may not be successful.

auditory memory Ability to retain and recall information that has been heard.

auditory modality The hearing mechanism or system which is used to receive an auditory signal and process the signal for meaning.

auditory motor function Movement resulting from *stimuli* or cues that have been heard; carrying out an activity in response to spoken directions.

auditory nerve The eighth *cranial* nerve; carries nerve impulses of sound from the inner ear to the brain.

auditory perception The ability to identify sounds; the assignment of meaning to a sound (e.g., *bark—dog*).

auditory sequential memory The ability to hear and remember a sequence of auditory materials. Also called **auditory sequencing**.

auditory training Instruction and practice in the development and use of auditory skills to enable an *acoustically handicapped* person to make maximum use of *residual hearing*. Auditory training is helpful in an individual's adjustment to a recently fitted *hearing aid*.

augmentative communication devices A variety of aids offering communication to non-oral children through the use of boards, mechanical or computer-assisted means. These devices allow children without oral language to make their desires known. (see also *nonoral communication*)

aura (or'-ah) A condition that occurs in some individuals with *epilepsy* just prior to a *seizure*. The person may see unusual colors, hear ringing sounds, smell peculiar odors, or experience other phenomena during this time. Knowledge of the aura can be useful as a warning, giving the person time to arrange for privacy and other optimum conditions.

aural (adv., **aurally**) Pertaining to the ear or the sense of hearing.

auricle (or'-ih-kull) The external *cartilagenous* portion of ear (also known as outer ear or *pinna*).

authoritarianism An approach to child management or administration in which the person in charge is very directive, autocratic, and makes the most of decisions that arise.

autism (adj., **autistic**) A severe disorder of communication and behavior that begins in early childhood, usually prior to 30 months but up to 42 months. The children lack meaningful speech (in almost half the group) and are described as withdrawn into themselves, uninterested in others, and/or affectionless. They sometimes have an interest in or attachment to animals or inanimate objects. The condition is also labeled *infantile autism* and *Kanner's syndrome.*

autoerotic Sexual gratification or arousal resulting from one's own ideas or actions.

automatic level functions Refers to *psycholinguistic* functions assumed to occur without the involvement of higher *language* processes. If someone says, "Johnny has an apple and Mary has two apples; how many apples do they have?" the child should make an automatic response of 3 without higher level thought.

automatism A *manneristic behavior* seen in some *severely handicapped, blind*, and *emotionally disturbed* children. May be expressed as rocking or other *self-stimulatory* movements or sounds; subtle and inappropriate repetitive movements such as lip smacking, chewing, and swallowing. (see also *blindism, stereotypic behavior*)

autonomic nervous system   The part of the nervous system that regulates involuntary muscles and glandular tissues.

autosomal dominant inheritance   A form in which the inheritance of a defective *gene* from one parent causes the disorder to be expressed in the offspring.

autosomal recessive inheritance   A form in which the inheritance of *genes* must come from both parents in order to be expressed in the offspring.

autotelic   Describes a system developed by O.K. Moore using typewriters and computers to teach academic skills.

autotopagnosia (aw-toe-top-ag-noe'-zee-ah)   The inability to recognize or orient various parts of the body correctly.

average daily attendance (ADA)   A figure arrived at by dividing the total number of days of attendance (of students) by the actual number of days school has been in session.

average daily membership (ADM)   A figure arrived at by dividing the total membership on a roll by the actual number of days in a session.

average intelligence   The range of *IQs* from 90 to 110 in which the largest number of individuals occur.

aversion therapy   A technique in which the escape from and avoidance of shock or other unpleasant stimulus is used to increase social interaction in *autistic* children.

aversive stimulus   An agent or a situation that a person typically avoids because it produces discomfort. Aversive stimuli cause the strength of a behavior to decrease when they are presented immediately after the behavior occurs.

avoidance learning   A term describing an individual's behavior when trying to avoid or escape consequences that are unpleasant.

B

babbling   A stage of *language* development that occurs very early and is characterized by the repetition of sounds. Babbling may be used as a technique in *speech therapy* in cases where repetition will help strengthen certain muscles or the development of certain sounds.

Babinski reflex   A muscular reaction that causes extension of the "big toe" when the sole of the foot is tickled or stimulated. Considered to be physiological or natural in infants but *pathological* in adults.

baby talk   Speech characterized by patterns of pronunciation imitating or carried over from earliest speech. The speech may involve *substitutions* of one sound for another, as in "witta" for "little," and it also may involve sound *distortions, omissions,* and *inflectional* patterns characteristic of a young child's speech.

backward (reverse) chaining   A process used in systematic teaching and *reinforcement* wherein the behavior just before the terminal behavior is used as the starting point, and each future step involves backing up in the sequence. In the example of teaching a child to put on a jacket, the sequence would be started just before the final pulling up of the zipper. The teacher would back up to the behavior just before pulling the zipper, etc. For the opposite approach, see *forward chaining.*

backward child   A term of British origin that refers to a level of *intellectual* functioning comparable to the educational classification of the *trainable mentally retarded.* The intellectual level, when assessed with an individual *intelligence* test, would involve *IQ* scores ranging from 20 to 50.

ballistic movement   A fast, easy motion of a limb caused by a single contraction of a muscle group with no *antagonistic* muscle group contracting to oppose it.

ballistograph (baa-lis´-toe-graf)   An instrument for measuring activity, incorporating a chair suspended by cables from a supporting superstructure (known as a stabilmetric chair). Movement causes a pattern to be recorded on a sheet of paper. The ballistograph has been used to study *hyperactivity* in children.

barbiturate (bar-bich´-er-ut)   A group of drugs derived of barbituric acid which act to depress the *central nervous system.* Barbiturates are used medically for relieving tension and *anxiety,* as an *anticonvulsant* in treating *epilepsy,* and for pain relief.

barotrauma (bare-oh-traw′-muh) Injury to the ear as a result of change in barometric (air) pressure.

barrier-free See *architectural barrier.*

barylalia (bar-ih-lay′-lee-ah) Poor *articulation* that produces thick, indistinct speech.

basal (bay′-zul) 1. Denotes the highest level of a test on which an individual can pass all items. 2. A program or *curriculum* for beginners, providing learning *fundamentals,* as in a basal reading series.

basal ganglia (bay′-zul gang′-lee-ah) The collection or mass of nerve cells at the base of the brain comprising the thalamus, corpus striata, and other structures. This is the general area affected in *athetoid cerebral palsy.*

basal reading(er) The main or primary reading series that a school system adopts for use in all elementary and middle grades.

base rate A percentage or frequency of occurrence of any behavior within a certain amount of time; e.g., number of times out of seat per 10-minute intervals.

baseline Beginning observations as a foundation for measurement prior to *intervention* or treatment; a beginning point for comparison of treatment effects. In some research designs, a second baseline is collected after treatment has been stopped, to analyze its effectiveness.

BASIC (Beginners All-purpose Symbolic Instruction Code) A computer *language* that is easy to learn. This is the language of most *microcomputers* used in the schools.

battered child syndrome (BCS) Any set of circumstances or *symptoms* indicating *child abuse.* Abuses may be physical, sexual, moral, emotional, medical, environmental, or educational. The battered child may be left with residual problems such as *emotional disturbance,* as well as physical or mental *handicaps.*

battery 1. An intentional *tort* in which the aggressor makes physical contact in wronging a person—e.g., grabbing, pushing, or striking. 2. A group of tests administered to an individual to determine the various characteristics as *assessed* by each test. May be used to refer to a group of tests *standardized* on the same population to allow comparison of results.

BEH (Bureau of Education for the Handicapped) See *Office of Special Education Programs.*

behavior analysis The science employing the principles of behavior to facilitate improvement of behavior or learning.

behavior coding A system for examiners or trainers to code subjects' behavior into defined categories. The examiner records observations by type of response in terms of the coded system.

behavior disorder (BD) A condition in which a person's actions are so inappropriate, disruptive, and possibly destructive that they may interfere with education and may require special services. This term has replaced *emotionally disturbed* in most government programs.

behavior management A collection of techniques and methodologies, one of which is *behavior modification,* used to change or control human behavior.

behavior modeling A procedure whereby the child or subject is offered a simulated or actual demonstration of the desired behavior, which the subject is expected to learn by copying or imitation.

behavior modification The *shaping* of one's behavior to minimize or eliminate negative behaviors and to emphasize and *reinforce* positive behaviors, through control of a learning environment with planned and systematic application of the principles of learning.

behavior rating scales Any of a number of measures or instruments that list specific observable behaviors and provide for ranking their severity or importance. Rating scales are one approach to identify and *assess* children with emotional or behavior problems.

behavior rehearsal An activity to influence behavior through practice of the desired behavior forms under simulated or highly structured conditions. As the desired behaviors gain in strength, the rehearsal settings may gradually take on characteristics similar to the natural situations in which the problem behaviors occurred.

behavior therapy An approach to treating emotional and behavioral problems that is based on learning theory or principles of *conditioning,* in which the primary objective is to modify the problem behaviors that brought the individual to treatment. This theory is based on the premise that undesirable behaviors are maladaptive habits, and if they are changed, the problems are removed because the behaviors have been unlearned or more appropriate behaviors are learned.

behavioral assessment A method of observing and recording behaviors over a specified time. Also referred to as *direct measurement.*

behavioral objective A statement of expected learning accomplishment for the child. Behavioral objectives must meet four *criteria:* (1) stating what the learner will do; (2) stating this in measurable terms; (3) stating under what conditions the performance will be demonstrated; and (4) including the criteria for judging the quality of a student's performance. Example: The student will recite the letters of the alphabet in correct order with no more than two errors in 1 minute.

behavioral repertoire The range of behaviors that a student is capable of performing.

behavioral rigidity Inability or difficulty in developing new, appropriate responses when introduced to unfamiliar situations. Behavioral rigidity often causes difficulty for individuals with *disabilities* when coping with new circumstances or learning new skills.

behaviorism A psychological theory based on the principle that behavior is the result of one's past experiences through which one has learned or been *conditioned.*

Bell's palsy A condition involving the peripheral branch of the facial nerve, resulting in *paralysis* of facial muscles; usually temporary, disappearing in 3 to 5 weeks.

benign (bee-nine′) Not tending to cause death; not recurrent or fatal. Opposite of *malignant.*

bi– A prefix denoting two, as in *bimanual.*

bibliotherapy   The use of reading (especially materials that include characters with whom an individual identifies) for *therapeutic* purposes.

bifurcate (by-fer'-kat)   To divide into two branches (verb); forked (adj.).

bilabial (by-lay'-bee-ul)   A term used to describe a *consonant* sound formed using both lips, as in *p, b,* and *m.*

bilateral   When used in reference to the body, means involvement of both sides.

bilingual education   A *concept* addressing the needs of students for whom English is not the primary *language.*

bilingualism (by-ling'-gwuh-liz-um)   The capability of speaking more than one *language* (such as Spanish and English). The percentage of bilingual children in *special education* has consistently been higher than their *prevalence* in the larger population. Some believe that bilingualism complicates the language development process; others believe that in some cases bilingualism can have a facilitory effect on language skills.

bilirubin (bil-ih-roo'-bin)   A compound resulting from the breakdown of free *hemoglobin* released from the destruction of red blood cells. A high content of bilirubin in the brain of a *fetus* is *toxic* and causes *kernicterus,* which results in *spasticity* of certain muscle groups and *mental retardation.*

bimanual   Refers to a skill or activity requiring the use of both hands; sometimes used in reference to the ability to use both hands.

binaural (by-nor'-ul) **amplification**   Magnification of sound in both ears simultaneously through use of *hearing aids.*

binocular vision   Ability to use the two eyes simultaneously to *focus* on the same object so that the two images fuse into a single shape. Inability to do this is termed *amblyopia.*

biofeedback   The process of measuring involuntary *(autonomic)* body functions such as blood pressure and brain waves, and employing techniques to exert control over selected functions for *therapeutic* value.

biogenic (adj.)   Refers to biological and *hereditary* factors; used in conjunction with *behavior disorders.*

biopsy (by'-op-see)   The removal of live body tissue and examination of the sample obtained, usually under a microscope, to establish precise *diagnosis* of disease conditions.

biosocial   A term describing something that possesses characteristics that stem from both biological and social processes or forces.

birth trauma   *Stress* that occurs at the time of birth. Birth trauma may leave a residual effect of physical or mental injury. (see also *brain injury*)

blend   A word or sound produced by combining other words, parts of words, or letters.

blind (blindness)   A descriptive term referring to a lack of sufficient vision for the daily activities of life. Legally defined in most states as having central *visual acuity* of 20/200 or less in the better eye with correction, or having the *peripheral vision* contracted to an extent in which the widest diameter of the *visual field* covers an angular distance no greater than 20 degrees.

blindism A behavior pattern, such as swaying the body back and forth or moving the head from side to side, that is a characteristic motion of *blind* persons. These behavior patterns are interpreted to be acts of involuntary *self-stimulatory behavior* resulting from a lack of meaningful activity. Because the *symptoms* are observed in *emotionally disturbed, brain injured,* and *retarded* children, the terminology is changing to *stereotypic behavior* or *manneristic behaviors.*

Bliss method A *nonoral* means of communication that requires one to point to abstract symbols that are associated with actual experiences or written words. These symbols are combined and modified to replicate the English *language.* The method is used primarily with individuals who have *severe handicaps* and *cerebral palsy* individuals with *mental ages* of 4 or above who are nonoral.

Bliss symbol scanner An *autotelic* device for teaching the Bliss symbol system to *severely handicapped* individuals.

block scheduling A technique used in *speech pathology* in which the amount of *therapy* time in one location is increased so the *therapist* can move on to another group or school at mid-year.

blocking Interference or stopping of the flow of thought or associations, which may affect communication or problem-solving ability. Blocking is often a temporary behavior, usually caused by unconscious conflicts that cause *anxiety* and tension. Blocking is closely related to *stuttering* behavior.

Bloom's taxonomy A conceptualization to explain the ways children learn, which emphasizes knowledge, comprehension, analysis, synthesis, and evaluation. The latter levels, considered to be the highest levels of cognition, are more appropriate for *gifted students.*

Bobath therapy A form of physical treatment emphasizing *reflex inhibition* as a basic form of treatment for *cerebral palsy.* Treatment evolved in England, emphasizing *positioning,* stimulation of muscle groups, and *physical therapy.*

body concept How one thinks he/she looks; one's opinion of the physical self.

body image (awareness) One's recognition of his/her body and consciousness of one's position in space and time.

body language An extension of oneself through physical movements and gestures in place of or in addition to speech. This represents a form of communication.

bone conduction Transference of sound waves to the inner ear by vibration of the bones of the skull. Bone conduction *audiometry* is especially useful in differentiating *conductive* versus *sensorineural* hearing loss.

bone conduction hearing aid An *amplification device* worn behind the ear to assist conduction of sound waves by vibration through the skull bones.

borderline intelligence The level of *intellectual* ability that falls between normal and *mildly retarded.* An equivalent term is *slow learner.* This level has been removed from the American Association on Mental Retardation Classification Manual.

brachycephalus (brock-ee-sef´-uh-lus) (adj., **brachycephalic**) Having a short, broad head.

bradycardia A condition in which the pulse rate is less than 60 beats per minute; may be of either physiological or psychological *etiology.*

braille (brayl) A *tactile* (touch) approach to reading and writing for *blind persons,* in which the letters are formed by combinations of raised dots in a cell two dots wide by three dots high. This approach originated in France by Louis Braille (1809–1852). Braille may be written by hand with a *slate and stylus* or with a mechanical *brailler,* or braille writer. In Braille Grade I, every letter is spelled out; in Braille Grade II, contractions are substituted for words according to certain definitive rules—this is the most widely used braille form in English-speaking areas.

brailler See *Perkins brailler.*

brailler, pocket See *pocket brailler.*

brain damage See *brain injury.*

brain disorder A loosely used term for a neurological disorder or *syndrome* indicating *impairment* or injury to brain tissue.

brain-injured approach Methodology applied to the education of children who display characteristics typical of *brain injury.* The philosophy is predicated on the belief that uninjured portions of the brain can be trained to perform functions of the injured portion.

brain-injured child A term used in the 1940s and 1950s by Alfred Strauss and others to indicate certain learning and behavioral problems that were postulated as resulting from injury to the brain. This terminology has largely given way to the term *specific learning disability.*

brain injury Any damage to tissues of the brain that leads to *impairment* of the function of the *central nervous system.* A brain-injured individual typically displays *hyperactivity,* short *attention span, impulsivity,* and *perseveration.*

brainstorming A problem-solving technique in which each member of a group contributes spontaneous ideas to the situation being discussed. This can be used to stimulate *creativity* and problem-solving activities, especially with *gifted* children.

breathiness (breathy) A quality of speech characterized by an excessive air flow or expiration of air that results in the excess air being unvocalized and wasted for speech purposes.

breech birth A *natal* condition in which the baby is in an *atypical* position, with the buttocks or feet appearing first, rather than the usual head-first (*vertex*) delivery.

Bright's disease A chronic disease of the kidneys; same as *nephritis.*

Broca's (broe´-kuz) **area** The portion of the brain designated as the center for articulated or *motor* speech. This area is located in the *posterior* portion of the left third frontal convolution of the *cerebrum.* Damage in Broca's area is believed to be a contributing factor in the speech and *language disorder* called *aphasia.*

bronchial asthma An *asthmatic* condition characterized by wheezing but no infection.

25

bronchography (brahn-kahg'-ruh-fee)   Radiographic examination of the bronchial passages of the lungs.

bruxism (bruk'-sizm)   The nonfunctional gnashing and grinding of teeth occurring during the day and night. The adverse effects have been noted in severe dental wear and damage to tissue, bone, and joints. In some *institutions* for *retarded individuals,* this condition has been recorded in over half of the individuals.

Buckley Amendment   See *Family Rights and Privacy Act.*

bulimia (boo-lee'-mee-ah)   A condition akin to *anorexia nervosa;* characterized by eating to excess (binge eating), then vomiting, and repeating the process. Associated with poor self-image.

Bureau of Education for the Handicapped (BEH)   See *Special Education Programs.*

burnout   A term increasingly used to indicate the disillusionment of teachers or human service workers who have perceived the work situation as being harmful, threatening, or unfulfilling over a period of time. The individual becomes fatigued and may express a variety of physical *symptoms.* A change in employment is often sought.

bursa (and **bursitis**)   A sac or pouch full of fluid located in various areas of the body where friction would otherwise exist; e.g., knee joint. Bursitis, or *inflammation* of the bursa, results in muscle pain and limited movement of the affected area.

C

caesarean (sih-zare´-ee-un) **section** A surgical procedure for delivering a baby by incision through the abdominal and *uterine* walls, as contrasted with the usual vaginal delivery; sometimes necessary to protect the health of the mother and prevent ill effects (including *mental retardation* resulting from oxygen deficiency at birth) on the baby.

Canterbury child's aid An electronic device used by *blind persons* to aid in *mobility.* It is worn on the head and emits sounds so that the individual can react to the echoes that signify tangible objects.

captioned Refers to a film that has been adapted for movies or TV in which the narrative or dialogue appears in print at the bottom of the screen or can be seen on a TV screen using a special electronic device. An aid to the *deaf* or *hearing impaired.*

carcinogen (kar-sin´-oh-jen) Any substance capable of producing cancer.

carcinoma (kar-sin-oh´-mah) A growth of *malignant* cells; cancer.

cardiac Pertaining to the heart.

cardiopulmonary resuscitation (CPR) A technique used to supply oxygen to the body and circulate the blood when these life systems have stopped. Administration of CPR requires the helper to compress the chest and breathe into the *respiratory* tract of the stricken person.

cardiovascular (kar-dee-oh-vas´-cue-lar) Refers to the circulatory system and its parts, including the heart and blood vessels.

career education An educational emphasis stressing teaching of the work ethic and job familiarity early in life, to be followed up throughout the child's schooling by training for some type of occupation(s). In *special education,* because of considerable emphasis already placed on vocational training and *habilitation,* this movement has facilitated stronger programs and preparation of *prevocational teachers* and job placement coordinators.

carrel (care´-ul) A booth or cubicle designed to keep external distractions to a minimum, where a child can go with the least possible interference.

27

carrier   A person with a *covert* disease condition that can be transmitted to offspring; e.g., in *muscular dystrophy* neither parent may have the condition but it may appear in their children if either parent is a carrier.

cartilage (adj., **cartilaginous**)   The tough, elastic substance between bones and joints, providing a slippery surface that permits the joints to *flex* smoothly. Injury to the cartilage may result in stiffening of the joint.

cascade of services   Schematic representation of the various administrative *delivery systems* in special education. The most often used is pyramid-shaped and is credited to Maynard Reynolds and Evelyn Deno, University of Minnesota.

case conference   A meeting of representatives of the professional *disciplines* working with a *handicapped* child, at which *diagnostic* findings are shared and future plans for education and treatment are made. Also referred to as a *staffing*. A case conference with the parents is required by *PL 94-142* to plan educational placement and develop an *individualized education program (IEP)*.

case finding costs   Those costs in *rehabilitation* that are necessary to "work up" a case for the counselor—e.g. *diagnostician,* medical treatment.

case history   An accumulation of pertinent data about an individual, such as family background, personal history, physical development, medical history, test results, and *anecdotal* records of behavior. The case history often is used in making decisions on treatment services.

case load   The number of individuals assigned to a given professional or agency to be worked with during a specific time period.

case work   The use of comprehensive studies of individual cases by *social workers* in their professional practice of assisting individuals or families to make better personal, social, or economic adjustments.

catalogia (kat-uh-log'-ee-uh)   Constant repetition of words, as displayed in some mental disorders. (see also *idiolalia; echolalia*)

cataract   A condition causing opacity of the *lens* of the eye, resulting in *visual* limitation or *blindness*. Surgical replacement of the lens is the most frequently used method of restoring or improving sight. Cataracts occur much more often among adults than among children; in children the condition may occur as a result of *rubella* (one form of measles).

catarrh (kuh-tar')   An *inflammatory* condition affecting any mucous membrane of the body by causing irritation of tissues and a fluid discharge. Inflammation of the nasal and air passages may be accompanied by a cough.

catatonia (kat-uh-tahn'-ee-ah) (adj., **catatonic**)   A form of *mental illness* characterized by a trance-like *stupor* that at times causes *rigidity* of muscles and may alternate with restless activity lacking in purpose and at times resulting in unwarranted excitement.

catchment area   The geographical region designated to be served by specified *mental health* or related programs.

28

categorical *Labeling* by specific classifications such as "mental retardation" and "learning disabilities" instead of more *generic,* or general, terms.

catharsis (kah-thar'-sis) A *therapeutic* approach toward relieving *anxieties* by encouraging an individual to tell anything he/she associates with his/her problem, freeing the mind of repressed memories that are causing the emotional conflict.

catheter (kath'-eh-ter) A narrow tube of rubber, plastic, metal, or glass, which can be inserted into the body to introduce fluids or to empty the bladder or kidneys, by a method known as **catheterization.**

cauterize To treat a condition by searing a body part with a special device such as an electric needle.

ceiling The upper limit of ability that can be measured by a test. If a test is too easy, it will not have enough "top" and the ceiling is too low to allow proper measurement.

ceiling age The age level on a test at which an individual cannot pass any of the items.

central deafness *Impairment* of hearing resulting from damage to the *auditory nerve* pathways or in the centers of hearing in the brain *cortex.*

central nervous system (CNS) The portion of an individual's nervous system that includes the brain and spinal cord. *Sensory* images are transmitted to the CNS, and *motor* impulses are given in response.

cerebellum (ser-eh-bel'-um) A part of the brain located at the lower rear; has the appearance of a walnut. Its function is to control *fine motor* coordination. Injury to this area sometimes results in *ataxic cerebral palsy,* causing difficulty in walking.

cerebral (ser-ee'-brul or sare'-eh-brul) Pertaining to the brain or the main *hemisphere* of the brain.

cerebral dominance The primary control of one *hemisphere* of the brain over the other in initiating or controlling bodily movements. Normally, this dominance resides in the left hemisphere in a right-handed person and in the right hemisphere in a left-handed person.

cerebral hemisphere The left or the right side of the brain; the largest portion of the brain in higher mammals.

cerebral palsy (CP) An abnormal alteration of human movement or *motor* function arising from a defect, injury, or disease of the tissues of the *central nervous system.* Three main types are usually described—*spastic, athetoid,* and *ataxic.*

cerebrospinal fluid The body liquid that surrounds and lubricates the brain and spinal cord.

cerebrum (ser-ee'-bruhm) The two *hemispheres* of the main part of the brain, located in the upper and forepart of the *cranium;* the organ of voluntary control, conscious sensation, and learning processes.

cerumen (seh-roo'-men) Ear wax.

chaining Refers to two or more performances linked by common *stimuli.* The stimulus linking two performances serves both as the *conditioned reinforcer* maintaining the frequency of the first, and as a stimulus for the second. (see *forward chaining* and *backward chaining*)

29

chancre (shang'-ker) An initial sore or ulcer associated with a disease, particularly a *venereal disease* such as *syphilis.*

character disorder A disturbance in one's personality manifested by destructive, *acting-out,* or *aggressive* behavior without apparent conscience or guilt. (see *conduct disorder*)

character neurosis A *deterioration* or disturbance in a person's nature that causes or may cause adjustment problems.

checkmark system A *reinforcement* program employed in *behavior management* programs in which the individual receives checkmarks on a special card for working on task, completing work, and several other *contingencies.* (see *engineered classroom; token*)

chemotherapy (kee-moe-thair'-uh-pea) The treatment for or prevention of disease by use of drugs for the purpose of destroying the disease agent.

CHI See *closed head injury.*

child abuse and neglect The physical or mental injury, sexual abuse, *negligence,* or maltreatment of a child under age 18 by a person who is responsible for the child's welfare.

child advocate A person (or group) who actively pursues and seeks support for a child's rights and entitlements. (see *advocacy*)

child-centered curriculum A school curriculum in which the pupil's *maturity,* interests, experiences, and needs in general are the main considerations in selecting materials and activities for the education program for that student.

Child Find An organized effort to identify children with *handicaps*; particularly active in regard to younger, preschool children. In the 1980s the terminology changed to "Child Serve."

child welfare Components or divisions of community agencies that plan and organize services for the physical, mental, and social well-being of children. New terminology refers to Health Service Agencies, Life Service Agencies, or Human Resources Agencies.

childhood schizophrenia A psychological disorder generally occurring before *puberty;* manifested in *atypical* body movements, *emotional disturbance, perceptual disorders,* and *hallucinations.*

children with special health care needs A term denoting children with medically related conditions in which the medical problem is either a threat to the child's survival or the medical condition causes extraordinary restrictions on the child's education. Sometimes called *medically fragile* children.

Chisanbop (chiz'-an-bop) A method using the fingers for math calculations. It has been used by the *blind* persons and other *handicapped* children who have difficulty with computation.

cholecystography (koe-leh-sis-tahg'-ruh-fee) A medical procedure for examining the gall bladder by injecting or having the patient swallow certain opaque substances that enter the bile, allowing the gall bladder to be visible on *x-ray.*

30

chorea (koe-ree'-uh) A nervous disorder characterized by spasmodic twitching of muscles; commonly referred to as "St. Vitus Dance."

choreiform (koe-ree'-ih-form) **movements** Characterized by difficulty in keeping the arms outstretched while the eyes are closed. A test for choreiform movements is used in *diagnosis* of *minimal brain dysfunction (MBD);* these movements are considered to be a *"soft" sign* of MBD.

chorioretinitis (koe-ree-oh-ret-ih-ny'-tis) *Inflammation* of two of the layers of the eye, the *choroid* and *retinal* layers.

choroid The layer of the eye between the *sclera* and *retina* that contains blood vessels that provide nourishment to the retina.

chromatin (krow'-muh-tin) The *genetic* material in the nucleus of body cells. The chromatin of every cell is controlled by principles of organization that determine inherited characteristics.

chromosomal anomaly (krow-moe-so'-muhl ah-nom'-uh-lee) Irregularity in *chromosome* material, which may result in the birth of an abnormal child. *Down syndrome* is an example.

chromosome The basic unit in the nucleus of the body cell that carries the *genes* or *hereditary* factors.

chronic Pertaining to a disease, condition, habit, or situation that is continuous or recurring and of relatively long duration.

chronological age (CA) The amount of time, usually expressed in years and months, that has elapsed since an individual's birth.

CIC See *clean intermittent catheterization.*

cineplasty (sin'-eh-plas-tee) The fitting of an *amputee* with a *prosthetic device* that allows the person to activate the *extremity* by a motor within the muscles of the stump itself.

cirrhosis (sir-oh'-sis) A *pathological* wasting away of connective tissues of a body organ, generally the liver.

citizens advocacy Interceding for the rights and entitlements of handicapped persons by individuals not related to those for whom they are interceding. (see also *advocacy*)

class action A legal suit brought on behalf of one person and all others with similar problems. For example, a parent of one *multihandicapped* child may sue for that child's rights and those of all other similarly *handicapped* children.

class size The number of children allowed by state statutes to be assigned to given types of classes. As an example, in some states the class size for a *self-contained special class* is a minimum of 10 and a maximum of 15.

classes One of Guilford's *products* of thinking, in which units of thought are grouped into categories. (see *structure of the intellect*)

classroom unit A measure used to determine support to schools under state-aid plans. The school verifies the number of classroom units in operation by reporting the number of pupils in *average daily attendance,* and the state reimburses a fixed amount of money to the district per unit verified.

claustrophobia   The fear of being in enclosed or narrow spaces.

clavicle   The collarbone.

clean intermittent catheterization (CIC)   A procedure used with *paraplegics* to drain urine from the bladder on a regular schedule. The procedure involves inserting a clean but not sterile tube through the urethra and into the bladder. Regular use may prevent infections and kidney damage.

clear type   A name used to denote the 18- to 24-point type size in which textbooks and other educational materials are printed for use with *visually impaired* students. The larger than usual print is more easily seen, and enhances *readability.* Also termed *large type.*

cleft lip   A split or opening of the upper lip, which is *congenital* and often associated with *cleft palate.* The condition is surgically correctable, especially if undertaken at an early age. "Cleft palate" is used if the cleft also involves the *hard* and *soft palate.*

cleft palate   A condition characterized by an opening in the roof of the mouth, involving the *hard* or *soft palate,* or both, and often extends through the upper lip. Usually attributed to faulty development before birth, but may occur as a result of injury or disease. The condition causes *nasal* speech, certain *articulation* problems, and sometimes additional physical problems. Cleft palate usually is treated by surgery and *speech therapy.*

client-centered therapy   Counseling wherein the counselor serves as a catalyst or facilitator in helping a client arrive at his/her own solutions to problems. Also referred to as the *nondirective approach.*

clinic   An agency or organization of *interdisciplinary* workers qualified to *evaluate* and *diagnose* more than one aspect of an individual or family in need of assistance and service. Clinics may be classified in many different ways, such as various kinds of medical clinics, speech clinics, *mental health* clinics, and reading clinics.

clinical   An approach for analyzing learning difficulties through use of a variety of tests, instruments, and technical aids in an attempt to detect specific needs and plan an educational program directed at *remediating* deficiencies.

clinical type   Any one of a number of handicapping conditions (especially pertaining to *mental retardation*) in which the physical traits and features are readily recognizable as being characteristic of the specific condition. Examples are *Down syndrome, cretinism, microcephaly,* and *hydrocephaly.*

clonic (klah'-nik) **block**   The involuntary jerking of speech muscles producing a repetition of parts of words or speech sounds. (see also *stuttering*)

cloning   The process of asexually producing *genetically* identical cells from a single cell.

clonus (kloe'-nus)   Any form of *seizure* characterized by rapid contraction and relaxation of muscles.

closed caption   Procedure for visually producing written text on a lower part of television screens, which is not visible without electronic decoders. The text allows deaf individuals to know the *auditory* portion of the program.

32

closed head injury   Documented traumatic head injury resulting in neurological damage that is most reliably detected by medical diagnostic methods. Characteristics include alterations in cognitive functions ranging from subtle to obvious. Medical history usually includes loss of consciousness and delayed behavioral residuals that occur up to several years after the original injury. Special education placement is usually in learning disabilities or other health-impaired programs.

closure   1. Achieving completion of a behavior or mental act. 2. Achieving a whole even though parts of the whole may be left out, especially as in *visual closure* or *auditory closure.*

cloze (close) procedure   A teaching method in which words or other *language* units are systematically deleted from reading material. The student is asked to fill in the missing parts. A teacher also may tape-record a reading lesson, then have the child listen and respond to pauses on the tape as in, "The man drove his car into the _____."

clubfoot   A *congenital* abnormality in which the foot (or both feet) is turned downward and inward at the ankle. If the condition is recognized early in the child's life and prompt corrective action is taken, the *prognosis* for minimizing any handicapping condition is good.

clumsiness   A characteristic of many children who have *minimal brain dysfunction* with a lack of neuromotor coordination in activities such as walking, running, throwing, climbing stairs, and dressing.

cluster grouping   Assigning groups of *gifted* children to a single teacher at each level.

clustering   A learning strategy involving training *learning disabled* students to group or categorize material to be learned. Clustering allows larger amounts of material to be remembered.

cluttering   A *speech disorder* characterized by rapid or excessive speech that is difficult to understand. Also termed *agitolalia.*

coccyx (kok´-six)   The small, triangular bone at the bottom of the vertebral column, formed by the union of four rudimentary vertebrae that terminate the tail end of the spinal column.

cochlea (kah´-klee-uh)   The snail-like coil of the organ of hearing located in the inner ear.

code learning   Responding to systematically occurring events so that rules can be established. Employed with the *deaf* in teaching *language.*

code of ethics   A set of moral standards written and approved to guide the conduct of a given group. The Code of Ethics for teachers is a statement of ideals, principles, and standards for professional conduct in the teaching profession.

cognition (kahg-nih´-shun)   1. Gaining knowledge through personal experience; the *perception* of knowledge that extends beyond a mere awareness. 2. One of Guilford's thinking *operations* in the *structure of the intellect* (i.e., to know, recognize, become aware of, understand, become acquainted with).

33

cognitive A descriptive term referring to the mental process of memory, reasoning, *comprehension*, and judgment.

cognitive behavior modification A behavior change method that teaches students new thinking strategies for controlling their own behavior or helping in the acquisition and *memory* of information. Students with *mental retardation* and *learning disabilities* are thought to particularly profit from this type of instruction. Also called *cognitive training*.

cognitive blindness A term to describe *language* competence of *deaf* persons, in which absence of spoken language or words interferes with the development of *concepts*.

cognitive deficit Below-average functioning on *intellectual* or *perceptual* skills. A student displaying a cognitive deficit generally is slow in learning academic subject matter.

cognitive dissonance A state in which two objects, thoughts, or *perceptions* have equal emphasis in one's mind but are conflicting in nature.

cognitive map (1.) A means of *memory* storage in which bits of information are stored in a nonlinear fashion that resembles the way places are coded into a map. Each bit of information in such a system is subject to direct access. (2.) A concept employed to help *blind* students visualize the environment and assist with *mobility.*

cognitive modeling A self-instructional training procedure in which a child uses his/her own *verbalizations* to control *overt* behavior. Based upon the work of Donald Meichenbaum, the process involves first an adult modeling the behavior, followed by the child modeling the behavior while speaking aloud. Gradually, the overt verbal control is faded out. (see also *cognitive behavior modification*)

cognitive style The approach an individual uses consistently in problem-solving and thinking tasks. Some individuals tend to see parts, and others tend toward *gestalt*—seeing things as wholes rather than being aware of components.

cognitive training See *cognitive behavior modification.*

COHI See *crippled and other health impaired.*

coin-click test A rough *screening* test of hearing. The person checking the hearing clicks two coins together near the pupil's ear and asks the pupil to indicate when he/she ceases to hear the clicks as the tester moves away. The tester should know the approximate distance at which a person with normal hearing would cease to hear the clicks, in order to recognize *hearing losses* in the population being tested.

coincidental teaching A procedure in which a teacher helps parents identify and use naturally occurring situations in the home and community to teach social skills and their *generalization.*

collaboration A term used in the late 1980s, referring to a need for *special education* and regular education to work more closely, especially in communicating about children. The term arose out of the *regular education initiative* and the implied need to bring the two disciplines closer together. Implies equally working together on common problems.

coloboma (kuh-low-boe'-mah)   A *degenerative* disease of the eyes, in which areas of the *retina* are not completely developed, resulting in impaired *visual acuity.*

colony system   A type of *institutional* organization in which the number of individuals in each cottage or unit is kept small and services offered are directed toward specific goals such as social living, vocational training, *self-help skills.*

color blind(ness)   A *hereditary* defect in vision characterized by a lack of color *perception* or an inability to *discriminate* between certain colors.

color coding   A method of preparing teaching materials using color to identify various elements of the material; based on the idea that such use of color aids identification of parts and functions and thus facilitates learning. For example, each of the parts of speech in a paragraph could be identified by a separate color (e.g., nouns-red, verbs-blue).

colostomy (koe-lahs'-toe-mee)   A surgical operation to create an opening between the colon and the body surface, usually in the side of the abdomen, to compensate for a bowel obstruction and enable elimination of solid bodily wastes.

coma   Complete, prolonged unconsciousness often brought on by a disease condition (as in *diabetic coma*). A person in this condition is said to be **comatose.**

combined method   A means of instruction used with *hard of hearing* or *deaf* persons in which procedures from both the manual and oral methods are used. (see also *manual method, oral method; total communication*)

communicable disease   A condition that can be transmitted readily from one person to another without direct physical contact (e.g., chicken pox, flu).

communication aide   A person who works under the supervision of a *speech and language pathologist* to provide therapy to students. The aide must be offered 50 hours minimum training and cannot serve children without parent approval.

communication board   Pictorial or symbol representations used in *nonoral* communication systems such as the *Bliss method.* In such a system, symbols denote thought components, and individuals with little or no speech are taught to communicate by pointing to symbols on the special board.

communication disorder   Any condition that inhibits communication, such as speech or *language* problems.

communication skills   Refers to the many ways of transferring thought from one person to another through the commonly used media of speech, written words, or bodily gestures.

communitization   The process of providing homes and developmental training environments for persons who are returning to the community from *institutional* living.

community-based instruction   That instructional environment where a student is taught to perform skills in the actual environment rather than being taught skills at school with an expectation for *generalization* and application on the job.

community center   A site or facility developed to provide services for people in the area who need them. Services are offered by *interdisciplinary* agencies and personnel from the community and are contained in various units such as *day schools, diagnostic* and consultation units, *sheltered workshops,* and *alternative living* units. (see also *alternative living* and *group home*)

community mental health center   A facility that provides comprehensive services and continuity of care for individuals with *mental illness* and *emotional disturbance.* The center provides *in-patient* treatment, *out-patient* treatment, partial hospitalization (day and/or night service), emergency services, and community consultation and education. The center functions as one administrative entity but may contract for hospital beds or other services.

compensation   A psychological adjustment technique whereby an individual reacts to conscious or unconscious feelings of inadequacy, inferiority, or incompetence by concentrating on and/or excelling in another area of activity; e.g., individuals with *learning disabilities* may develop certain skill areas to **compensate** for deficiencies in other areas.

compensatory activities   1. Refers to programs substituted for those in which handicapping conditions would interfere with satisfactory achievement. 2. The educational means necessary to repair harm done to an individual previously denied the right to an education, regardless of present age.

compensatory education   A term for programs that emphasize circumventing a learning problem. In *special education* an attempt is made to teach through strengths rather than remediating deficiencies. In regular education compensatory education usually refers to all the efforts made to remediate cultural disadvantagement or academic underachievement.

competency   Mastering or reaching specific level of performance for success that has been set in a subject area.

competency-based instruction (CBI)   Teaching derived from specific *criteria* that have been set prior to the instructional period. The goal of the instruction is to achieve the competencies that are spelled out in the criterion.

compound fracture   A break of a bone in which an external wound is associated with the break.

comprehension   Understanding the meaning of spoken or printed *language* (as contrasted with perceiving or pronouncing words without understanding their meaning).

comprehension monitoring   One of the *concepts* employed in teaching *cognitive* strategies; emphasizes self-evaluation of memory processes.

comprehensive plan   A document produced by a *local education agency* or a state that describes how it intends to meet the needs of all *exceptional children* within its jurisdiction, as mandated by federal or state law.

compulsion (adj., **compulsive**)   An irresistible impulse to perform an irrational act.

compulsive behavior   A *neurotic* form of behavior in which an individual has an irresistible impulse to perform a controversial behavior that might be against his/her better judgment or will.

compulsory school age range 'The ages required by law for children to attend school. This range varies according to the state code; in many states it is from ages 6 to 16.

computer assisted instruction (CAI) The use of computers for instruction. Microprocessors/microcomputers have come into increasing use to teach children and adults who have *handicaps*.

concave lens A lens (as in eyeglasses) that has one flat side and one side curved slightly toward the middle, producing a "hollow" effect. A concave lens expands the light rays entering the lens, thus lengthening the distance of *focus*. Concave lenses are used to correct *myopia* (nearsightedness). For comparison, see *convex lens*.

concave-convex lens A lens that is concave on one side and convex on the other. (see *concave lens*; *convex lens*)

concentration 1. Giving close attention to a specific learning situation. 2. The combination of all forces, mental and physical, exerted in an effort to solve a problem or participate in an activity.

concept 1. An accumulation of all that is conveyed to one's mind by a situation, symbol, or object. Sometimes used to refer to a thought, opinion, or general idea of what something should be. 2. The set of characteristics common to a class of objects; e.g., triangularity includes all three-sided figures.

conceptual (conceptualization) Describes the integration of two or more sets of characteristics that are isolated by a process of abstraction and united by a specific definition.

conceptual disorders Difficulties in generalizing, abstracting, and reasoning, as well as storing and retaining past experiences. These disorders may become apparent by an individual's lack of ability to remember ideas, *concepts*, rules, or regulations that appear reasonable for the individual's *intellectual* level.

concrete Describes an idea or an image of a situation, symbol, or object that can be perceived by the senses and derives from an experience that makes it familiar.

concrete mode A person's learning or *cognitive style* characterized as learning most efficiently by use of objects and tangible items.

concrete operations An interpretation of a level of individual functioning proposed by Piaget. At this level the individual structures reality as completely as possible by remaining close to reality in its raw form and without isolation of variables. A lower or simpler level of functioning than a more complex *abstract* level.

concussion The shock produced by bodies or objects crashing together. Concussion also is commonly used to refer to the injury, with a lowering of functional activity, resulting from a fall, a blow, or similar injury (as a brain concussion).

conditional aversive stimulus An agent that is not in itself unpleasant to a person but becomes so when repeatedly paired with an agent that does disturb the person.

conditioned reflex (response) (CR) A learned response to an external *stimulus* that has been developed by training structured to teach a specific response.

conditioned reinforcer A *stimulus* that typically has no reinforcing qualities but acquires them as a result of being repeatedly paired with strong reinforcers.

37

conditioning The process of building up the association of a *stimulus* with a response so that in the future the stimulus can produce the response.

conduct disorder One of the classifications of behavior disorder in Quay's dimensional classification system. It describes individuals who have *aggressive* and other behaviors that are all negative (e.g., boisterous, bullying).

conduct problem A term proposed as being applicable to students who do not show signs of *emotional disturbance* but instead represent behaviors of "normal" students who choose to break socially defined rules. Educators who support this concept would not have *special education* serve "conduct disordered" students.

conductive hearing loss A form of hearing loss characterized by obstruction along the sound conduction pathway leading to the inner ear. This reduces the sound transmission through the outer and middle ear, causing a flat *audiogram* and generally a hearing loss of less than 70 *db*. This form of hearing loss is the most preventable and treatable.

confidentiality One of the requirements under *PL 94-142*; protects the privacy of student and parent information, including protection of student files, as well as teachers and others not using the student's name in open discussions.

configuration clue In reading, a hint toward the identity of a word that can be gained from examining its physical characteristics or general outline, in contrast to examining its detailed and specific parts.

conformity Adjustment to a social environment by acting within the dictates of the behavior standards of that environment. Teachers sometimes seek conformity of students through classroom control and management.

confrontation A direct verbal or physical response to inappropriate behavior. On the teacher's part this involves a willingness to enforce rules that have been established.

congenital (kun-jen'-ih-tal) Describes the presence of a condition or characteristic in an individual at birth. The meaning of this term does not limit causes of the condition to *hereditary* factors. Examples are congenital *deafness* and congenital heart defects.

congenital amputee See *amputee*.

congenital anaphthalmos (ann-ahf-thal'-mos) Lack of development of the eyes and associated parts of the brain necessary for vision; usually associated with *mental retardation*.

conjunctiva (kon-junk-tie'-vah) A thin, transparent membrane that lines the eyelids and covers the front of the eye. In diseases such as pinkeye, the conjunctiva is *inflamed*.

conjunctivitis (kon-junk-tih-vie'-tis) *Inflammation* of the mucous membrane that lines the inner surface of the eyelid and covers the forepart of the eyeball.

consent agreement A legal term denoting an agreed-upon stipulation regarding an individual's treatment, involvement in research, or other action, based on that person's capacity to make decisions, having adequate information, and in the absence of force or coercion. *Informed consent* means that the individual is apprised of all rights and the consequences of consent.

consent judgment   A contract acknowledging in open court a mutual agreement binding on both parties as fully as other judgments.

consonant   An alphabet letter representing a speech sound articulated by narrowing the breath channel enough to cause a brief stoppage of the breath stream or an audible friction (for example, *f, g, l*).

constitution   The basic make-up of an individual including the factors of physical well-being, health, and vitality.

constitutional disorder   Any illness or condition an individual has as a result of his/her unique mental or physical structure. This may be inherited or *chronic* or longstanding but does not include conditions acquired after birth as a result of accident, disease, or environmental situation. Constitutional disorders can affect the way individuals view themselves, to the extent that they can be considered *handicapped* in some instances.

construct   A *concept* invented for purposes of theory. Constructs generally are not directly observable.

consultant (consulting teacher) (CT)   One type of resource person in special education, offering *diagnostic* and other help and support to teachers, rather than direct services to students.

content validity   A measure of the appropriateness of a test to determine how well the material represents the goals the developer had in constructing it. Usually used with *achievement tests* to determine if the subject content really represents the *curriculum.*

contents   One of the elements of thinking in Guilford's model (see *structure of the intellect*). Contents include figural, conceptual, symbolic, and behavioral.

context   1. The written or spoken material in which a specific word, phrase, or statement is found which helps explain the phrase or statement's meaning. 2. May be used to refer to the environment or circumstances in which something is found or occurs.

contextual clue   1. A hint toward the meaning or identity of a word that can be gained from adjacent words in the passage or sentence. 2. May refer to a hint toward social behavior that can be gained from the environment or particular circumstances in which social behavior might be observed.

contingency (kuhn-tin'-jen-see)   A structured relationship between behaviors and delivery of subsequent events. A **contingency contract** is one in which the parties involved (e.g., teacher-student, parent-child) develop an agreement (usually written) specifying the positive or negative consequences of specific behaviors. The contract is signed by all parties to verify their commitment to meeting terms of the contract.

contingency contracting   A procedure in which a student and teacher write up an agreement stating the consequences that will result if a given behavior or performance occurs.

contingency management   The manipulation of consequences in an individual's environment to achieve target behaviors.

39

contingent reinforcement A planned consequence that is forthcoming when a specific response is anticipated from a behavior.

continuing education Learning opportunities offered to youth and adults through special programs, schools, centers, institutes, or colleges, emphasizing specific areas of knowledge and skills rather than traditional course sequences. The programs often are provided to individuals who have completed or have withdrawn from full-time educational programs.

continuous reinforcement A schedule whereby every response is rewarded, or reinforced.

continuum of alternative placements See *service delivery system*.

continuum of services See *service delivery system*.

contract An agreement between two parties stating the conditions under which a consequence will occur. For example, "If Mary stays in her seat for 15 minutes, then she will receive 15 minutes of "free time."

contract plan An educational program especially suited to accommodate individual differences in children. The course content is divided into a number of assignments given one at a time, in sequence, to the pupil. Upon completion of a contract, the student is allowed to proceed to the next contract, thus allowing time to proceed at the most suitable rate for each individual. Same as *Dalton plan*.

contracture Shrinking or shortening of a muscle, tendon, or other tissue, which may result in distortion or disfiguration of the area of the body involved. If not treated with *physical therapy*, surgery, or other means, it becomes increasingly severe and eventually irreversible.

control braces Devices designed to regulate and direct movement of students with *physical handicaps* (rather than for support). May be used to eliminate purposeless movement or to allow movement in only one or two directions.

control group A unit of individuals used in research; it does not receive the experimental treatment but may be exposed to another treatment or no treatment at all. Use of control groups provides a reference or index against which the experimental group(s) can be compared.

controlled competition A classroom technique that structures activities in a way so that rivalry among individual pupils or groups is kept to a minimum or at the level the teacher allows.

convergence The ocular mechanism that allows the two eyes to look at an object and to see only one. (see also *fusion*)

convergent thinking 1. Reaching conclusions that appear to be optimum, drawing from available information (as contrasted with *divergent thinking*). 2. One of Guilford's thinking *operations*. (see *structure of the intellect*)

convex lens A lens (as in eyeglasses) that has one flat side and the other side curved outward on the exterior surface, causing a bulging effect. Convex lenses compress light rays entering the lens, thus shortening the distance of *focus*. Convex lenses are used to correct *hyperopia* (farsightedness). For comparison, see *concave lens*.

40

convulsion   A violent, involuntary contraction or series of contractions of the bodily muscles; often present in the more severe *seizures* of *epilepsy,* causing the body to thrash about in a uncontrolled manner.

convulsive disorder   A clinical *syndrome* characterized by frequent *seizures* and loss of consciousness.

cooperative learning   A grouping and instructional technique becoming popular as we move into the 1990s emphasizing cooperative goals which only can be reached if all members of the group work together. Students may contribute and work at different levels which makes this popular with mainstreaming proponents.

cooperative plan   A *service delivery* approach in which students are enrolled in *special classes* and attend regular classes for a portion of the day. Used primarily with children who cannot be totally mainstreamed. This term has been largely replaced by *resource room* and *mainstreaming,* although this usage is not correct in describing the cooperative plan. (see also *shared services*)

cooperative work-study program   A school arrangement that functions under an established formal agreement between the local school and the state *rehabilitation services,* providing work training in community business.

coping behavior   The actions or strategies individuals use in dealing with their environments. If the individual is able to deal effectively with the environment, this may be referred to as "good coping behavior."

cornea (kor′-nee-uh)   The clear, transparent, outer coat of the eyeball forming the covering of the *aqueous* chamber.

coronary thrombosis   A condition in which a blood clot forms or lodges in one of the arteries that nourish the heart's muscles.

correctional counselor   See *probation officer.*

corrective braces   Physical support structures used for straightening bones (generally leg bones) and allowing joints to move by supporting a part of the body weight. Referred to loosely as *orthopedic* braces.

corrective physical education   Programs that involve specific activities or exercises selected to change or improve the function or structure of the body. Often a segment of rehabilitative programs in *rehabilitation* hospitals.

correlation   A statistic showing the relationship between two scores or characteristics. The tested relationship may occur frequently and be referred to as having a "high correlation," or it may occur infrequently and be referred to as having a "low correlation."

cortex   The outer layer of gray matter cells of the *cerebrum* and *cerebellum* (brain parts).

counselor-centered therapy   *Intervention* wherein a counselor gathers information before the session and takes charge during the session in describing what the information means in terms of client action. Also referred to as the *directive approach.*

counter-conditioning   A process in which the aversive quality of certain *stimuli* is reduced or eliminated by associating the negative events with positive experiences; e.g., fear of animals might be reduced by conditioning pleasant experiences with fuzzy or furry items.

covert Refers to an action that cannot be observed. Opposite of *overt*.

crack A slang term for a derivative of cocaine. Its use has physical, behavioral, and emotional manifestations.

craft-centered curriculum An approach formerly used in a limited number of classes for those with *mental retardation*. It prepared them for specific trades. Craft-centered activities alone, however, were found to not meet the needs of retarded pupils because they were isolated skills that became ends in themselves rather than preparing the retarded to understand life experiences and solve persistent life problems.

cranial (n., **cranium**) Pertaining to the head or skull.

cranial anomaly (kray´-nee-ahl ah-nah´-mah-lee) A *malformation* of the *cranium* (i.e., abnormal shape of head), usually because of an inherited condition.

craniostenosis (kray-nee-oh-steh-no´-sis) Premature closure of the *cranial* sutures during development of the skull, which results in a shortening or narrowing of the cranium.

cranium bifidum (biff´-ih-dum) A *hernial* protrusion of spinal, or more appropriately, *cranial* (brain) tissue through the skull because of improper closure of the skull cavity; usually results in *retardation, paralysis, hydrocephaly,* and complicated educational and health care problems. (see also *spina bifida*)

Cranmar abacus An adaptation of the Japanese *abacus* used by individuals who are *blind* to conduct math calculations.

creativity (adj., **creative**) The ability to produce a large number of original and unusual ideas, to have a high degree of *flexibility* in responses, and to develop ideas and activities in detail. Possessed by most children to some extent; particularly considered as one characteristic of *gifted* children.

creeper A device, usually a flat, rectangular board with movable wheels at each corner, which may enable an individual with *physical handicaps* lying *prone* on it to push himself/herself about by use of the arms.

cretinism (kree´-tih-nizm) A *clinical type* of *mental retardation* resulting from a *thyroid* deficiency; becomes evident early in life, and is characterized by thick, dry skin, roundness of face, *hoarseness* of voice, listlessness, and dullness. If treated early enough, a person having this condition can be helped to develop normally, and mental retardation and associated conditions may be prevented.

cri-du-chat syndrome A french word meaning "cry of the cat," one characteristic of a growth disorder involving the fifth *chromosome;* the resulting condition often results in *severe mental retardation* and *microcephaly.*

crippled and other health impaired (COHI) A term used for years to refer to *orthopedic handicaps* and medical conditions (e.g., heart abnormalities, *muscular dystrophy*). The term has been replaced largely by *physical handicap.*

crisis intervention An immediately available service to meet crucial needs of individuals who present themselves for help in emergency situations.

crisis teacher A *resource teacher* or *itinerant teacher* of children with *emotional disturbances.* This term came about because the teacher was to respond to behaviors that might be a real threat to the regular classroom but, if dealt with properly, might allow a student to be *mainstreamed.*

criterion (pl., **criteria**) The goal set in a learning situation or a test to which the student must perform before he/she is considered to have learned the required material or met the minimum requirements of the test.

criterion-referenced A term describing tests designed to measure specific knowledge or content a student has learned and not learned, in contrast to *norm-referenced* tests, which compare an individual's performance to that of a norm group.

cross-age tutoring See *peer tutoring.*

CRT An abbreviation for *criterion-referenced* testing.

cued speech A method of communication, developed by Orin Cornett, used with *deaf* persons, in which a combination of hand signals near the chin supplements and clarifies *lip reading* and speech variations. Cannot be used as a *total communication* system.

cueing A signal to aid a student in remembering a correct behavior. The teacher signals the correct behavior just before action is expected so there is less chance of incorrect performance.

cuisenaire (kwih-zen-air′) **rods** An instructional device utilizing various sized colored wooden rods to teach *arithmetic processes.*

cultural deprivation The cumulative effect on a child living in an environment of low socioeconomic status, disorganized family life, isolation, crowded conditions, or lack of stimulation, which tends to contribute to one's inability to function adequately.

cultural-familial Describes a condition in which an individual is *diagnosed* as having *mental retardation* without evidence of *cerebral pathology,* but having a family history of *intellectual* subnormality and *cultural deprivation.*

culture-fair or **culture-free tests** Instruments designed or constructed in an attempt to minimize or eliminate the effects of one's culture on performance. The preferred term is now *nondiscriminatory testing.*

cumulative record A continuous individual written account of a child's educational experiences, kept by the school. These experiences may include subjects studied, achievement, health, information about the home, attitudes, and other data.

curriculum (adj., **curricular**) A systematic grouping of activities, content, and materials of instruction offered under school supervision for the purpose of preparing students to learn and live effectively.

curriculum based assessment (CBA) See *curriculum-based measurement*; the two terms are interchangeable.

curriculum-based measurement (CMB) A system of repeated measurements of achievement with a prescriptive orientation toward *remediation.* The system involves small samples of reading and other subject matter that has previously been taught. The combination of instruction and measurement has been effective in improving the academic functioning of children with and without handicaps.

curriculum consultant   A professional person who has had special training in a specific *curricular* field and devotes an allotted amount of time to consult with and aid school faculty in that area.

curriculum development   The cooperative study of goals and procedures for modifying and improving learning activities and *curricular* content of a school program.

cursive writing   A method of handwriting characterized by connected letters and flowing lines. In *special education*, cursive writing may be the preferred and only method of handwriting taught to some children with *perceptual disorders*, to the exclusion of *manuscript printing*.

custodial   A term formerly applied to persons with *profound retardation* who required constant care and supervision. This term implied nursing care and fell into disuse before 1970.

cutaneous (kyew-tane´-ee-us)   Pertaining to the skin or to the skin as a sense organ (cutaneous sense).

cyanosis (sy-ah-no´-sis)   A condition characterized by blueness of the skin resulting from a lack of oxygen in the blood; often observed in children with severe *cardiovascular* disorders.

cycloplegia (sy-kloe-plee´-juh)   *Paralysis* of the ciliary muscle of the eye, with resulting loss of ability to constrict the *pupil*.

cystic fibrosis (sis-tik fibe-roe´-sis) **(CF)**   The most common, and usually fatal, *hereditary* disease of childhood; affects most body organs, particularly the lungs and *pancreas*. Abnormal mucus secretions obstruct bodily functions, especially the body's ability to clear the lungs, which results in excessive coughing.

cytogenetics (sy-toe-jeh-net´-iks) (adj., **cytogenic**)   The study of *chromosomes* and their relationship to *heredity*. Often concerned with the relationship between chromosomal *aberrations* and *pathological* conditions.

D

dactylology (dak-til-ol´-oh-jee) See *fingerspelling.*

daily living skills See *ADL.*

Dalton plan See *contract plan.*

dance therapy The use of dancing for *habilitation* purposes in treating mental and emotional disorders, based on the premise that improved coordination, posture, and rhythm in bodily movements create inner feelings of confidence and greater security.

day school A facility attended by children during part of the daylight hours but who spend the remainder of their time elsewhere.

db See *decibel.*

deaf (deafness) Defined as a condition in which the *auditory* sense is not the primary means by which speech and *language* are learned and the sense of hearing is so lacking or drastically reduced as to prohibit normal function as a hearing person.

deaf-blind Describes a person whose vision and hearing are so deficient as to require specialized methods of communication different from those used in the fields of the deaf or the blind. Such individuals may not be equally *handicapped* in each *modality* and in fact might not meet the legal definition of either *deafness* or *blindness.* In teaching, *residual vision* and *residual hearing* are used in conjunction with the sense of touch.

decibel (db) A unit of measurement expressing *intensity* of sound; a unit of hearing or audition. Extent of hearing is expressed as the number of decibels necessary for the person to hear pure tones above the *baseline* used to measure normal hearing.

deciduous (deh-sid´-you-us) **teeth** The first set of teeth, 20 in number, called "baby teeth"; these are shed between ages 5 and 14 and are replaced by "permanent" teeth.

decoding 1. Receptive habits in the *language* process that allow meaningful use of what is received either *auditorially* or *visually.* 2. Breaking down a complex structure into the simplest understandable units, or translating something that is not understood into something that is comprehended.

decubitus (deh-kue´-bih-tus) **ulcer** Any breakdown of tissue and skin in which the sense of feeling is absent. Also called bed sores or pressure sores, these ulcers are common among *quadriplegics* and *paraplegics.*

45

deductive thinking   A term used by learning theorists to describe the process of reasoning from the general to the specific, in which the conclusion is reached by following logical inferences from the beginning. Opposite of *inductive thinking.*

defective syntax   A condition in which an individual can use words or short phrases for self-expression but is not able to organize complete sentences for adequate communication.

defense mechanism   A general term describing behavior used to reduce tension and *anxiety.* The behavior may be *aggressive,* retiring, diversional, destructive, or any other form that achieves the purpose. Often, the individual's defense mechanism against admitting failure is to place the blame elsewhere.

deficit   A term denoting that an individual is behind age peers in certain basic developmental processes. A deficit in memory skills, for example, means that the individual is lacking in that area and indicates redirection of *curricular* efforts to focus on reducing that deficit.

deformity   Any distortion of the body or a specific part of the body that is considered disfiguring, ugly, and at times is accompanied by loss of function.

degeneration (adj., **degenerative;** v., **degenerate**)   A breaking down or deterioration, usually of a progressive nature. Degeneration of body tissues is accompanied by a steady loss of vitality.

deinstitutionalization   A practice arising from the principles of *normalization* and *least restrictive environment,* in which individuals with *mental retardation* and *emotional disturbance* are moved out of *institutions* into community *alternative living* arrangements.

delayed recall   The ability to remember learned material after a lapse of time.

delayed speech   Any condition in which the development of speech is slower than the normal rate for the various stages of speech development.

delinquency (adj., **delinquent**)   Offenses against the legal and social standards of society; refers to unacceptable behavior in youth. (see *juvenile delinquency*)

delirium   A mental disturbance of short duration marked by illusions, *hallucinations, delusions,* incoherence, and physical restlessness. This condition often accompanies infection and high fever.

delivery model (system)   An administrative arrangement to provide services. *Special education* models include *resource room, special class, itinerant* program, and others. (see *service delivery system*)

delusion   A mental image an individual accepts and defends as true or real but in reality is false or unreal.

delusions of grandeur   A trait exhibited in some *psychotic* conditions, in which the individual has an exaggerated misconception of importance, position, abilities, wealth, or accomplishments.

delusions of persecution   A trait exhibited in some *psychotic* conditions, in which the individual believes that another individual(s) is trying to belittle, injure, or harm him/her in some way.

46

dementia (dih-men'-chuh) Acquired *mental deficiency* or disorder as opposed to *congenital* mental deficiency or disorder. (British usage)

dementia praecox (dih-men'-chuh pree'-cocks) A form of mental disorder that results in deterioration of the mind, a loss of interest in people, and incoherence of thought and action, culminating in loss of touch with reality. (Not preferred terminology today.)

demographic Descriptive term applied to statistical studies of physical conditions or vital statistics of populations (births, marriages, health, etc.).

denasal speech A condition resulting from obstruction of the nose, characterized by the absense of *resonance* in the voice, as sometimes is noted in the common cold.

denial reaction Behavior of a *handicapped* person who refuses to admit any limiting effects associated with the handicap.

deoxyribonucleic acid See *DNA.*

dependence A situation in which one is unable to function independently and make decisions without the assistance of another. **Dependency** is a common problem for persons with *handicaps.*

depopulation A procedure for reducing the number of persons in an *institution,* under the *deinstitutionalization concept.* Theoretically, the concept means reduction of population to zero residents.

depression (depressed) A psychological/psychiatric term referring to a dejected mood, despondency, *psychomotor* retardation, reduced vitality and vigor, and despair. Mild depression may come and go with no long-term effects, but severe depression is considered a serious *mental health* problem.

depth perception Accurate recognition of distances to or between objects in the environment; enhances ability to *orient* one's self in relation to objects.

deregulation A term that has taken on more meaning in the last few years as the government reduced the restrictiveness of regulations governing implementation of laws. **Deregulatory** actions, for example, were attempted against *PL 94-142.*

dermal Pertaining to the skin.

dermatitis (der-mah-tie'-tiss) *Inflammation* of the skin.

dermatologist A medical doctor who specializes in the *diagnosis* and treatment of skin conditions and disorders.

desensitization A *behavior therapy* technique in which the individual is exposed gradually and systematically to objects, events, and situations that evoke fear, the purpose of which is to reduce fear.

desired learner outcomes (DLO) Terminal *instructional objectives* as defined in the Education Sciences Program developed by Jack Cawley. Includes objectives written in behavioral terms; e.g., student will be able to make change correctly for any combinations up to $1.00. (see also *behavioral objective*)

47

detachment (of retina) A condition in which the inner layers of the retina of the eye become separated from the pigment epithelium, where it is normally attached, resulting in *visual impairment* or *blindness.*

detoxification A treatment process for alcoholism involving controlled withdrawal of alcohol from the person being detoxified. Sometimes shortened in the vernacular to "detox."

developmental approach A *concept* that holds that individuals learn in the same way and in the same general sequences but that they vary in the rate of learning. Proponents of this theory hold that children with *mental retardation* learn the same way as normal children, but at a slower rate. The developmental approach emphasizes *Piagetian, cognitive* and *sensorimotor* stages of *intelligence* and the normal sequence of acquisition of *language* skills. For comparison see *nondevelopmental approach.*

developmental disability (DD) A term that came into usage with the Nixon administration to include developmental disorders occurring before 18 years of age, such as *mental retardation, epilepsy,* and *cerebral palsy.* The definition was broadened with *PL 94-103* to include *autism* and severe *learning disabilities* if the cause originates from mental retardation. In 1979 PL 95-602 expanded the concept to include *physical handicaps* and severe childhood *emotional disorders.*

developmental dyslexia A type of severe reading disorder that is different from acquired dyslexia and is not caused by brain injury or known agent; often seen in children of above average intelligence.

developmental lag Functioning at a level lower than that expected of one's *chronological age* when compared to *age norms.*

Developmental Language Disorder, Expressive Type (315.31) A classification in the *DSM* III System; denotes difficulty or inability to express one's wishes. Another term for this is *expressive aphasia.*

Developmental Language Disorder, Receptive Type (315.31) A classification in the *DSM* III System denoting difficulty in understanding the spoken word. Another term for this is *receptive aphasia.*

developmental maximation unit A small *residential* facility located near state *institution(s)* and used for intensive treatment and training of institutionalized individuals being prepared to return to the community.

developmental period The time between conception and 18 years of age, during which physical and mental growth occurs. The period in which *developmental disabilities* originate.

developmental retardation A term that has been suggested as a replacement for *mental retardation.* Proponents believe it emphasizes the correct elements of mental retardation and would remove some of the confusion with *mental health* and *mental illness.*

developmental therapy   A *psychoeducational* curriculum approach to treatment of students with *emotional disorders*, emphasizing developmental milestones. This approach, by Mary Wood, emphasizes four basic curricular areas: behavior, socialization, communication, and academics.

developmental training home (DTH)   A group residence for adults with *handicaps* who require a moderate amount of supervision and support in *self-help skills,* training development, and so on. (See also *group home*)

deviancy model   An approach in educational, *mental health,* and social programs, in which a child who does not achieve, behave, or adapt as expected receives certain *interventions* set up to correct the variance the individual expresses.

deviate (v.) (adj., **deviant**)   To turn aside or stray from a standard, principle, or *norm.* Describes a person who varies noticeably from societal norms in some personal characteristic—mental, emotional, moral, or physical.

diabetes (die-uh-bee′-tess) (adj., **diabetic**)   A *metabolic disorder* in which the body is unable to properly utilize carbohydrates in the diet because of failure of the *pancreas* to secrete an adequate supply of *insulin,* or failure of the insulin secreted to function properly in the digestive process, resulting in an abnormal concentration of sugar in the blood and urine. *Symptoms* are excessive thirst, excessive urination, weight loss, slow healing of cuts and bruises, pain in joints, and drowsiness.

diabetic coma (or **reaction**)   Uncontrollable drowsiness and muscular pain, possibly resulting in unconsciousness, resulting from too little *insulin* in the system. This condition could become serious if the individual is not administered insulin soon after onset of *symptoms.*

diabetic retinopathy   A condition associated with *diabetes,* in which the blood supply to the *retina* of the eye is faulty and which results in *blindness.*

diagnosis (adj., **diagnostic;** v., **diagnose**)   1. The act of recognizing disease or conditions by *symptom* identification and/or testing. 2. The resulting judgment after critical scrutiny. In *special education,* diagnosis usually is made by an *interdisciplinary* team that analyzes the cause or nature of a condition, situation, or problem.

diagnosogenic (die-ag-no-so-jen′-ik) **theory**   A premise that attributes *stuttering* in individuals to influences in the child's early environment, specifically by significant persons in that environment who call attention to normal *dysfluencies* and label them as stuttering.

diagnostic-prescriptive center   A setting emphasizing short-term *assessment* and teaching with the expressed purpose of determining a student's strengths and weaknesses and developing a specific teaching plan.

diagnostic-prescriptive education   See *diagnostic prescriptive teaching.*

diagnostic-prescriptive teaching (DPT)   An approach to instruction of students on an individual basis, with attention to strengths and weaknesses, followed by teaching prescriptions designed to remedy the weaknesses and develop the strengths.

diagnostic test   A measure designed to analyze or locate an individual's specific areas of weakness or strength to receive attention in future instruction. A **diagnostician** may conduct this testing.

dialect   A noticeable variation of any *language,* differing from the standard or traditional form in characteristics such as pronunciation, voice *inflection,* choice of words and terms, or phraseology. May be the customary speech of a social class, a geographic region, a nationality, or an ethnic or cultural group.

Diana v. State Board of Education   A landmark court case in California that set the precedent for students to receive testing, placement, and similar considerations based not only on the English *language,* but the primary language of the home.

diaphragm (die´-ah-fram)   The muscular partition that separates the thoracic or chest cavity from the abdominal region of the body and has an important function in breathing.

dichotic (die-kot´-ik)   Simultaneous *auditory* stimulation of both ears by different *stimuli,* usually by use of ear phones and two channels of a tape recorder.

diction   One's choice of words and *enunciation* to express oneself *orally* with clarity and effectiveness.

Dictionary of Occupational Titles (DOT)   A publication that gives an extensive listing and classification of jobs in the United States. Published by Superintendent of Documents, Washington, DC 20202.

didactic (die-dack´-tik) **method**   Any approach to teaching that uses materials that are practical or instructive in and of themselves. The Montessori method is especially noted for its emphasis on practical self-instruction.

differential diagnosis   An *evaluation* that attempts to distinguish between similar disorders or conditions by identifying features that are characteristic of only one of them.

differential education   Educational experiences uniquely designed to involve the capacities and needs of the *gifted* which, in general, are beyond the reach of and not appropriate to the capacities or needs of persons not gifted or endowed with unusual potential for productive or *creative* thinking.

differential reinforcement   Providing rewards for behavior in the presence of one *stimulus* situation and not reinforcing in the presence of other stimulus conditions.

differential threshold (JND—just noticeable difference)   The smallest amount of difference between two *stimuli* that can be detected by use of a receptor, or sense organ.

digraph   The *phonetic* combination of two letters to spell a single sound, as *sh* in "shoe."

dimensional classification   A system of categorizing school-age *behavior disorders,* developed by Herbert Quay.

diopter   The unit of measurement for refractive power of a lens, as used in testing the eyes and prescribing eyeglasses.

diphthong (dif´-thong)   A result of uniting two *vowel* sounds to produce another sound, as *oy* in boy.

50

diplegia (die-plee´-juh) *Paralysis* of the body in which both sides are affected; a result of injury to both *hemispheres* of the brain.

diplopia (die-ploe´-pea-ah) Commonly called "double vision," a *visual* defect in which single objects are seen as two. Also termed *ambiopia.*

direct consent An agreement elicited by a person directly involved in a research project, information or data gathering, etc. to use some aspect of that work in a specific way. (see also *substitute consent, consent agreement*)

direct instruction A method of teaching academics to students with learning handicaps that emphasizes teaching skills rather than remediation of psychological processes.

direct measurement A method of collecting data in which tangible behaviors can be observed and counted. (see also *behavior assessment*)

direction taking The act of a *blind* person locating a line or course that better facilitates traveling in a straight line toward an objective.

directionality One's ability to differentiate the basic directions involved in the environment, such as right from left, up from down, front from back. Young children express a normal deficiency in this capacity, but older children who lack directionality may have learning problems.

directive approach or **therapy** See *counselor-centered therapy.*

directive teaching An instructional approach with emphasis on instruction in basic skills combined with systematic measurement and collection of data on children's academic performance. Directive teaching is an extension of *prescriptive teaching* and *applied behavioral analysis,* emphasizing intentional academic instruction.

dis– Prefix meaning opposite or absent.

disability A physical, psychological, or neurological deviation in an individual's makeup. A disability may or may not be a handicap to an individual, depending on one's adjustment to it. The terms *disability* and *handicap* often have been considered and used synonymously, but this is not accurate, as a handicap actually refers to the effect produced by a disability. (see also *presumptive disability*)

discipline 1. Management of youngsters so as to prevent unnecessary disruptive behaviors and incidents and promote positive experiences. 2. An area of training in professional services; e.g., psychology, teaching.

discrepancy formula A means of expressing the difference between expected and actual achievement to determine if the difference is large enough to warrant special services. In *learning disabilities* a special formula is applied to determine if the child is to be labeled *LD.*

discrimination (v., **discriminate**) The ability to make judgments regarding sameness or differences between at least two *stimuli.* This ability is of great importance in academic work, for judging form, shape, right or wrong, large or small, etc.

disguised rejection An apparent attitude of caring or loving that actually is a "cover" for feelings of guilt or other negative emotions. For example, a parent who appears to be overly concerned in showing love and is oversolicitous of a *handicapped* child may have really rejected the child and, because of guilt feelings, *compensates* by overly expressing love and concern.

disinhibition The inability to restrain oneself from reacting to distracting *stimuli;* loss of effects of conditioned *inhibition.* Disinhibition may be exhibited by *brain injured* children, causing them to respond to or be distracted by all stimuli.

disorientation Loss of ability to keep one's bearings in the surrounding environment, with reference to right and left, location, time, recognition of acquaintances, and in more severe instances, recognition of one's own identity.

displacement A psychological *defense mechanism* in which an individual substitutes another form of behavior or thinking for what is expected, with the intention that the new behavior will be more acceptable.

dissociation A mental condition in which ideas or desires are separated from the main stream of consciousness or from one's personality to a degree that they are no longer accessible to memory or consciousness. The individual has difficulty or is unable to perceive things or situations as a whole, but instead tends to respond to *stimuli* in terms of parts or segments.

distal Far from the point of attachment or origin; often used with reference to *physical disabilities.* Opposite of *proximal.*

DISTAR An *acronym* for Direct Instruction System for Teaching Arithmetic and Reading; one of the most systematic instructional methods derived from the *early childhood* movement. Developed as an outgrowth of the work of Bereiter and Engelmann.

distinctive features A term used to describe individual characteristics of a sound—voiced sound, voiceless sound, duration, tenseness, etc.

distortion (in speech) An *articulatory* disorder in which speech sounds are altered, as in "shled" for "sled."

distractibility (adj., **distractible**) A behavioral characteristic, often present in children with *central nervous system* disorders, in which the child is unable to refrain from responding to *stimuli* that are essentially unnecessary to immediate adjustment. As a result, the child is unable to direct attention to stimuli that are important to adjustment or learning.

diuretic (die-you-ret´-ik) A general term describing the properties of any drug that reduces the amount of water retained in the body and increases the flow of urine.

divergent thinking 1. Reaching conclusions in a manner not entirely determined by available information. In divergent thinking, one's thoughts may go in different directions, sometimes searching and seeking variety so that a number of different responses are produced. Also, a reorganizing of known facts into new relationships. 2. One of Guilford's thinking *operations* in the *structure of the intellect.* (see also *convergent thinking,* in contrast.)

diversion The act of turning a person or things aside from the course being followed. Often used with *exceptional children* in reference to changing a negative or nonprofitable activity or goal into a positive or profitable activity or goal.

divestiture in special education   A term of the early 1980s indicating that special education ought to get out of the business of serving *mildly handicapped* children. In the late 1980s this has been replaced with the *regular education initiative (REI)*, which recommends total *mainstreaming* with support from special education *consulting teachers.*

dizygotic (die-zie-got'-ik)   A descriptor of twins resulting from the simultaneous fertilization of two separate eggs rather than the division of one (*monozygotic*) egg. These twins are referred to as fraternal rather than identical.

DNA (deoxyribonucleic acid)   The principal constituent of *chromosomes* and the prime carrier of *hereditary* factors.

Doman-Delacato method   A neurophysiological approach to the treatment and education of *cerebral palsied* and other *handicapped* individuals developed by Doman and Delacato of the Center for Development of Human Potential. This method is best known for *patterning,* in which children are physically aided through developmental activities such as creeping and crawling.

dominant genes   Those in which the *genetic* make-up provides expression of characteristics that prevail over *recessive genes.*

Doppler effect   A term used to describe the changes in *pitch* of an object as it gets closer. This phenomenon aids *blind* persons in judging distance and navigating the physical environment.

double interlocking reinforcement   A *contingency* arrangement whereby a member of a group is rewarded for specified social responses, and the group in turn is reinforced for social responses directed toward the specific individual.

Down syndrome   A *clinical type* of *mental retardation* resulting from a specific abnormal *chromosomal* arrangement. Individuals with Down syndrome have *intelligence* in the *moderate-mild* range of retardation.

drug addiction   A condition in which the body becomes physically dependent on a substance and, as tolerance increases, larger amounts may be needed to produce the desired results.

drug therapy   1. Any prescriptive use of medication to modify behavior, to aid in education, or to help improve social acceptability. 2. In medicine, use of substances in the traditional sense to treat illness or disease.

DSM (Diagnostic and Statistical Manual of Mental Disorders)   Classification system of the American Psychiatric Association. This system is widely used, primarily by medical and *mental health* clinics.

dual diagnosis   A term indicating that a person has more than one handicap. The term has been used especially to describe individuals who have both *mental retardation* and *mental illness,* which occurs frequently and poses unique educational and treatment needs.

Duchenne (due-shane') **disease**   A childhood form of *muscular dystrophy,* which usually starts between ages 2 and 6 and is characterized in early stages by waddling, walking on toes, or difficulty in running. (see also *pseudohypertrophy*)

due process A principle of law that protects the rights of children and parents in *identification, evaluation,* and placement; provides prior notice, parental consent, impartial hearing, appeals, written decision and *surrogate parents.* (see also *procedural due process*)

dull normal A term used to designate pupils who function just below average or normal in general *intelligence.* Used in classification systems such as that of Terman. A more common and desirable term is *slow learner.*

dullard A term commonly used during the 19th century in reference to an individual who was unable to function as well as his/her peers, or academically at school; a child of moderately subnormal *intelligence.* (This term is not currently acceptable and is relegated to slang usage.)

dwarf (dwarfism) An individual of unusually small stature, and in which bodily proportion varies from the norm.

dynamic assessment An emerging term in the 1980s that is being used to describe a new type of *intellectual* testing; the American approach to the measurement of *intelligence,* which is similar to Feuerstein's (Israel). Its essence is the measurement of ability by finding out the maximum that children can do with help. In this approach children are given clues or prompts to assist their maximum assessment.

dynamometer (die-nah-mah´-meh-tur) An instrument used to measure the power in a muscular contraction.

dys– Prefix meaning bad, difficult, or abnormal.

dysacusis (dis-ah-kyew´-sis) A *sensorineural* condition in which an individual has difficulty understanding speech; equivalent to the reading disorder *dyslexia,* which produces difficulty in deriving meaning from the printed word. Classified under the general category of *aphasia.*

dysarthria (dis-are´-three-uh) A defect in the *central nervous system* that results in faulty *articulation* of speech sounds; usually observed in *cerebral palsy.*

dyscalculia (dis-kal-kyew´-lee-uh) Impaired ability to calculate or manipulate number symbols; often associated with a pattern of *learning disabilities.*

dysfluency More commonly called *stuttering;* hesitations or interferences with smooth speech, which may or may not constitute a handicapping condition. Some dysfluency is normal in all persons. (see also *fluency disorder*)

dysfunction Partial disturbance, *impairment,* or abnormality in a particular bodily activity.

dysgraphia (dis-graf´-ee-ah) A *learning disability* characterized by difficulty in writing; often associated with neurological *dysfunction.*

dyskinesia (dis-kih-nee´-zee-ah) A physical condition caused by partial *impairment* of the coordination of voluntary muscles, which results in obvious clumsy movements and poor physical control.

dyslalia (dis-lay'-lee-ah) A speech disorder of *articulation* caused by abnormal use of external speech organs rather than damage to the *central nervous system.*

dyslexia (dis-leck'-see-ah) An *impairment* in reading ability, or partial inability to read; often associated with *cerebral dysfunction* or *minimal brain dysfunction.* An individual with this condition does not understand clearly what he/she reads. A more *generic* term for learning problems including dyslexia is *learning disability.*

dyslogia (dis-loe'-zhuh) A *linguistic* disturbance characterized by faulty formulation or expression of ideas in the spoken form. Dyslogia may accompany *mental retardation* or *emotional disturbances.* (see also *aphasia*)

dysmetria (dis-meh'-tree-ah) A "*soft*" *sign* of *minimal brain dysfunction,* in which the child being tested has difficulty directing the finger to the nose with eyes closed.

dysnomia (dis-noe'-mee-ah) The partial loss of ability to comprehend, organize, or express ideas or names in speech, writing, or gestures.

dysphasia See *aphasia.*

dysphemia (dis-fee'-mee-ah) A *speech disorder,* such as *stuttering,* related to *psychoneurosis.*

dysphonia (dis-fone'-ee-ah) A *voice disorder* characterized by faulty *phonation* or *resonance* and *pitch* deviations.

dysplasia (dis-play'-zee-ah) Abnormal development of the body or cells.

dyspraxia (dis-prak'-see-ah) An *inhibition* of the ability to coordinate body movements, especially speech. (see *apraxia*)

dysrhythmia (dis-rith'-mee-ah) A *malfunction* of the neuromotor system, which causes poor rhythm or a loss of ability to move with rhythm.

dystonia (dis-toe'-nee-ah) A rare disease of the *central nervous system* that affects young children, causing a loss of muscle tone and use.

dystrophy (dis'-troe-fee) See *muscular dystrophy.*

ear defenders Protective devices or objects used to cover and protect the ears from loud noises and dangers.

ear drum See *tympanic membrane.*

early childhood education A practice of teaching or intervening with children before traditional schooling begins, to aid subsequent learning in youngsters thought to be *at-risk* or identified as having some problem. It can be applied from birth and emphasizes preventive *intervention.* (see also *preschool education*)

early infantile autism A term first used by Kanner in 1943. (see *autism*)

eccentric gazing A behavioral characteristic of some *visually impaired* students who see more clearly by using *peripheral vision* and thus not looking directly at instructional material or teachers. This behavior should not be viewed as daydreaming and should not be discouraged.

echocardiograph Examination of the function of the heart by means of ultrasound equipment.

echoencephalography (ek-oh-en-sef-ah-log´-ruh-fee) Examining or measuring the internal structure of the *cranial* cavity of the skull by means of ultrasound equipment.

echolalia (ek-oh-lay´-lee-uh) A speech condition characterized by involuntary repetition of words, syllables, or sounds spoken by others, as if echoing them. A common characteristic of *severe mental retardation.*

echolation A technique used by *blind* persons of emitting a sound and interpreting the qualities of the reflected echo to aid in *mobility* and *obstacle perception.*

echolation device An aid to *blind* persons, invented by Kay and developed by Bower, that emits high-frequency sound waves that bounce off objects. The loudness of the returning signals indicates the size of an object, and the *pitch* indicates distance.

eclectic (ek-lek´-tik) **method** A teaching and counseling approach in which the teacher uses methods from various systems and philosophies that are most appropriate to the situation, the child, and the classroom.

56

ecological approach One of the treatment *concepts* used with individuals who have *behavior disorders,* in particular. It emphasizes that the child is not sick but, rather, an interaction of the child and his/her environment results in the child's behavior. In this approach, a change in the environment is one method of bringing about a change in the individual.

ecological inventory A listing of activities and skills that individuals with severe handicaps are required to perform in a living, working, and school environment.

ecological model See *ecological approach; ecosystem.*

ecosystem (or **ecological system**) The combination of all forces existing in the environment or in a certain realm, as in the "family ecosystem." In the *ecological approach,* the ecosystem is believed to determine the behavior of individuals within it; thus, the focus on a disturbed child would be away from internal factors and toward external environmental factors.

ectomorphic (ek-toe-more'-fik) One of the body types *(somatotypes)* in Sheldon's classification system; this type is characterized by slender stature and slight muscular development.

eczema (ek'-zeh-mah or ek-zee'-mah) An *inflammatory dermatitis* (skin condition) characterized by redness, itching, tiny postules, oozing, crusting, and later scaling.

edema (eh-dee'-mah) Swelling caused by localized fluid in the tissues.

edible reinforcer Any food preferred by pupils that can be used as a reward for appropriate behavior.

educability The capacity of an individual to learn by experience and to use learning to adjust to one's environment.

educable Capable of learning to a degree that exceeds mere repetition, as in the *educable mentally retarded.*

educable mentally retarded (EMR)/educable mentally handicapped (EMH) The term ascribed to the highest level of *retardation,* including individuals capable of becoming self-sufficient and learning academic skills through upper elementary grades. EMR is the equivalent of *mildly retarded* in the American Association on Mental Retardation classification system. The most accepted *IQ* range is 2 to 3 *standard deviations* below the *mean* on an individually administered *intelligence* test, or an IQ of approximately 55–70.

educateur A professional employed in France and parts of the United States to provide an educational and treatment program for children with *behavior disorders.*

Education for All Handicapped Children Act of 1975 (PL 94-142) A federal law that has been described as a "Bill of Rights for the Handicapped," which includes many provisions and special features including *free appropriate public education,* definitions of the various *handicaps,* priorities for *special education* services, protective safeguards, and procedures for developing the mandatory *individualized education program (IEP).*

educational diagnosis   Using tests and evaluative instruments to determine the academic level of students and how they learn. Information collected through educational diagnosis is used in selecting services for the students and in planning educational activities for them.

educational potential   The theoretical maximum academic performance an individual will reach at *maturity.*

educational retardation   Failure to develop in academic achievement as rapidly or as far as expected for one's *chronological age* even though one may not have *mental retardation.*

educational therapist   A term often used in *clinical* teaching programs for *exceptional children* when referring to an educator who does educational *assessment* and prescribes educational activities accordingly.

educationally blind   A term that means vision is reduced to such a degree that education must occur though *braille,* listening, and other nonstandard means. This term has not gained wide usage. (see also *functionally blind*)

educationally handicapped (EH)   A term used in some state educational codes to refer to children with difficulties at school that result from either learning or behavior disorders or a combination of the two. This term has been replaced in some states by *learning handicapped,* which includes *mild mental retardation, behavior disorders,* and *learning disabilities.*

educationally subnormal   A term of British origin referring to a level of *intellectual* functioning comparable to the educational classification of *educable mentally retarded* or *mildly retarded.*

EEG   See *electroencephalogram.*

effective instruction   Those practices that research has shown to be of unusual significance in demonstrating increased learning among regular and special education students; a statement of rationale for fast-paced instruction, time on task, allotted time for instruction, and summary of instruction.

efferent (ef'-er-ent) **nerves**   The nerves of the body that convey impulses outward from the nerve centers or the *central nervous system.*

efficacy (ef'-ih-kah-see)   The producing of a desired outcome, or power to produce desired outcomes. Often used in *special education* to refer to studies that seek to evaluate effectiveness of *special class* programs or educational methodology.

efficiency   The ability to produce an effective operation in achieving desired results, as measured by a comparison of cost in time, energy, and money against the amount of work accomplished.

egalitarianism (ee-gal-ih-tare'-ee-an-izm)   A legal principle under which persons with unequal physical and mental abilities are granted equal opportunities.

ego   A term first discussed in Sigmund Freud's writings on *psychoanalytic theory* in the 1890s; the aspect of one's being that serves as an arbitrator between one's inner needs and wishes and the external demands of the environment, thus helping one to better perceive reality; the conscious subject of one's experiences that provides awareness of personal identity.

egocentric   A characteristic of being self-centered in which one regards everything as it relates to oneself and does not heed the needs or rights of others.

EKG   See *electrocardiogram.*

elaboration   One of Guilford's *products* of *creative* thinking, which provides for constructing more complex objects or organizations from available information. (see *structure of the intellect*)

Elective Mutism (313.23)   One of the classifications of the *DSM* III System in which the individual refuses to speak. The person may appear to be incapable of hearing or speaking.

electrocardiogram (eh-lek-troe-kar'-dee-oh-gram) **(EKG)**   A graphic record of the electric charges caused by contraction of the heart muscles as recorded by an **electrocardiograph.**

electrocautery (e-lek-troe-caw'-ter-ee)   See *cauterize.*

electrodermal audiometry (EDA)   A form of *audiometry* used to test the hearing of hard-to-test children and adults. The test is based on measuring skin resistance when responding to sounds. This form of testing is nearly obsolete.

electroencephalogram (eh-lek-troe-en-sef'-ah-loe-gram) **(EEG)**   A mechanical tracing made by an **electroencephalograph** that depicts electrical output of brain waves. An EEG is useful in studying *seizures* accompanying brain injuries, *epilepsy,* etc.

electrolarynx   A mechanical device used by individuals who have had *laryngectomies;* simulates the actions of the *larynx* that has been removed, allowing the person to produce speech.

electromyographic   Describes an *intervention* strategy employing *biofeedback* that is used to control *hyperactivity.*

electroretinograph (ee-lek-troe-ret-in'-oh-graf)   An instrument used to measure the electrical response of the *retina* of the eye when stimulated by light.

electroshock therapy   Treatment of *mental illness* through administration of electrical current, which induces neurological reactions.

Elementary and Secondary Education Act (ESEA)   The first general support of education by the federal government. This act, passed during the Johnson administration, included support for Titles I through Title V, and Title VI was added to cover persons with *handicaps* with provisions similar to the previous five titles.

eligibility   The process of an *assessment* team deciding if an individual meets the criteria, according to state rules and regulations, to be classified according to one type or another handicap. Also the determination process for deciding if a client meets the requirements for rehabilitation services.

ELP   See *estimated learning potential.*

embolism (em'-boe-lizm) The sudden clogging of an artery by a clot or foreign object.

embryonic The second stage of *fetal uterine* development, which lasts from about the end of the second week to the 8th week after conception.

EMH See *educable mentally retarded*.

emmetropia (em-eh-troe'-pea-ah) Refractive condition of the eye perfectly focused for distance so the image of an object focuses directly on the *retina*, without *accommodation*. Condition of the normal eye.

emotional disorder (disturbance) A term applied to individuals who are not able to control their emotions well enough to maintain behavior within an acceptable range. Mildly disturbed students may be served through continued placement in regular classes with supporting service from an *itinerant teacher* or *crisis teacher*. A comparable term used in many states is *behavior disordered*.

emotional lability A condition in which an individual displays unstable moods often characterized by rapid shifts from one extreme to another.

empathy A mental reaction in which one identifies himself/herself in a positive manner with another individual or group. This trait often is cited as being important in relating to or teaching *exceptional individuals*.

empirical Describes the use of observation or experience, sometimes without research design, to gather data to support a conclusion.

employee assistance programs Counseling and *therapy* services offered within agencies and private companies, enabling employees to deal with drug and/or emotional problems and thus have a chance to retain their jobs.

EMR See *educable mentally retarded*.

encephalitis (en-sef-ah-lie'-tis) 1. Any condition that causes *inflammation* of the brain. The condition may result in residual neurological or physiological *disabilities* that inhibit a child's *educational potential*. 2. Also, a disease of the brain caused by a *virus* infection that is contagious; commonly referred to as "sleeping sickness."

encephalography (en-sef-ah-log'-rah-fee) *X-ray* examination of the head following removal of *cerebral spinal fluid* and replacement with air. This *diagnostic* technique allows *x-rays* of the air spaces of the brain that otherwise would not be possible. Also called *pneumoencephalography*.

encephalopathy (en-sef-ah-lop'-ah-thee) Any *degenerative* disease of the brain.

enclaves A term referring to a group of three to four severely handicapped workers who are placed as a group in a supportive employment situation with a job coach.

encoding A *psycholinguistic* process that involves expressing ideas in symbols. An individual may encode by speech or writing. A simpler, synonymous term is *expression*.

encopresis (en-koe-pree'-sis) Inability to control one's bowels; *incontinence* of feces that is not attributable to *organic* defect or illness.

ENCOR   An *acronym* for Eastern Nebraska Community Office of Retardation, which developed a comprehensive system of services and model program. Professionals may refer to the "ENCOR standards."

endocarditis (en-doe-kar-die'-tis)   *Inflammation* of the **endocardium,** or membrane lining, of the heart. This condition especially involves the heart valves.

endocrine (en'-doe-krin) **gland**   One of the ductless glands that produce chemical substances such as *hormones* that pass directly into body fluids. These substances help regulate body functions. Examples: *thyroid gland, pituitary gland.*

endogenous (en-dodge'-eh-nus)   Describes conditions resulting from internal rather than external factors, and includes *hereditary* conditions. In the field of *mental retardation,* usually refers to inherited mental retardation. Opposite of *exogenous.*

endomorphic   One of the body types *(somatotypes)* in Sheldon's classification system; this type is characterized by a fat, stout body and large abdomen, squatness and general roundness of form, with little or no muscle definition.

endorphins (en'-dore-fins)   A class of brain peptides that plays a role in neurochemical aspects of learning, memory, pain, and behavior.

engaged time   A term used in effective instruction indicating the minutes the child is actually paying attention and working.

engineered classroom   A program developed by Frank Hewett and others for students with educational or learning problems. Pupils are assigned specific work based on prior achievement. As new work is completed, a *checkmark system* and *reinforcement* are employed. Cards filled with checkmarks can be exchanged for tangible items or special privileges. The program derives its name from the structure and systematic reinforcement system.

enrichment   The most common approach to teaching *gifted* pupils; *curricular* activities or experiences are expanded into greater depth of understanding and application than those of other students. Enrichment may include resource reading, *creative* projects, community application, special assignments, small group work, and other adaptations of instruction.

entering behavior   A student's behavior before receiving instruction. Instruction or *therapy* should start with reference to these behaviors.

enucleation (ee-noo-klee-ay'-shun)   Removal of the eye, usually necessary when a disease does not respond to treatment and results in *blindness* or when the eye is severely injured by an accident. Treatment may include fitting of an artifical eye to improve appearance and prevent *deterioration* of the eye socket.

enunciation (eh-nun-see-ay'-shun)   Pronouncing words with a distinctness of *articulation* that makes them clearly intelligible to the listener.

enuresis (en-yuh-ree'-sis)   A condition in which an individual involuntarily discharges urine.

environmental deprivation   The concept that lack of stimulation in certain environments can reduce a person's learning capacity.

environmental engineering The use of circumstances and space around a person or group to provide a better learning environment or to effect better control of individual or group behavior. The term *ecological* or *ecosystem* refers to the systematic study of the effect of environment on individuals and groups; this field of investigation demonstrates that factors affecting learning may not relate only to the student or teacher, but that other noninstructional factors can have a strong influence.

environmentalism A school of thought that minimizes *heredity's* effect and emphasizes the influence of one's cultural, physical, and psychological surroundings on one's development and life.

enzyme (en'-zime) An *organic* compound of protein content that serves as a catalyst in producing change in substances. Bodily enzymes are important in the digestive process of converting food to energy, and cellular processes.

epicanthus (ep-ih-kanth'-us) **epicanthal fold** A vertical fold of skin on either side of the nose, which covers the innermost portion of the eye. The presence of this fold gives individuals with *Down syndrome* the appearance of slanted eyes.

epidemiology (ep-ih-deh-mee-ahl'-oh-jee) The branch of medicine that deals with the origin and treatment of epidemic diseases. In *mental retardation* or any field, an **epidemiological** study would deal with search for causes.

epiglottis A lidlike *cartilaginous* structure in the back of the throat that overhangs the *larynx* and prevents food from entering the windpipe.

epilepsy (adj., **epileptic**) A *chronic* condition of the *central nervous system,* characterized by periodic *seizures* accompanied by *convulsions* of the muscles and, with the more severe attacks, loss of consciousness. (see also *grand mal, petit mal, akinetic seizure,* and *myoclonic seizure*)

epiphysis (eh-pih'-fih-sis) The ends of long bones in which growth takes place. Injury to this area may slow or stop growth in a leg or arm.

equal protection The principle set forth in the Fourteenth Amendment that guarantees the same rights and benefits to all citizens with respect to government, unless the withholding of rights and benefits has a justifiable reason—e.g., an *epileptic* person with regular *seizures* may not be allowed a driver's license and certain other rights, to protect others.

equivalent form Describes a test or measure that closely parallels another measure with respect to content, number and difficulty of items, and on which an individual can be expected to obtain similar scores.

erythroblastosis (air-ith-roe-blast-oh'-sis) A condition originating before birth as a result of incompatibility of mother's and baby's blood; characterized in the infant by *anemia, jaundice,* and possibly *kernicterus.* (see also *Rh factor*)

erythrocytes (air-ith'-roe-sites) The red blood cells that perform the important function of carrying oxygen to body cells.

esophageal (eh-sahf-ah-jee'-ul) **speech** A form of speech developed by persons who have had *laryngectomies.* This form of speaking has limited volume and *pitch* but is adequate for communication.

esophagus The tube in the alimentary canal that connects the *pharynx* and stomach. Its primary function is to carry food to the stomach.

esophoria (es-oh-for'-ee-ah) **esotropia** (es-oh-troe'-pea-ah) A muscular defect causing one or both eyes to turn inward. (see *strabismus*)

estimated learning potential (ELP) A term employed in the System of Multicultural Pluralistic Assessment to indicate the expected learning capacity of individuals when compared to children of similar sociocultural levels.

etiology (ee-tee-ahl'-oh-jee) The study or assignment of causes, reasons, or origins, especially of diseases or conditions such as behavior/learning disorders.

eugenics (you-jen'-iks) The science that studies influences for improving inborn or *hereditary* qualities of a race or breed; application of the knowledge of heredity to improve the human race.

eustachian (you-stay'-shun) **tube** A passageway connecting the middle ear with the *posterior* part of the *nasal* cavity *(nasopharynx);* serves to equalize air pressure on both sides of the *ear drum.*

euthanasia (you-thuh-nay'-zee-ah) Painlessly putting one to death, particularly individuals suffering from a fatal, unbearable disease or condition. (see also *infanticide*)

euthenics (you-then'-iks) The science dealing with improvement of living conditions, especially physical aspects such as food, clothing, light, ventilation, and shelter, for the purpose of producing more efficient human beings.

evaluation 1. An appraisal or estimation of certain specific characteristics, such as *intelligence,* personality, or physical aspects of an individual. 2. In Guilford's model (see *structure of the intellect*), judgment of the suitability of information that has been cognized, memorized, or generated.

event recorder A mechanical device for counting the frequency of specific occurrences in a given time period.

event recording A system of taking observational data in which the number of times a behavior occurs is noted. If rocking were the behavior, for example, the teacher would count the number of times the rocking occurred.

evoked-response audiometry A form of *audiometry* based on the changes in brain-wave activity when the brain's response to sounds is measured by an *electroencephalograph.*

exacerbation (egg-zas-er-bay'-shun) Increased severity, as in a disease or *symptoms.*

exceptional child(ren) (exceptionality) One who deviates markedly, either above or below the group *norm,* in mental, emotional, physical, social, or *sensory* traits, to a degree that special services are required to help the individual profit from educational experiences.

excess costs That portion of the annual expenditure for the education of an *exceptional child* that exceeds the average expenditure for a nonexceptional child. Some states fund services under this system.

63

exocrine glands Glands that secrete through a duct, as contrasted with ductless *(endocrine)* glands.

exogenous (egg-zah'-jen-us) Describes a condition resulting from external factors, such as a physical, nonhereditary condition. Opposite of *endogenous.*

exophoria (ek-so-for'-ee-ah) **exotropia** (ek-so-troe'-pea-ah) A deviation in the alignment of one or both eyes so that one or both turn outward. Opposite of *esophoria* and *esotropia.* (see also *strabismus,* a broader term)

exophthalmos (ek-sof-thal'-moss) Abnormal bulging or protrusion of the eyeballs from their sockets.

expectancy table A design measure used to predict how persons with one set of scores will perform. In planning and setting goals for students, ability often is compared to expectancy in achievement.

experience chart A summary of the important knowledge, facts, or principles involved in a topic of classroom discussion or unit that is developed cooperatively by the class, usually written on large sheets of newsprint, often illustrated with pictures, and held on an easel for display.

expression See *encoding.*

expressive aphasia Defect in or loss of the power of expression by speech, writing, or gestures, resulting from injury or disease of the brain centers. *Dysgraphia* (writing disorder) is one form.

expressive language The aspect of communication whereby messages are conveyed verbally, symbolically, or in writing. In contrast, see *receptive language.*

expressive therapy A form of *psychotherapy,* used in treating *behavior disorders,* in which the emphasis is on the individual's talking out or through his/her problems.

expulsion The forced removal of a student from a school program for more than 10 days because of behaviors which are highly disruptive or dangerous. Expulsion necessitates a revision of the student's IEP and must be used with caution with handicapped students.

expunction of records The legally protected review of a child's school records for error and elimination of any errors found.

expungement (egg-sponge'-ment) A process whereby parents and *handicapped* individuals can have previous school, court, and other inappropriate records destroyed.

extended care Provision of prolonged or continuous supervision, care, protection, or custody of an individual.

extended family A term of sociological origin referring to the implications of a home or living environment that includes not only the primary family unit, but grandparents, aunts, uncles, cousins, etc. This larger family unit was common among some ethnic groups in the past but does not usually characterize the modern family.

extended program A *special education* program that goes beyond graduation or past the traditional school age, many times having *vocational education* or *sheltered workshop* elements. Also may be used to refer to extended day programs that exceed the normal school day in length.

64

extended school year (ESY)   A term referring to school programs for handicapped children that extend beyond 180 days; came into wide use in the 1980s with litigation to extend the school year for some handicapped youngsters.

extensor   A muscle that functions to straighten or extend a joint.

extensor thrust reflex   A reaction by some *cerebral palsied* individuals who are overly sensitive to being supported by the back part of the head during feeding or dressing; causes them to stiffen the body and possibly slide out of the chair.

external locus of control   A hypothetical *construct* that holds that one's life, destiny, success, and failure are perceived to be controlled by outside forces. Opposite of *internal locus of control.*

external otitis (oh-tite′-iss)   Often called "swimmer's ear"; an infection of the skin of the external *auditory* canal of the ear.

extinction   The dying out or extinguishing of a specific behavior; may occur as a result of a planned adjustment of goals or needs or removal of *reinforcement* for a response.

extracurricular activities   Programs organized and sponsored by the school to provide exercise of pupil abilities and interests not a part of the regular required *curriculum* (and not accredited). At the secondary level, particularly, *special education* pupils should have the opportunity to be involved in extracurricular activities of their interest and for which they are suited.

extralinguistic   Describes non-language activities such as failure to *discriminate visual* tasks, *distractibility, stereotypic* or self-destructive behaviors that are noncommunicative.

extrapunitive   Descriptive of one's blaming others or expressing one's own anger against others.

extremities   Limbs of the body; the arms and legs.

extrinsic motivation   The use of *incentives* external to the activity involved but valued by the learner, with the intent of improving or facilitating performance of the activity; often involves offering prizes or material rewards for outstanding work.

extrovert (extravert)   A person who is predominantly interested in the external world and social life, as contrasted with an *introvert,* who is predominantly concerned with mental processes involving deep understandings such as reflections or *introspections.*

eye coordination   The ability of an individual's eyes to work together to *focus* on a single *visual* image.

eye-hand coordination   The ability of an individual to combine and coordinate functions of the eyes and the hands in carrying out manipulative activities involving the hands.

facial vision A term used to express the ability of the *blind* to "feel" objects or to perceive their presence with the face.

facio-scapulo-humeral dystrophy A type of *muscular dystrophy* that usually begins in the muscles of the face, shoulders, and upper arms; *symptoms* may vary in intensity, but weakness of facial muscles is usually the most noticeable.

fading Gradually changing or reducing a *stimulus* or *reinforcement* as an individual acquires the desired skills.

Fair Labor Standards Act Commonly known as the Federal Wage and Hour Law; establishes minimum wage, child labor control, overtime, and equal pay standards for employment.

false imprisonment In education, usually refers to teachers' exceeding their authority in confining a student with no reasonable exit. This may involve misuse of *time-out* procedures.

familial (adj.) Occurring in members of the same family and across generations.

familial mental retardation Retardation that is not *diagnosed* as a *clinical* type or caused by *organic brain injury,* but rather having arisen from causes such as cultural inheritance, common exposure to agents associated with social customs, transmission of deleterious *genes,* economic poverty, and factors related to social structure (even when unrelated to economic level).

family care service A term sometimes used in place of *foster home*; includes an expanded role for contract care of persons with *handicaps* to live in the community.

family involvement program An educational innovation developed by Merle Karnes and others emphasizing parents, family, and home as instructional units.

family neurosis A mental disorder that affects all members of a family group to some degree. Members show tension, *anxiety, hysteria, phobias,* obsessions, and, in general, unusual mannerisms.

Family Rights and Privacy Act (Buckley Amendment) A law that gives parents of students under 18 years of age and students over 18 the right of access to the student's school records. The *local education agency* must maintain confidential students' records and make them available within 45 days of a request by an eligible person to see them.

family therapy A counseling or *therapeutic* method in which problems are viewed as being those of the entire family and therefore are treated in the *context* of a family unit.

fantasy A product of a vivid imagination usually dealing with fictitious images. Fantasy can be a means of adjusting to strong desires or emotions. In moderation, it may be satisfying, but when allowed to replace constructive thoughts, it can become an educational interference.

FAPE Acronym for *free appropriate public education,* one of the major provisions of *PL 94-142.*

farsighted(ness) See *hyperopia.*

FAS See *fetal alcohol syndrome.*

febrile (feb'-ril) Accompanied or marked by fever.

feces (fee'-seez) (adj., **fecal**) Waste matter discharged from the body during bowel movements; stools.

feeblemindedness A term of British origin that refers to a level of *intelligence* comparable to the educational classification *educable mentally retarded* or the American Association on Mental Retardation's classification *mild mental retardation.* The *intellectual* level when assessed with an individual intelligence test would involve *IQ* scores ranging from 50 to 70. (This term is no longer used in the United States or in current literature.)

feedback Transmittal of information that allows improvement of *motor* or *cognitive* responses based on previous information or response.

femur The large bone located between the hip and the knee.

fenestration (fen-eh-stray'-shun) **operation** Surgery in which an opening is cut in the bone between the *ear drum* and the inner ear to replace an obstructed natural opening that was causing *hearing impairment.*

feral (fear'-uhl) **child** One who has been reared in isolation or by animals in the wild and is, therefore, uncivilized. Some 23 cases have been recorded, of which the most noted was Victor, with whom Itard worked.

Fernald method A *multisensory* approach to learning reading words. The words to be learned are written in large letters on newsprint or in sand. The child then traces the letters with the index finger while saying them aloud. The combined *visual, tactile,* and *auditory* stimulation increases the potential for learning the words. (see also *VAKT*)

fetal alcohol syndrome (FAS) A condition found in some infants of alcoholic women, marked by low birth weight, *retardation, cardiac* and physical defects.

fetal stage The time period from about the 8th week of pregnancy until birth.

fetoscopy (fcc'-toe-skop-ee) A *diagnostic* technique used during the *prenatal* period to visually examine the *uterine* environment. A needlelike device with a light and lens is inserted through the abdomen to allow examination of disorders not picked up by *amniocentesis* and *alpha-fetoprotein* tests.

fetus The developing organism during the period of pregnancy from the 8th week after conception until birth; often applied to all pre-birth existence.

fibrosis (fie-broe'-sis) The formation of fibrous tissue, as in *cystic fibrosis.*

fibula (fih'-byew-luh) The smaller of the two bones of the lower leg, situated to the outer side of the larger bone, the *tibia.*

field defect A blind area in the *field of vision;* the individual does not see in that portion of the eye.

field of vision The entire area one can see without shifting the gaze. In *visually impaired* individuals, a reduction in field of vision can be considered a handicapping condition.

figural One of Guilford's materials of thought (see *structure of the intellect*), which includes *visual* objects with their properties of shape, size, color, etc.; *auditory* elements in the form of rhythms, melodies, speech sounds; *tactual* and *kinesthetic* materials.

figure-background disturbance The tendency to confuse immediately important components of the environment, which are referred to as figure, with less important aspects of the environment, which are referred to as background or ground. This disturbance may cause pupils to show poor judgment in selecting figures, or they may completely reverse the background and figure, which interferes with problem-solving activities.

filial therapy *Nondirective,* or *client-centered, therapy* conducted by parents under the direction of a professional *therapist.*

fine motor Refers to skills involving the small muscle groups, primarily of the hands. Fine motor skills are involved in drawing, etc. In contrast, see *gross motor.*

fingerspelling A method of communication used by the *deaf;* a process of using different combinations of the hands and fingers to indicate letters in spelling words. Also termed *dactylology.* Used to facilitate *manual communication* by spelling out letter by letter proper names, etc., that lack manual signs.

First Chance Programs established by Congress in 1968, giving opportunities for educational training for young children with *handicaps* and their families, encouraging further training in the model procedures used, and stimulating development of new programs for these young children.

first priority children Defined by *PL 94-142* as school-aged *handicapped* children and youth who are not receiving any education and must be served first educationally.

fissure Any opening or failure to close, as in *cleft palate.*

Fitzgerald key A system of teaching *language* structure by classifying parts of sentences according to function. The key was developed for use with *deaf* children, but its application has broadened to programs for other *handicaps* as well.

68

fixed interval reinforcement   A system of rewards in which the reinforcement is given following the lapse of a specified amount of time (e.g., reinforcement is given every 5 minutes if the desired behavior is apparent).

fixed ratio reinforcement   A schedule of rewards in which the reinforcement is given after a behavior has been successfully performed a specified number of times (e.g., reinforcement is given after three math problems have been answered correctly).

flaccid (flack'-sid) **(flaccidity)**   Describes poor muscle tone in which the muscle is flabby, soft, weak, and considered unhealthy. In contrast, see *tonus*.

Flanders interaction analysis system   A procedure for observing a classroom in which interactions between the teacher and pupils are recorded and analyzed to determine how well the teacher is interacting with the pupils.

flex (v.)   To bend, as in flexing a joint or muscle in a continuous *reciprocal* motion.

flexibility of thinking   One of Guilford's factors in *creative* thinking, representing the variety of ideas produced by a person. (see also *structure of the intellect*)

flow-through funds   Monies available under *PL 94-142* that are passed through the *state education agency (SEA)* to the *local education agency (LEA)*.

fluency   1. Uninterrupted smoothness and rapidity, as in reading or speaking. 2. In Guilford's *structure of the intellect,* the factors in *creative* thinking that represent the quality and the number of ideas produced.

fluency disorder   One of the types of communication or speech problems, characterized by interrupted flow or rhythm of speech. The best example is *stuttering.* (see also *dysfluency*)

focal length   The distance from the eye to the object in line of sight.

focal seizure   A malfunction that begins with a twitching in a specific part of the body (e.g., finger), which is associated with a *lesion* in the corresponding *motor* area of the brain and which may generalize to *grand mal* seizures. (see also *Jacksonian seizure*)

focus   (n.) The point at which light rays converge to project a clear image (as on the *retina* of the eye). (v.) To adjust a lens system to produce a sharp, clear picture.

follow up   To provide later *diagnosis* and treatment after the initial diagnosis and treatment of a condition. Also, to continue supervisory and training services after an individual leaves a vocational *work-study* or *rehabilitation* program. Also used as a noun and an adjective, and more *generically* to denote any contact or service subsequent to the first one.

following technique   The act of a *blind* person lightly holding on to a sighted person's elbow while walking. Also called *sighted guide technique.*

fonator   An electronic device that converts spoken words into vibrations or vibrator speech patterns, which can be used by *hearing impaired* children as an aid to their "hearing" and learning of speech; this adds *tactual* information to the *visual* signals already received.

69

fontanel (fon-tah-nel') The soft-spot area in the skull, or *cranium,* of a newborn child that has not yet become *ossified* and hardened. Sometimes called "birth spot."

footedness Preference for using one foot (either right or left) over the other, especially for performing tasks that require use of only one foot. (see *lateral dominance*)

form constancy The ability to recognize letters or other basic shapes regardless of color, size, or variations. This is extremely important in reading when different type faces and styles are used.

formal assessment (testing) A procedure in which normed or *norm-referenced* tests are used to measure specified characteristics. These tests, usually produced and sold commercially, are often referred to as *standardized tests.* The individual's score is compared to the norm or how other children perform.

forward chaining Teaching behaviors by beginning with the first behavioral segment and adding each behavioral segment in natural order. *Reinforcement* is provided for larger and larger component sequences until the entire behavior pattern is maintained by the final reinforcing event. In contrast, see *backward chaining.*

Foster Grandparents A program initiated in 1965, using older Americans in volunteer programs for children, particularly individuals who have *mental retardation* and are in *institutions.*

foster home A living environment other than one with the parents, in which a child may be placed for rearing, usually by a family or welfare agency. (see also *family care service* and *developmental training home*)

foster parent An individual who assumes legal responsibility for rearing a child and takes the place of the child's parents for a period of time but does not necessarily adopt the child. (see also *advocacy/advocate*)

fovea (foe'-vee-ah) A small area of the *retina* of the eye in which vision is the most distinct or clear.

fracture A break of a bone. (a) compound—fracture with external wounds; (b) comminuted—bone crushed or splintered; (c) compression—joint jammed together; (d) greenstick—fracture on one side of bone and other side bent; (e) impacted—one fragment driven into another.

fragile X syndrome A familial form of *mental retardation* resulting from a *genetic* marker on the X *chromosome.* Affects males, and females are carriers of the condition.

fragmented perception Having only partial or incomplete understanding of information received, in conjunction with a *learning disorder.*

free appropriate public education (FAPE) One of the key requirements of *PL 94-142,* which requires an educational program for all children without cost to parents. This does not mean the best possible education but, when combined with *least restrictive environment,* implies that the individual is to receive the education and *related services* that will bring about an adequate program.

free association A technique to encourage *creative* thought or to appraise thought processes, which requires the reporting of thoughts as they come to mind.

Freedom for All A series of Acts incorporating the principle of restoring rights to the physically, mentally, and *sensory handicapped* by repealing all other Acts or portions of Acts that restrict their rights. Such Acts reinstate the rights of the *epileptic* to marry, to vote, etc.

freedom from peonage A principle based on the Thirteenth Amendment that guarantees all persons freedom from having to work without pay; as applied to persons with *handicaps,* they do not have to work unless they so choose and, if so, are assured fair labor standards and a decent wage.

frenum A fold of skin under the tongue which, if attached too near the end, has been referred to as "tongue-tied." The condition can be corrected early in life through simple surgery.

frequency In the area of hearing, the physical parameter of sound that refers to the number of vibrations of a sound in one second. Frequency is expressed in *hertz (Hz).*

frequency distribution When counting behaviors, the record of the number of times that a behavior occurs in a given time interval or intervals.

fricative (frick'-uh-tiv) A *consonant* sound produced by forcing voiced or unvoiced breath through a limited opening (such as *f* in *fat, sh* in *shut*).

Friedreich's ataxia A *hereditary* disease of children that causes hardening of the spinal cord and results in *paralysis* of the lower limbs and *impairment* of speech. The condition affects males and females equally with onset usually in the 7 to 10 years after birth. The disorder is progressive, usually resulting in death by 30 years of age.

Frölich's syndrome A combination of conditions including *retardation*, obesity, small stature, and failure of sexual development resulting from *pituitary hypothalmic dysfunction.*

frustration-aggression hypothesis A theory holding that frustration leads to aggression as a natural consequence.

FTE Stands for "full-time equivalent"; incorporated in some state financial formulas in which teacher loads for six periods are used to figure teacher allotment.

functional Denotes nonorganic or without apparent structural cause. In *retardation,* it signifies lack of *brain injury.*

functional curriculum An educational program for mildly *mentally retarded* persons that emphasizes preparing students to cope with and solve persistent life problems, to be able to live successfully in the community. (see also *community education*)

functional hearing loss Inability to hear, stemming from psychological problems rather than from *impairment* of the ear, or *auditory* mechanism.

functional language A communication system that is usable and allows an individual to make known his/her needs. The term is used primarily with reference to *severely handicapped* persons to connote a language goal or function the teacher is seeking to develop.

71

functional literacy   The level of communication ability that is necessary to live adequately in society. An individual usually has to read above the fourth grade level to have much chance for success in independent living.

functionally blind   The condition of *visual impairment* in which the individual is not able to use print as a reading medium. (see also *educationally blind*)

fundamentals   The basic knowledge or skills of an area of study or activity, such as the fundamentals of arithmetic.

fusion   In vision, the process of combining images seen by both eyes into one image.

G

galactosemia (gah-lak-toe-see′-mee-ah) A *hereditary* disease identified by the body's inability to convert the galactose part of the lactose molecule in milk to glucose in a normal way for proper body use. If not identified and treated by a controlled diet, results in *mental retardation* and, sometimes, *cataracts* and liver damage.

Gallaudet (gal-uh-det′) **College** A federally supported institution of higher learning for *deaf* students; located in Washington, DC.

gamma globulin (gam′-ah glob′-you-lin) The part of the blood *plasma* that contains *antibody* activity to fight infection and diseases.

gargoyle, gargoylism (gar′-goil-izm) See *Hurler's disease.*

gastric Pertaining to, originating in, or affecting the stomach.

gene Specific part of the *chromosome* that carries *hereditary* characteristics.

geneology (jee-nee-ahl′-oh-jee) The study and recording of descent of an individual or a family from its ancestors.

general learning disability (GLD) A term to be used in preference to *educable mental retardation* and implying generalized learning problems as opposed to a *specific learning disability. This term has not received wide usage.*

generalization (of learning) A statement of or a process of forming a conclusion based on or inferred from a number of specific facts or instances. Lack of ability to generalize learning to situations other than that in which the learning occurred is characteristic of children with reduced *intelligence.*

generalization training Instruction designed to help pupils transfer knowledge or skills learned in one situation to other situations.

generic (jeh-nare′-ik) (adv., **generically**) Having to do with a group of similar things and inclusive of all things in the group or class in general. Usually used in reference to a set of materials or teaching techniques applied with children of differing diagnoses.

genetic (jeh-net′-ik) Pertaining to *heredity,* or features transmitted by *chromosomes* from parents to their offspring. Certain characteristics such as skin, hair, and eye coloring, and conditions such as *Down syndrome* are **genetically** determined.

73

genetics (and genetic counseling) The systematic study of biological inheritance. Genetics has become an integral part of counseling for family planning when there is concern that offspring might inherit a disabling condition; genetic counseling reveals the likelihood of handicapping conditions, based on probability statistics, *chromosome* studies, *amniocentesis,* and other factors.

genius An individual who demonstrates exceptionally high mental ability. No specific *IQ* score has been universally accepted as indicating such a level; however, an IQ of 150 or more would in most cases be considered as genius level.

genotype (jee´-noe-tipe) The total inherited characteristics of an individual. This *genetic* endowment establishes a range within which behavior can develop in relation to the individual's environment.

geriatrics (jare-ee-at´-rix) **gerontology** (jare-un-tol´-oh-jee) The study of problems accompanying old age and the treatment of diseases during this period of life.

German measles (rubella) A disease caused by a *virus* infection. Infection of a woman during early stages of pregnancy results in a high *incidence* of severe *handicaps* in the offspring including *mental retardation, cardiac* abnormalities, *cerebral palsy,* and *sensory* (hearing and vision) handicaps. Vaccinations for rubella are now routinely given to children.

gestalt (geh-stawlt´ or geh-shtalt´) A theory based on the viewpoint that events or behaviors do not occur through summation of separate parts, but that the whole becomes more than the sum of the parts.

gestation (jeh-stay´-shun) The time period in which a developing baby is carried in the *uterus;* the period of pregnancy.

gifted(ness) A designation for an individual who possesses unusually high ability. No specific *IQ* has been universally set to indicate the *intellectual* level of giftedness; however, an IQ of 130 or more sometimes has been used as a standard, in conjunction with other traits such as *creativity.*

gifted and talented A more encompassing term than "gifted," to include high ability in the creative and performing arts.

Gillingham method A highly structured *phonic* system of teaching reading; begins by teaching the sounds of letters and builds these letter sounds systematically into words.

glaucoma (glaw-koe´-muh) A condition of the eye in which internal pressure causes hardening of the eyeballs; if not treated, it results in *impairment* of vision or *blindness.*

global intelligence Refers to the combined effects of all the traits in one's *intellect.*

glottis (glot´-iss) One's vocal apparatus, consisting of the vocal cords and the space between them.

glycemia (gly-see´-mee-ah) The presence of glucose in the blood. (see also *hyperglycemia*)

gonococcus (gon-oh-kok´-us) The individual microorganism that causes *gonorrhea.*

74

gonorrhea (gon-oh-ree'-ah) A *venereal disease* occurring in both sexes; may lead to *cutaneous lesions, arthritis,* and sterility. A *fetus* may contract gonorrhea from an infected mother at birth.

Gower's sign A symptom of *Duchenne* type *muscular dystrophy,* in which a weakness of back and stomach muscles causes a child to "walk up" his/her legs using the hands to facilitate reaching an upright standing position.

grade equivalent A way of expressing what a particular *raw score* represents in terms of average school achievement. Thus, a raw score of 24 may be interpreted as being most like children at the fifth month of the fourth grade—4-5. (see also *age equivalent*)

grade level An indication of educational *maturity* designated by the school grade corresponding to an individual's achievement record. Usually, grade level can be established by subtracting 5 from *chronological age.*

grade norm See *grade equivalent.*

Grade I braille The first, or introductory, level of *braille,* in which every word is spelled out.

Grade II braille The advanced level of *braille,* in which students are taught to use or read contractions of words and phrases. It improves the speed of reading and transcription because it is a shortened form.

grand mal A severe form of *epileptic* seizure involving loss of consciousness and extreme *convulsions.*

grapheme (graf'-eem) A written symbol representative of a spoken *language* sound. The printed representation of a *phoneme.*

graphesthesia (graf-es-thee'-zee-ah) The ability to recognize letters traced on the skin. Lack of this ability may be considered a *"soft" sign* of *minimal brain dysfunction.*

gross motor Refers to large muscle activity. Activities such as rolling, crawling, walking, running, throwing, and jumping are examples of the use of gross motor skills. In contrast, see *fine motor.*

group home A form of *alternative living* arrangement in which *retarded* and *multi-handicapped* individuals live in a community setting rather than in an *institution.* (see also *developmental training home*)

group intelligence test Any instrument, designed to measure *intelligence,* that can be administered to several persons at a time as opposed to being administered individually.

group therapy An approach to *psychotherapy* in which small units of individuals are treated at the same time. Positive factors of this approach are that it is financially economical, uses professional personnel more efficiently than the one-to-one approach, and allows individuals in the group to help each other.

guardianship A legally sanctioned relationship between a competent adult and a minor or handicapped individual. The guardian has the authority and duty to make and effect decisions within the limits set by the court.

guide dog A trained dog used by blind persons in *mobility*. Also called lead dog or seeing eye dog (the latter is least preferred).

guttural speech A speech and *voice disorder* in which the *pitch* is likely to be lower than normal and the voice gives the impression of falling back into the throat; sometimes referred to as "raspy."

gynecology (guy-neh-kahl'-oh-jee) A branch of medicine that deals with treating females and their unique diseases.

habilitation The process of training and providing services for the improvement of an individual's total range of function. Habilitation implies development of skills for successful living or employment, in most cases, whereas *rehabilitation* implies that the person once had normal functioning or employment and is being retrained or rehabilitated.

habilitation plan A program for each individual receiving *developmental disabilities* funds; includes a written *assessment* and treatment plan.

halfway house A temporary *residential* unit usually operated by an *institution* for the purpose of training participants to live with a greater degree of independence than is provided within the institutional setting, and which may be directed at preparing an individual to live independently within the community.

hallucination An abnormal mental condition in which a person has the impression that imaginary things are real. The person also may see or hear nonexisting objects or sounds.

hallucinogen (adj., **hallucinogenic**) Any drug that causes *hallucinations.*

halo effect Any impression given by an individual or group (as in research studies) that causes a rater's estimate of specific abilities or traits of that individual or group to be consistently too high or too low.

handedness The preference of either the right or the left hand to be used predominantly in performing tasks, particularly tasks requiring the use of only one hand.

handicap (adj., **handicapped**) The result of any condition or deviation, physical, mental, or emotional, that inhibits or prevents achievement or acceptance. (see also *disability*)

handicapism A term referring to prejudice, stereotyping, and discrimination against the *handicapped.*

haptic A term first used by Victor Lowenfeld to refer to the *kinesthetic* and *tactile feedback* that a child receives through movement and touch. Includes all the sensations derived from the skin receptors for contact, pressure, pain, warmth, and cold. If the haptic sense is impaired, individuals may have difficulty making the correct *motor* responses. Some children with *learning disabilities* appear to have haptic deficiencies.

hard of hearing   A condition of reduced *auditory acuity* to the degree that special services, such as auditory training, *speech* (or lip) reading, speech therapy, or a *hearing aid* may be required. With proper adaptations, many hard of hearing individuals can be educated as effectively as hearing children.

hard palate   See *palate.*

hardware   Pieces of equipment used in providing a service; e.g., teaching machines, *microcomputers,* amplification equipment. Utilizes *software.*

harelip   See *cleft lip*, the preferred term.

Head Start   A nationwide program instituted in 1965 to provide preschool experiences for economically disadvantaged children.

health impairment   A condition that may result in a child's requiring *special education.* Any condition or disease that interferes with an individual's state of optimal physical, mental, or social well-being. Often used in reference to diseases that result in low vitality or progressive *deterioration.*

health service system   New terminology for all health, medical, and *related services* coordinated by one agency or plan.

hearing acuity   How well one can hear. Commonly measured by audiometric testing *(audiometry).*

hearing aid   Any of a number of devices used for collecting, conducting, and amplifying sound waves, to help the user utilize his/her hearing capacity to the maximum.

hearing loss (impairment)   A deficiency in one's ability to hear. May range from a mild loss to a total lack of hearing ability *(deafness).* At the level of severe loss, defined as 70–90 *db,* measured on an *audiometer*, **hearing impaired** individuals require extensive training in communication methods.

hearing officer   A person who is trained by the State to conduct *due process* hearings and render decisions. Many hearing officers are lawyers, but the primary requirement is that they are not employed by the school system.

hearing threshold   The level at which the individual can detect sound 50% of the time. The hearing level is measured in *decibels (db)* on an *audiometer.*

heart defect   Any of a number of *cardiac* conditions resulting from *malformations,* mechanical imperfections, or injuries to the heart, its muscles, or vessels leading to and from it. Heart defects most often are classified as congenital or acquired. *Congenital* conditions are usually malformations or mechanical defects, and acquired conditions may be injuries or residual effects of diseases such as *rheumatic fever.*

Hebb's theory   A viewpoint of *conceptual* and *perceptual* neural organization that advocates that a *stimulus* of a sense organ activates a chain of upper *central nervous system* cells called a "cell assembly" that, upon repetition, produces a stable perception. A series of cell assemblies produced by related stimuli forms a "phase sequence," which allows sequential perceptions while the relating of the stimuli to previously learned perceptions is handled by another *neural* organization called "phase cycles." Hebb's theory often has been applied in *mental retardation* as a basis for instructional technology and research.

Heller's disease (dementia infantilis) A *degenerative metabolic* disorder involving *atrophy* of the brain and nerve cells. This condition usually occurs at about 3 or 4 years of age, at which time the child becomes irritable, negativistic, and disobedient.

hematology (hee-muh-tahl'-oh-jee) The study and science of the composition and function of the blood.

hematoma (hee-mah-toe'-mah) A tumor filled with blood.

hemiatrophy (hem-ee-at'-roe-fee) The *degeneration* or wasting away of an organ or muscular portion of the body on one side only. The word stems from hemi (half) and *atrophy* (wasting away).

hemi– A prefix meaning half.

hemiplegia (heh-mih-plee'-juh) **hemiparesis** *Paralysis* of the arm and leg on one side of the body. The latter term implies lesser severity.

hemisphere One half of any spherical body structure or organ. Either half of the brain, for example, is called a hemisphere (right or left).

hemoglobin The red pigment in the red blood cells that performs the function of carrying oxygen.

hemophilia (hee-moe-fee'-lee-ah) A condition, usually *hereditary,* characterized by failure of the blood to clot following an injury. Profuse bleeding, internal as well as external, occurs from even slight injuries. Found primarily in males, because of hereditary determination factors. An individual with this affliction is called a **hemophiliac.**

hemorrhage An abnormal discharge of blood from a blood vessel, usually caused by an injury, but may be caused by rupture, or break, of a vessel under undue pressure changes.

hepatitis (hep-ah-tie'-tiss) Any of the disease conditions in which the primary characteristic is *inflammation* of the liver. (see also *infectious hepatitis*)

hepatolenticular (hep-ah-toe-len-tih'-cue-lar) **degeneration** See *Wilson's disease.*

heredity (adj., **hereditary**) The biological *genetic* process by which an organism produces offspring of similar or comparable structure. Significant in *special education* because of the number of traits or types of deficiencies transferred to offspring by *genes.*

hernia A result of the breaking down of specific muscles, allowing protrusion of a part of an organ or tissue through an abnormal opening of the body.

herpes (her'-peez) A *viral disease.* The most common type results in cold sores or fever blisters. Another type causes ulcers on the adult genitalia, which may infect an infant progressing down the birth canal. Herpes in infants attacks the brain and in many newborns is rapidly fatal. If the baby lives, *brain damage* usually is profound. Herpes in the newborn may be prevented by good *prenatal* care and delivery of the child by *caesarean section.*

herpes simplex One of several types of organisms that cause infection on the lips and genitals. Pregnant mothers with the genital type of infection can give birth to children who have *mental retardation.*

79

hertz (Hz)   A unit of measurement of *frequency,* or vibrations per second of sound waves; formerly, cycles per second (cps).

heterogeneous (het-er-oh-jee'-nee-us) **heterogenous** (het-er-ah'-jen-us)   Consisting of dissimilar parts that may come from a wide range of sources and not have uniform quality throughout; e.g., a group of students with a wide range of abilities. Opposite of *homogeneous,* or *homogenous.*

heterophoria (het-er-oh-fore'-ee-uh)   A general term for a defect in the muscle balance of the eyes, in which the deviation is latent and not as apparent as in *strabismus.* When the eyes pull toward the nose, it is called *esophoria;* when the eyes pull away from the nose, it is called *exophoria;* when the eyes tend to pull up, it is called *hyperphoria;* down, it is *hypophoria.*

"high grade" mental retardate   An archaic term of *institutional* origin, classifying individuals with less severe retardation as "high grade" (in contrast to those with more severe retardation as "low grade"). Comparable to the preferred term *mild mental retardation.*

high-risk   Describes children who come from families with a record of *disabilities* or *handicaps.* The risk may have *genetic* origins or result from a lack of activities that stimulate development. (see also *at-risk*)

hirsutism (her'-suit-izm)   Abnormal hairiness, often an adverse reaction to certain kinds of *drug therapy.* In contrast, see *hypotrichosis.*

histidenemia (hiss-tih-deh-nee'-mee-ah)   A *metabolic* disorder sometimes resulting in *mental retardation,* retarded growth, and speech *impairment.* The condition results from an abnormal level of **histidine** in the blood because of a deficiency of the *enzyme* **histidose.**

HIV   Human immunodeficiency virus, the agent that causes *AIDS.*

hives   An eruptive skin condition usually caused by a reaction of the body to a specific substance or sometimes considered to be of emotional origin.

hoarse(ness)   A *voice disorder* characterized by harshness and a grating, breathy quality comparable to that otherwise accompanying a cold or other irritation of the *larnyx.*

Hodgkin's disease   A *malignant* condition involving a painless, progressive enlargement of the *lymph* nodes and spleen. Related *symptoms* may be loss of appetite, weight loss, fever, night sweating, and *anemia.*

holophrastic (hoe-loe-fras'-tik) **speech**   Use of the single word to express an underlying complex intention or situation. For example, a child may say "bottle" and mean, "I want my bottle." Also called *kernel sentence.*

homebound instruction   Teaching provided for students who are unable to attend school. Home instruction represents one of the options in the *service delivery system* of *special education.*

homeostasis (hoe-mee-oh-stay'-sis)   A condition of stability in body functions. This is achieved by a system of control mechanisms that are activated when the functions become unbalanced.

homogeneous (hoe-moe-jee'-nee-us); **homogenous** (hoe-mah'-jeh-nus) Consisting of similar parts and having a uniform quality throughout. For example, a *self-contained class* would be more homogenous than a regular *mainstreamed* classroom. Opposite of *heterogeneous,* or *heterogenous.*

homophones (adj., **homophonous**) (hoe-mah'-fuh-nus) Different sounds that are identical in terms of external appearance on the lips. Homophones cannot be distinguished by *hearing impaired speech readers* (e.g., pan, pen, pin.)

honeymoon period The time period when a new program starts when students may not express the behaviors they were referred for. Research and data collection during such early stages may yield inappropriate or misleading research.

Honig v. Doe A landmark case in which the Supreme Court set forth limitations on suspensions and expulsions of handicapped students from schools.

honor society or **honors program** A selective system of membership recognizing individuals with a high level of academic achievement. Often a part of a school's provision for *gifted* students. A student who achieves at or above a specific high level, as designated by school policy, may receive the designation of **honor student.**

Hoover cane A long, thin cane designed by Richard Hoover to assist *blind* persons in safe and effective *mobility,* or movement from one place to another. Also called *long cane.*

hormone A chemical substance produced by the ductless glands of the body, secreted directly into the bloodstream, and involved in helping to regulate body functions.

hortitherapy A term coined by Carl Menninger in the 1930s to describe the beneficial effects to disabled individuals of growing and working with plants. The *therapeutic* benefits led to establishment of the National Council for Therapy and Rehabilitation through Horticulture (NCTRH).

hospital/homebound instruction The teaching of students who are hospitalized or confined to their homes because of illness, accident, recuperation following surgery, or any handicapping condition that doesn't allow them to attend regular school.

houseparent A person employed to provide supervision and guidance to children, adolescents, or adults as a *surrogate* mother or father in a *residential* setting such as an *institution,* a *group home,* or a *halfway house.*

human service system New terminology used to refer to educational, *rehabilitative,* medical, welfare, and other needs combined into a unified program to reduce confusion in services.

humanistic education An approach to teaching or instructing people that emphasizes the dignity and worth of each individual and holds that a person has within himself/herself the ability to correct the imbalance between an individual and his/her environment. Incorporates the thinking of Carl Rogers and others.

Huntington's chorea (koe-ree'-uh) A *hereditary* condition that results in a wide variety of rapid, jerky, involuntary movements.

Hurler's syndrome A *hereditary metabolic* disturbance that may cause *mental retardation* and general progressive physical *deterioration* until, if not treated, death occurs. Characterized by physical abnormalities including thickened lips, broad bridge of nose, and many other identifiable characteristics. Sometimes called *gargoylism.*

huskiness A voice quality characterized by roughness in tone and generally of a relatively low *pitch.* Could be a *symptom* of a *voice disorder.*

hyaline membrane disease A condition that affects the lungs of newborn, especially, premature infants, caused by the formation of a membrane between the lung capillaries and the tiny air sacs (alveoli), interfering with passage of oxygen into the blood and of carbon dioxide out of the body after it returns as waste from the lungs. Sometimes results in death.

hydrocephalus (hydrocephaly) (hie-dro-sef'-uh-lus) (-lee) A condition of excess *cerebrospinal fluid* accumulation in the *cranial* cavity, causing undue pressure on the brain and resulting in an enlarged head. Formerly referred to sometimes as "waterhead." Now, surgical procedures such as *shunting* are used to reduce fluid pressure and head enlargement. If unchecked, the condition usually causes *mental retardation.*

hydrotherapy A method of treating *disabilities* or disease using water, as in creating pressure by a forced flow of water.

hyper– A prefix designating an excess, more than desirable.

hyperactive (adj.) (n., **hyperactivity**) Describes behavior characterized by abnormal, excessive activity or movement. This activity may interfere with a child's learning and cause considerable problems in managing behavior.

hyperglycemia (hie-purr-glie-see'-mee-ah) A condition of excessive sugar in the blood, resulting in excessive thirst, frequent urination, weakness, rapid breathing, and sometimes *coma.* In contrast, see *hypoglycemia.*

hyperhemolytic (hie-purr-hee-moe-lit'-ik) **crisis** An abnormal destruction of red blood cells resulting in loss of *hemoglobin* and interfering with nourishment of cells, as in *sickle cell anemia.*

hyperkinetic (adj.) (n., **hyperkinesis**) (hie-purr-kin-ee'-sis) Characterized by excessive *motor* activity, inattention, and *impulsivity.* This terminology is used in the medical field with reference to *hyperactive* and *distractible* children.

hyperlexia Calling words by sight with little or no *comprehension* of their meanings.

hypermetropia See *ametropia.*

hypernasal (hypernasality) Describes excessive sound emission through *nasal* passages during speech, as in *cleft palate* speech.

hyperopia (hie-purr-oh'-pea-ah) **(farsightedness)** Poor vision at close range, because of shortened eyeball from back to front so the light rays tend to focus behind the *retina.* Hyperopia most often is corrected by using *convex lenses,* which bend the rays so they will focus on the retina. In contrast, see *myopia.*

hyperoxia (hie-purr-ock'-see-ah) An excess of oxygen in the body.

hyperphoria A muscle defect of the eyes, causing a deviation in which the eyes pull up. (see also *heterophoria*)

hyperplasia (hie-purr-play'-zee-ah) An abnormal multiplication of elements comprising a part of the body, such as cells of an organ or a tissue.

hypertelorism A condition characterized by an abnormally great distance between the eyes and broadening of the base of the nose. In itself, hypertelorism is not a disease, but it is associated with several forms of *mental retardation.*

hypertension A condition characterized by abnormally high arterial blood pressure. An individual with hypertension may have no symptoms or may have symptoms such as headaches, dizziness, or nervousness. Hypertension may lead to a *stroke.*

hyperthyroidism A condition characterized by excessive activity of the *thyroid* gland, which may result in weight changes, *hyperactivity,* nervousness, and similar behaviors.

hypertonia Excessive muscular tension.

hypertrichosis (hie-purr-trik-oh'-sis) A condition characterized by excessive body hair. (see also *hirsutism*)

hypertrophy Abnormal enlargement of a body organ or part. Hypertrophy of the gums is a possible side effect from using the drug Dilantin.

hyperventilation Excessive respiration characterized by short, rapid breath, and possibly loss of consciousness. The condition causes (usually temporarily) an abnormal loss of carbon dioxide from the blood.

hypnosis (adj., **hypnotic**) An induced state of passivity in which the subject has increased responsiveness to suggestions and commands provided that they do not conflict with the subject's conscious wishes.

hypnotherapy The use of *hypnosis* to change behavior or treat a disease.

hypo– A prefix designating lower or less than desirable.

hypoactive Showing an obvious loss or absence of physical activity. Opposite of *hyperactive.*

hypochondria (hie-poe-kahn'-dree-ah) A state of being unusually anxious about one's health, often accompanied by imaginary illnesses.

hypodermic Describes administration of medicine under the skin, as an injection.

hypogenitalism (hie-poe-jeh'-nih-tah-lizm) Decreased growth of sexual organs and secondary sexual characteristics.

hypoglycemia (hie-poe-glie-see'-mee-ah) Low glucose content in the blood caused by an increase in *metabolism* resulting from too much exercise, too much *insulin* (insulin reaction), not enough food, or nervous tension. In contrast, see *hyperglycemia.*

hypokinesia (hie-poe-kih-nee'-zee-ah) Abnormally reduced *motor* activity with possible appearance of laziness.

hypolexia Low reading level or ability in a person of high *intelligence.*

83

hypometabolism Body *metabolism* of well below normal rates and an abnormally decreased utilization of material by the body.

hyponasality See *denasal speech*

hypophoria A defect in the eye muscles, causing the eyes to pull down. (see also *heterophoria*)

hypoplasia (hie-poe-play´-zee-ah) A term referring to decreased or arrested growth of an organ or tissue. In some forms of *mental retardation,* the genitals do not develop normally and the person is said to have hypoplasia.

hypotension Below normal blood pressure. This is often a result of shock but may derive from other causes.

hypothalamus (hie-poe-thal´-ah-mus) (adj., **hypothalmic**) A nerve center of the brain that lies beneath the thalamus on each side. It encompasses regulatory centers of *autonomic* (involuntary) body functions.

hypothyroidism A condition caused by an abnormally low secretion level of the *thyroid* gland. If this condition occurs to a severe degree during early childhood and is not treated, *cretinism* may result.

hypotonia A neuromuscular disorder characterized by weak, *flaccid* muscles.

hypotrichosis Less than the usual amount of bodily hair.

hypoxemia (hie-pok-see´-mee-ah) Reduced oxygen supply in the blood.

hypoxia (hie-pok´-see-ah) A condition characterized by a low content of oxygen in the air being inhaled, which results in a deficiency of oxygen carried by the blood.

hysteria (adj., **hysterical**) An outbreak of wild emotionalism, which can become *chronic.* If hysteria persists as a *psychoneurotic* condition, it may become a *functional* nervous disorder with varying manifestations of an emotional, mental, and physical nature including *blindness, deafness,* or *paralysis.*

Hz See *Hertz.*

I

–ia Suffix denoting *pathology,* as in *kleptomania.*

iatrogenic (aye-at-roe-jen´-ik) Describes the condition when a patient becomes worse as a result of the medication or treatment.

ichthyosis (ik-thee-oh´-sis) A *congenital hereditary* skin disease that produces dryness and scaling.

id A term first discussed in Sigmund Freud's writings on *psychoanalytic theory* in the 1890s; represents or contains components of one's instinctual life. The two basic instinctual drives are, first, the fixed quantity of sexual energy available to an individual from birth, called *libido,* and a second, called *aggression.*

IDEA See *Individuals with Disabilities Act.*

identification 1. A *defense mechanism* in which an individual associates himself/herself with other persons, groups, or organizations in an attempt to be more secure and to relieve frustrations. 2. A method for effecting behavior change and learning, whereby the pupil is led to think, feel, and behave as though the characteristics of another person or group belong to him/her. Identification with the model of the other person or group may be done consciously or unconsciously. 3. Pinpointing the need of an individual for further treatment, assessment, or training.

idiolalia (id-ee-oh-lay´-lee-ah) A form of spoken communication that consists of invented *language.* It occurs most often between twins, who can understand their own language while no one else can. It may delay normal communication to the extent that some **idiolalic** children have been misidentified as *retarded.*

idiopathic (id-ee-oh-path´-ik) Descibes a condition of unknown causes, as in certain *epileptic seizures.*

idiot (old usage) A term of British and *clinical* origins that refers to a level of *intellectual* functioning comparable to the educational classification of *severe mental retardation* or the American Association on Mental Retardation's classification of *profound mental retardation.* The intellectual level, assessed with an individual *intelligence* test, would be estimated at *IQ* scores ranging from 0 to 20.

idiot savant See *savant syndrome.*

85

IEP   See *individualized education program.*

IEP manager   The person agreed upon at the IEP conference to monitor overall implementation of the child's *individualized education program.*

IIP   See *individual implementation plan.*

ileostomy (ill-ee-ahs'-toe-mee)   A surgical procedure for diverting the urine via an *ilioconduit,* through a *stoma* exiting on the abdomen.

ilioconduit (ilial loop)   Refers to the means of diverting urine from the bladder out through a *stoma* on the abdomen. With *paraplegics* and *incontinent* individuals, this helps prevent kidney damage. (see also *ileostomy* and *clean intermittent catheterization*)

illiteracy   The inability to read and write at a functional reading level, usually considered to be below fourth grade.

imagery   *A learning strategy,* used especially with *learning disabled* and *retarded* children. The individual is encouraged to make a *visual* picture of the *stimulus* item. The interaction between the stimulus item and *visualization* is what improves learning.

imbecile (old usage)   A term of British and *clinical* origins that refers to a level of *intellectual* functioning comparable to the educational classification of the *trainable mentally retarded* or the American Association on Mental Retardation's classification of *moderate mental retardation.* The intellectual level, *assessed* with an individual *intelligence* test, would involve *IQ* scores ranging from 20 to 50. The term has negative connotations in the U.S.

immitance testing   A measurement made by *audiologists* to determine the flexibility of the ear drum and pressure in the middle ear. This is not a *hearing acuity* measure but a determination of the possible cause of a *conductive hearing loss.*

immunity   The body's ability to resist a particular disease or infection, as in immunity to chicken pox.

impaction   A state in which a material becomes firmly wedged or lodged, as in wax impaction in the ear or *fecal* impaction in the rectum.

impairment   A general term indicating injury, deficiency, or lessening of function. For example, *visual* impairment indicates a condition less than normal.

impedance (imm-peed'-ans) **audiometry**   An approach to measuring middle ear function by determining the reaction in the middle ear to changes of pressure in the *auditory canal.* The preferred term is now *immitance testing.*

imperception   Lack of ability to understand or interpret *sensory* information accurately; involves *impairment* of *cognitive* functions rather than sensory impairments.

impulsivity   Responding abruptly without consideration of consequences or alternatives.

in loco parentis (in-low'-koe pair-ent'-iss)   A legal term referring to situations in which teachers are allowed to act in place of parents. This authority varies according to state law, but in most states it may be exercised only when the situation bears a reasonable relationship to the order of the school and the teacher is acting without excess emotion.

in-school suspension (ISS)   A practice in which disruptive students are removed from the regular classroom and receive individually oriented instruction in skills and knowledge areas in which low achievement levels are contributing to the students' adjustment problems. ISS has been a response of school systems in the 1980s toward keeping students with behavioral problems in school in preference to suspending or expelling them.

in-school work experience   A prescribed method of eliciting information about pupils' *incentives* and attitudes toward productive labor and preparing them for ultimate placement on a job in the competitive market, by assigning supervised duties within the school. An in-school work program is most valuable when it emphasizes factors that may be generalized to any type of employment (e.g., punctuality, socialization, completion of tasks, respect for authority).

inborn error of metabolism   Any one of the inherited disorders caused by absence of certain *enzymes,* which results in a metabolic block or incomplete metabolism.

incentive (in-sen'-tiv)   Anything that incites action toward achieving an objective; can be tangible or intangible.

incidence   The number of cases of a given condition identified and reported for a population (e.g., the number of children born with Down syndrome), usually reported as a numerical ratio (say, one child with Down syndrome per each 1,000 live births) or expressed as the number or percentage to have a given condition at some time in their life. (see also *prevalence*)

incidental learning   Acquisition of knowledge that takes place not as a primary goal but as a part of the peripheral effects of the experience.

incontinence (incontinent)   The inability to control bladder or bowel functions. Opposite of *continence.*

incorrigible   Describes behavior that is rebellious and unmanageable.

incus (ing'-kus)   The second of the three small bones of the middle ear that conduct vibrations from the *tympanic membrane* (ear drum) to the inner ear. This bone is sometimes referred to as the anvil. The other two bones are the *malleus* and the *stapes.* These three bones are called the *ossicles.*

independent living rehabilitation services   Programs for individuals who have *severe handicaps* and require training and support to allow them to live and work in the community with or without supervision.

independent living skills (ILS)   Practical learning imparted to persons with *mental retardation* so that they can function in home or community environments. (see also *ADL*)

individual family service plan (IFSP)   A feature of *PL 99-457;* an expanded *individualized education program (IEP)* for preschool children with *disabilities* and their whole family. The plan outlines the family's strengths and needs related to enhancing the child's development.

individual implementation plan (IIP)   The portion of the *individualized education program (IEP)* that states the *short-term objectives* and specific strategies for *intervention.*

individual reading inventory (IRI)   A nonstandardized procedure teachers use to establish a student's reading level for independent and assisted instruction; involves selecting reading passages from which the student reads and the teacher computes the number of errors. (see also *informal reading inventory*)

individual services plan (ISP)   An organized statement of proposed services to guide the service provider and client throughout the duration of service. Similar in meaning to the *individualized progress plan (IPP)*.

individual test   A measure designed to be administered to one person at a time as contrasted with administering to a group in one setting.

individualized education program (IEP)   A component of the *Education for All Handicapped Children Act* that requires a written plan of instruction for each child receiving special services, giving a statement of the child's present levels of educational performance, *annual goals, short-term objectives,* specific services needed by the child, dates when these services will begin and be in effect, and related information. The program is undertaken by a team including *parent involvement.*

individualized instruction   Teaching and study approaches selected specifically for adaptation to a given pupil's interests, needs, and abilities.

individualized planning conference   A meeting for the purpose of developing, reviewing, or revising a child's *individualized education program (IEP)*.

individualized program plan (IPP)   Approximates an *individualized education program* or *habilitation plan.* Any program plan that specifies the appropriate instruction, *therapies,* etc. needed by an individual child or adult.

individualized progress plan   A plan of instruction or *habilitation* called for in *PL 94-103* (Developmental Disabilities Act of 1975). (also see *individually prescribed instruction*)

individually prescribed instruction (IPI)   Teaching based on an *individualized education program* or *habilitation plan.*

Individuals with Disabilities Act (IDEA)   An act passed and implemented at the beginning of 1990 encompassing civil rights provisions similar to those previously provided to other minorities.

inductive learning   Acquisition of knowledge through guided discovery. In this approach, students are presented with several illustrations of a rule or occurrence and are then asked to infer the principle involved.

inductive thinking   A term used by learning theorists to describe the process of reasoning from parts to the whole, often resulting in a general principle inferred from particulars in the environment. Opposite of *deductive thinking.*

infant education   With the passage of *PL 99-457,* a shift in emphasis to include many more children with *handicaps* in programs from birth to age 3.

infanticide   A term similar to *euthanasia* except that it is exclusive to young children; refers to the act of letting defective babies die by withholding treatment, withdrawing treatment, and/or withholding sustenance.

infantile   Describes behavior that tends to revert to characteristics of an infant.

infantile amaurotic family idiocy   See *amaurotic family idiocy* and *Tay Sachs disease.*

infantile autism   See *autism.*

infantile (progressive spinal muscular) atrophy   A severe and rapidly advancing neuro-muscular disorder of infants.

infantile schizophrenia   See *childhood schizophrenia.*

infectious hepatitis   An *inflammation* of the liver caused by a specific *virus.* Early symptoms are nausea, vomiting, and pain in the upper abdomen; *jaundice* may or may not be present. This disease may infect anyone but usually occurs in children between ages 5 and 15.

infectious mononucleosis (mah-noe-new-klee-oh´-sis)   A condition thought to be caused by a *virus;* characterized by fever, sore throat, chills, headache, stomach pain, body rash, initial enlargement of the *lymph* nodes, possible *central nervous system* involvement, and low vitality. Treatment involves bed rest and restriction of activity.

inferiority complex   A psychological term indicating a lack of self-confidence sometimes to the degree of causing *introvertive* tendencies. Usually stems from experiencing failure, but may result from frustrating self-love experiences as a child.

inflammation (adj., **inflammatory**; v., **inflamed**)   A condition of body tissues characterized by pain, redness, and swelling, and resulting from infection, injury, or overexertion.

inflection (adj., **inflectional**)   The changing degree of loudness and rise and fall of *pitch* during speech, which gives different shades of meaning to words and phrases.

influenza (flu)   An epidemic disease caused by any number of *virus* infections, often characterized by *acute inflammation* of the throat and bronchi, usually accompanied by aching muscles and fever. If a woman contracts influenza during early pregnancy, the chances of having an impaired baby are increased.

informal assessment (testing)   A procedure in which the assessment utilizes instructional materials that have not been *normed.*

informal reading inventory   A procedure in which graded materials are used to *assess* a student's reading level. The inventory is not normed or *norm-referenced,* but is designed to provide a basis for beginning instruction.

information theory   A broad view of communication that emphasizes a computer-like approach to the treatment of knowledge; emphasizes input and output variables and mathematical probabilities in the production of information.

informed consent   See *consent agreement.*

inhibition   The process whereby an individual restrains an impulse or activity by utilizing an opposing internal force. Inhibition is not always the result of a conscious effort but may be the result of some force or experience of which the individual is not aware.

innate response system The unlearned *motor* instincts with which a child is endowed at birth.

inner speech Mental images of words in terms of *visual, auditory,* and *kinesthetic* sensations.

inservice training In the context of this book, special instruction conducted by a school district for its employed teachers. Inservice training has been heavily emphasized to improve teaching *competencies.* Current vocabulary favors the term *staff development.*

insight A characteristic of being able to quickly grasp, apprehend, or understand a situation. This quality often is evident in *gifted* children and often lacking in children with *mental retardation.*

institution(al) A public or private facility or building(s) providing specified services to persons on a 24-hour *residential* basis.

institutionalization Placement and residence within a specialized structure, particularly with reference to persons who have *mental retardation* or *emotional disturbance.* Such placement may have an inhibiting effect on development, because of limited *sensory* stimulation and personal experiences, and has been shown to result in loss in *intellectual* functioning in some instances.

instructional materials center (IMC) 1. Any of the regional offices forming a national network designed to gather, evaluate, store, and make available materials for use by individuals involved in teaching. 2. *Generically,* a name often applied to settings in which the above function is performed; also termed *resource center* or *learning resource center*—now part of the national Area Learning Resource Centers (ALRC).

instructional objective The outcome toward which teaching effort is directed.

instructional plan The part of the *individualized education program (IEP)* that states *short-term objectives* and specific strategies for *intervention.*

instrumental enrichment The term used by Feuerstein in his training of persons with *mental retardation,* to indicate the nature of the *curriculum.* The goal of this curriculum is to change the overall *cognitive* structure by transforming passive and dependent cognitive styles into independent and autonomous thinking. It is a paper-and-pencil curriculum administered three to five times a week over a 2- or 3-year period, with each lesson lasting about an hour.

insulin A *hormone* produced by the *pancreas.* It is extracted from the pancreatic glands of animals (or produced synthetically) for use in treating *diabetes.*

insulin shock A reaction brought on as a result of receiving too much *insulin,* not eating enough food, or participating in too much exercise, if one has *diabetes;* characterized by feelings of hunger, trembling, perspiring, and muscular contractions. The body needs sugar, so eating candy, pure sugar, or an orange will relieve the condition.

integrated life experience curriculum An approach used to instruct *educable mentally retarded* students. Units, *experience charts,* dramatizations, and other means of pupil participation provide firsthand experiences to help them better understand their environment and solve persistent life problems.

integrated plan An administrative approach to assigning *exceptional children* for educational experiences whereby the pupil is carried on the roll of a regular classroom, with a specially trained teacher available to assist in a *special class* or *resource room*. Terminology largely has been replaced by *resource room* and *mainstreaming*.

integrated skills method An approach to teaching reading, developed out of the work with talking typewriters, in which reading is independent of any specific traditional program or approach. The program integrates pupil needs with teacher knowledge, skills, and teaching styles, and emphasizes three major components—a beginning skills unit, integrated skills lessons, and applied reading.

integration The placement of children with *handicaps* in educational programs also serving children without *handicaps*. A similar term is *mainstreaming*.

intellect(ual) The substance of a person's thinking or *intelligence,* represented by abilities such as observing, reasoning, comprehending, judging, and understanding.

intelligence The ability to understand, comprehend, and adapt rapidly to new situations and learn from experiences. Also, degree of ability, as displayed by performance on tests constructed for the purpose of measuring mental development level.

intelligence quotient (IQ) The numerical figure commonly used to express level of mental development. The IQ is computed by dividing the *mental age* (as measured by performance on an intelligence test) by the *chronological age* and multiplying by 100.

intensity 1. Magnitude or degree of tension, activity, or energy. 2. The physical parameter of sound expressed in *decibels* (the psychological correlate is loudness).

intensive training residence (ITR) A term for a community *residential alternative;* a further extension of the *group home concept* but emphasizes training in skill acquisition and the elimination of unsocialized behavior. ITRs were started to provide the added expertise necessary for the remaining "hard core" *deinstitutionalization* cases.

interdisciplinary A term describing members of two or more professions sharing a function or goal; e.g., a *diagnostic* team consisting of a physician, a *psychologist,* a *social worker,* and a special educator. Similar to *multidisciplinary.*

interindividual differences A *concept* based on the idea that each person is unique. The term is used in describing differences among children in weight, height, reading ability, learning capacity, etc. Compare with *intraindividual differences* (within a person).

interjacent child A term originated by Edgar Doll in the 1950s to refer to students now called *learning disabled.*

intermediate district See *shared services.*

intermediate level 1. A school grade placement equivalent to the fourth, fifth, and sixth grades. 2. A grouping for *special education* classes involving pupils approximately 9 through 12 years of age.

intermittent reinforcement A procedure whereby only selected, not all, responses are rewarded periodically during training. This strategy builds more resistance to *extinction* than does *continuous reinforcement.*

internal locus of control A hypothetical *construct* in which individuals believe they are largely in control of their own destinies. Opposite of *external locus of control.* (see also *locus of control*)

international phonetic alphabet (IPA) A system of representing speech sounds, in which each sound is represented by a single written character. (see also *phonetic alphabet*)

internship A period of continuous, full-time participation directly working in the profession for which one is being trained, during which time the **intern** receives direction and supervision—in the case of teaching or administration, from a local supervising teacher or administrator, as well as a supervisor from the college or university granting credit for the experience.

interpersonal relations The linkage between a person and others with whom he/she interacts, such as *peer group,* family, and authority figures. One's effectiveness in this regard seems to be related closely to one's ability to recognize and respond to the needs of others in the surrounding environment.

interpreter (for the deaf) A person who uses *sign language* and/or *fingerspelling* to translate spoken communication so *deaf* individuals can understand it.

interrelated A term used in some states which is equivalent of *mildly handicapped* serving those students with mild retardation, mild learning disabilities and mild behavior disorders.

intersensory integration An interdependent and facilitating relationship among several *sensory modalities,* which can result in sensory processing superior to that of one sense alone.

interservice transition plan (ITP) A proposal in recent years for a team of school, community, and agency personnel to write a transition or employment plan for a *handicapped* student before his or her leaving school.

interval recording Keeping an account, at regular, equally spaced times, of the occurrence of behavior.

intervention The interception of unproductive or undesired behaviors or conditions and changing or directing them in ways that are more advantageous.

intonation (in-toe-nay'-shun) The speaking patterns of *inflection* and vocal *pitch* variations that create inferences for various meanings, or the characteristics of various *languages.*

intracranial Located within the skull.

intraindividual differences A *concept* applied to the comparison of abilities and *disabilities* within a person, as opposed to *interindividual differences* (between persons).

intrauterine growth retardation (Warkany's syndrome) A condition characterized by a small *placenta* and low birth weight.

92

intrinsic motivation   The property causing improved performance in a given task through *incentives* within the task itself; i.e., a child's interest in learning or performing the task motivates him/her to do it.

introjection   Making an occurrence or characteristic a part of oneself or turning hostility felt toward another against oneself.

introspection (adj., **introspective**)   Examining one's own thoughts and feelings; self-analysis.

introvert (intravert)   One who tends to shrink from social relationships and becomes involved with himself/herself, sometimes in *fantasy* and the *symbolic;* inner-directed rather than outer-directed; *introspective.* Opposite of *extrovert.*

invalid   One who is seriously, usually *chronically,* disabled by ill health. An invalid is often dependent upon others, limited in getting around, and may have negative, *depressed* feelings as a result of these limitations. The term has been used most often with reference to disabled elderly people.

invasion of privacy   A situation in which information (say, concerning a handicapped individual) is shared with a third party without a *consent agreement.*

inventory   A questionnaire or checklist used to elicit pertinent information. A skills inventory, for example, often is used to determine arithmetic knowledge in a nonstandardized manner, or an inventory may be used to measure personality characteristics.

inversion   Reversal in order, form, relationship, or position. An example is a change in the normal sentence structure, such as placing a verb before its subject; this is observed sometimes in those whose primary *language* is different from the one in which the inversions occur.

IQ   See *intelligence quotient.*

iris   The colored portion of the eye, which contracts or expands involuntarily depending upon the amount of light entering the eye. The iris functions similarly to the shutter of a camera.

iritis (eye-rih′-tis)   A condition marked by *inflammation* of the *iris* of the eye and in which one experiences pain and discomfort from light.

Ishihari color plates   Specific materials developed to identify and measure *color blindness.* Certain colors used in the plates are visible to persons who are not color blind but cannot be discriminated by those who are color blind.

ISO standard   The normal listener's average *threshold* levels to sound pressure from which *hearing acuity* is determined, as set by the International Standard Organization. This standard has been used to determine a slight *hearing loss* to be from 25 to 40 *decibels* (db), a mild loss to be 40 to 55 db, a marked loss to be 55 to 70 db, a severe loss 70 to 90 db, and an extreme loss +90 db.

ita (initial teaching alphabet)   A system of representing speech sounds in which each sound is represented by a single written character. (see also *phonetic alphabet*)

itinerant teacher/therapist   A professional person who renders service in small groups or individually, traveling to more than one school. Usually applied to *speech and language pathologists* and teachers of low-incidence *exceptionalities* such as visual impairment.

J

Jacksonian seizure   A form of *epileptic* activity in which muscular contractions begin in one part of the body (e.g., left hand) and may subside without loss of consciousness or may spread to the entire body and develop into a *grand mal seizure*. (see also *focal seizure*)

jactitation (jack-tih-tay´-shun)   Jerking and twitching of the body.

Jaeger chart   An aid to determine *visual* competence utilizing different sizes of print, and to conclude the best print size for *visually impaired* individuals.

jargon   Speech characterized by an unintelligible jumble of syllables; may occur in early speech development of infants or in speech efforts of individuals who have *profound mental retardation*.

jaundice   A condition in which an abnormal presence of bile pigments in the blood and tissue causes yellowness of the skin and eyes, and a deep yellow color of the urine. May occur in young children; if caused by the *Rh factor* (see *erythroblastosis*), it can result in *retardation*.

Jena (hay´-nuh) **method**   A procedure to teach *lip (speech) reading* to those with *hearing impairment* based on exposing them to the sensations of movement during the production of speech.

jig   A device specially designed to help workers perform tasks faster, more accurately, and with greater ease. Jigs are often used in *sheltered workshops* for persons with *retardation* to limit or control work operations so the workers can perform them under conditions of minimum supervision and reduced hazards.

job club   A type of organization enabling *prevocationally* handicapped and nonhandicapped individuals to share job experiences and suggestions on how to look for a job.

job coach   A person designated as a supervisor for a person with *severe handicaps* in competitive employment. The job coach serves in an instructional capacity, working and modeling alongside the individual with disabilities.

job-coached employee   A worker with *disabilities* who is placed on the job in competitive employment with a supervisor or other supportive person to help the disabled person cope and be successful on the job.

94

job sample A selected sampling of a standard work activity that involves all or part of the total operations required by a given job. Job samples often are taken to evaluate or determine if a worker or workshop can accomplish certain things, prior to hiring or setting up the complete workshop.

Jukes family The subject of a study by Richard L. Dugdale, published in 1875, which popularized the position that people living under poor social conditions would *degenerate* from generation to generation, and thus emphasized the *familial* aspects of *mental retardation.*

juvenile court A court of law that hears only cases involving minor, or underage, children. Many cases brought before these courts involve neglected, dependent, or *delinquent* children.

juvenile delinquency The adjudged behavior on the part of young people, classified by state as under-age, that causes them to be charged as law breakers.

juxtospinal Close to the spinal column.

K

Kallikak family The subject of and title of a book published by Henry H. Goddard in 1912, supporting the position that *mental retardation* is *hereditary*. Goddard studied the *geneology* of an *institutional* patient and found that the patient's great-great grandmother had 480 descendants, of which approximately three fourths were considered "degenerates" of some type. The patient's great-great grandfather, however, later married a woman of normal *intelligence* and produced 496 direct descendants, all of whom were considered responsible individuals and of normal intelligence.

Kanner's syndrome See *autism*.

karotype An analysis of *chromosome* make-up for an individual or a systematic array of metaphase chromosomes of a single cell arranged in pairs in descending order of size.

keratitis (kare-ih-tie′-tiss) *Inflammation* of the *cornea* of the eye with residual scarring.

kernel sentence See *holophrastic speech*.

kernicterus (kur-nik′-ter-us) A condition resulting from blood incompatibility of the mother and developing *fetus*. The consequent *allergic* reaction causes a breakdown of the red blood cells, which releases large amounts of *bilirubin* (the red pigment in the red blood cells). Residual effects of kernicterus may include *mental retardation, cerebral palsy,* and other *impairments*.

ketone (kee′-tone) Any compound containing the carbonyl group. Ketone bodies are usually found in the blood and urine of those with uncontrolled *diabetes*. Any condition in which ketone bodies are found in the urine is called **ketonuria.**

kinesthesis (kih-nes-thee′-sis) The sensation of movement from muscles, joints, or from the *vestibular* mechanism in the inner ear.

kinesthetic See *haptic*.

kinesthetic method An approach to teaching reading and related skills in which symbols are traced in the air, in clay, or on paper. This use of the senses enhances learning in some children who have had difficulty with other forms of instruction. (see *VAKT*)

kinesthetic sense A general term referring to *tactile* sensations and muscle movement in any part of the body. Described as a receptive *feedback* of information to the brain in the interest of *sensorimotor* coordination and planning for immediate action. Activities such as reading, writing, and speech depend tremendously on accurate kinesthetic information.

kleptomania (klep-toe-may'-nee-uh) A persistent impulse to steal articles that are often of little or no value, and monetary profit is not a motive.

Klinefelter's syndrome A condition *(clinical type)* occurring in males, caused by sex-*chromosome aberrations.* At *puberty,* boys affected by this condition develop feminine-like breasts and have sparse beards and scant pubic hair. The individual is usually sterile and frequently has *mental retardation.*

knee-jerk reflex Involuntary movement of the quadriceps muscle causing extension of the leg when the tendon below the kneecap is tapped. Absence of this reflex is an indicator to physicians of the presence of certain conditions.

kolytic (koe-lit'-ik) Describes a calm, self-controlled temperament with a tendency toward being passive.

Kurzweil machine (curz'-well) A device useful to *visually impaired* persons that optically reads print and reproduces it as *synthetic speech.*

kwashiorkor (kwash-ee-or'-core) A condition caused by severe protein deficiency, characterized by retarded growth, skin and hair pigment changes, *eczema* (a skin disorder), *pathological* changes in the liver, and mental *apathy.*

kymograph (kye'-moe-graf) An instrument used to record variations in any physiological or muscle process.

kyphosis (kye-foe'-sis) A condition in which the back around the shoulder is rounded, causing a curvature of the spine in a stooped position.

L

labeling (or **labelling/label**)   The practice of attaching a generalized name to a person with a handicapping condition—such as *mentally retarded, cerebral palsied, learning disabled.* Although labels may entitle an individual to special services, they carry the risk of creating stigmas and nowadays tend to be discouraged as much as possible.

labial (lay'-bee-uhl)   1. Pertaining to the lips. 2. Describes a speech sound produced with the aid of the lips (e.g., *p, b*).

lability (lah-bill'-ih-tee) **of affect**   A behavioral/emotional characteristic, often noticed in *brain injured children,* in which a child overreacts to minimal stimulation; for example, bursting into tears upon completing a certain task, giggling when insecure, or other indications of unstable control of impulses.

lacrimal (lak'-rih-mal) **gland**   Located just above the outer corner of each eye, it has the function of secreting tears.

lahlophobia (lah-loe-foe'-bee-ah)   An abnormal fear of speaking.

lallation (lah-lay'-shun)   An ear-voice *reflex* occurring in children of about 6 months of age, in which the *stimulus* of hearing a spoken sound is sufficient to set the vocal mechanism into operation to produce the sound again, which again stimulates the ear, which again stimulates the speech mechanism, etc. This reflex explains why a child may say "da-da-da-da-da."

lalopathy (lah-lop'-ah-thee)   Any *speech disorder.*

laloplegia (lah-loe-plee'-jah)   *Paralysis* of the speech organs.

landmark   1. Any familiar object, sound, odor, temperature, or *tactual* clue that a *blind* person can easily recognize as having a known and exact location in the environment and can be used for direction taking. 2. A store, factory, or other object used by instructors to train individuals with *mental retardation* in bus or rapid transit travel. The store or other landmarks serve as the stimulus that it is time to pull the cord for disembarking.

language   1. A system of words or symbols and the rules for putting them together to form a method of communication among a group of individuals. (see also *functional language*). 2. A code used by a programmer for purposes of organizing a computer's circuits so the machine will perform specific tasks on demand.

language bifurcation (bie-fer-kay'-shun)   Inadequate learning of both the primary and secondary language by *bilingual* or ethnic minority individuals.

98

language development The growth in an individual's ability to communicate through use of vocal and written symbols.

language disorder A communication problem in comprehending, expressing, or otherwise functionally utilizing spoken language.

language-experience approach The teaching of reading and other language skills incorporating the pupils' experiences. This method frequently uses an *experience chart* dictated by the pupils and recorded by the teacher, which becomes material for teaching language and reading.

large type A print, usually produced to aid *visually handicapped* individuals in reading, that is approximately twice as large as regular print. (see also *clear type*)

Larry P. v. Riles A landmark court case in which California schools were ordered to not use *IQ* as the primary determinant for placement in *EMR* classes. The case was brought because blacks in *special education* far exceeded their percentage in the general population, and tests to determine IQ were considered culturally biased.

laryngectomy (lair-un-jek'-toe-mee) Surgical removal of the *larynx* (voice box) because of a diseased condition or *trauma* to the vocal folds.

laryngitis (lair-en-jite'-iss) Temporary *inflammation* of the *larynx* (voice box), which includes *hoarseness* and soreness of the throat and sometimes loss of voice.

laryngologist (lair-en-gahl'-oh-jist) A medical doctor who *diagnoses* and treats disorders of the throat, *pharynx, larynx,* and *nasopharynx.*

laryngology (lair-en-gahl'-oh-jee) The branch of medicine dealing with the throat, *pharynx, larynx* and *nasopharynx.*

laryngoscope (lair-in'-go-skope) **laryngoscopy** (lair-en-gahs'-koe-pee) An instrument designed for direct *visual* examination of the interior of the *larynx* (voice box) through the process known as laryngoscopy.

larynx (lair'-inks) The organ of voice, located in the upper part of the *trachea* (windpipe), that contains the vocal cords and essential musculature for production of speech.

laser cane An electronic device that emits a sound that aids *blind* persons with *mobility.* As the individual approaches an object, the pitch rises.

latchkey Contemporary term applied to children from homes in which the parents work and the children are unsupervised from the end of the school day until the parents get home. Some research has indicated that these children have a much greater chance of becoming *socially maladjusted* than do children who have supervision.

laterality (or **lateral dominance**) One's preference for using either the right or left side of the body and correctly interpreting the position and sidedness of the body.

lazy eye See *amblyopia.*

LD See *learning disability.*

LEA See *local education(al) agency.*

lead dog   See *guide dog.*

lead poisoning   A *toxic* condition resulting from ingestion of lead. Results in *central nervous system* damage and *retardation.* Most often caused by ingestion of lead paint from old houses.

learned helplessness   An evolved state in which an individual does not attempt to do a task or solve a problem although he/she has the ability to do or solve it. This occurs because the person has come to feel that his/her efforts are useless or unimportant to the outcome.

learning curve   A graphic presentation of progress or achievement as indicated by the graphing of periodic *evaluation* during presentation of the *curricular* sequence; often used to allow pupils to keep a record of their achievement in a specific area.

learning disability (LD)   A lack of achievement or ability in a specific learning area(s) within the range of achievement of individuals with comparable mental ability. Most definitions emphasize a basic disorder in psychological processes involved in understanding and using *language,* spoken or written.

learning disorder   A *diagnosed* physical or neurological *impairment* that interferes with academic achievement.

learning handicapped   A term used in California pertaining to a category of *service delivery* in which students with *mild handicaps* formerly labeled *educable mentally retarded, behaviorally disordered,* and *learning disabled* are served within the same program through a *resource*-type rather than a *self-contained* program.

learning resource center   See *instructional materials center.*

learning strategies   Techniques, principles, or methods that help a student in the acquisition, manipulation, storage, and retrieval of information. Learning strategies are particularly needed by those who lack thinking, attention, or memory skills and consequently have difficulty with academic learning.

learning strategies approach   An instructional method that advocates teaching students skills that will aid them in their learning. Because students with *learning disabilities* and similar *handicaps* seem to lack skills that are *prerequisite* to academic skills, the instruction emphasizes thinking, memory, and listening skills—"how to learn" rather than teaching basic content.

learning style   Refers to the way a child learns; two different meanings have been applied: 1. Preferred sensory modalities and how a child learns relative to the use of *visual, tactile,* and other *sensory* modes. 2. Personality characteristics that have implications for behavioral patterns in learning situations.

least prompts   A teaching method that advocates the fewest possible means of assistance. In teaching a task, the teacher helps only to the extent necessary for the child to get to the next learning stage. Includes *modeling* and physical prompts.

least restrictive alternative   A legal term that antedates the term *least restrictive environment* but is presently essentially synonymous. The term was first used in 1918 in relation to branch banking but has subsequently been employed in cases such as *Wyatt* v. *Stickney* (1971) and *PARC* v. *Commonwealth of Pennsylvania* (1971).

least restrictive environment (LRE) A *concept* expressed by the courts in the 1970s, *mandating* that each person with a *handicap* should be educated or served in the most "normal" setting and atmosphere possible. This led to the concept and practice of *mainstreaming*. Under *PL 94-142* it includes educational placement as similar to that of nonhandicapped children as possible.

legal advocacy Activities by an individual or group to promote desired changes to benefit another individual or group, whereby one or more of the three legally constituted avenues of government—legislative, administrative, and judicial—will be convinced to react concretely upon these desired changes. (see also *advocacy*)

legal blindness A term for the level of *visual impairment* at which eligibility for special consideration, services, or funding is set. Defined as 20/200 in the better eye after correction or if vision does not exceed 20 degrees in the visual field.

legal commitment A court order requiring specified care, confinement, or treatment for an individual.

Legg-Calve-Perthes (leg-cav-perth'-ez) A disease of the circulatory system that can result in destruction of the head of the femur. It occurs most often in boys between 5 and 9. Its effects can be prevented by immobilization.

leisure life skills (leisure time activities) Tasks taught to persons with *handicaps* to assist them in wise, pleasant use of time when they are not working or attending classes. Because many are restricted in work and other uses of time, effective use of free time is an important area for development. Other terminology is *outdoor education*.

Lekotek (lek'-oh-tek) The name of a worldwide system of play libraries for the handicapped. The centers were first established in Sweden. Their primary role is to provide consultation and to lend toys and instructive materials so that young children with *severe retardation* can be maintained and their early education accomplished in their homes.

lens (of eye) The transparent component of the eye between the *posterior* chamber and the *vitreous* body that functions in focusing light rays and images on the *retina*.

lesion (lee'-zhun) Any change in the structure of organs or tissues as a result of injury or disease.

lesson plan An orderly, detailed schedule of the important points of a teaching session, giving *objectives* to be achieved, order of presentation, materials to be used, teaching methods, and student assignments.

leukemia (lew-kee'-mee-uh) A disease of the blood-forming organs, marked by an increase in number of white blood cells and resulting in progressive *deterioration* of the body. Great strides have been made in treating this condition.

life experience unit A teaching block of related skills and facts based on real-life situations and problems. This unit is commonly included in educational programs for *educable mentally retarded* students.

life space Commonly used in reference to the immediate environment in which an individual functions.

101

life-space interviewing   A form of treatment advocated by William Morse and others in which the teacher or *crisis teacher* serves as a nonjudgmental recorder of events and helps children work out what response they should make in similar situations.

lifelong career development   A systematic approach for persons with *handicaps* to acquire skills and resources they need to maintain the maximum degree of independent living throughout their life.

limited guardianship   A legal arrangement under which the guardian of an individual with *developmental* or other *disabilities* has prespecified restricted authority and responsibility. The extent of guardianship is determined by the court and is dependent upon extent of *adaptive behavior, intellectual* level, and *self-care skills,* as well as the capabilities and qualifications of the limited guardian.

lingual (ling'-gwuhl)   A speech sound basically formed by the tongue and in which the tongue is considered to have the major *articulatory* role.

linguistics   The science or study of *language* and human speech, which includes the origin, structure, and *semantics* of language.

lip reading (speech reading)   A skill taught to *deaf* and *hard of hearing* persons through which they can understand much of what another person says by observing the context of the situation and *visual* cues of speech production such as movements of the lips and facial muscles.

lisp   An *articulatory* defect of speech in which the sounds of /s/ and /z/ are improperly produced with an accompanying emission of air, such as "thaw" for saw or "thebra" for zebra.

listening ear dogs   Animals trained to assist *hearing impaired* individuals. The dogs learn to respond to bells, alarms, sirens, a baby's cry, and other audible signals.

literacy   The ability to read and write, usually considered to be *functional* reading above fourth-grade level.

local education(al) agency (LEA)   An administrative arrangement referred to by federal and state legislation to designate the entity responsible for providing public education through 12th grade—usually a school district.

lock-step education   Describes a rigid, structured system of pupil progress from grade to grade, regardless of ability or need to progress more rapidly or more slowly. (see also *social promotion*)

locus of control   A hypothetical *construct* used to describe the expectations for the occurrence of behaviors. *Gifted* children generally score high on *internal locus of control.* Many individuals with *handicaps* have a low or *external locus of control.*

logical consequences   A treatment procedure that has a *contingency* logically related to the misbehavior (e.g., losing freedom to move around the classroom after disrupting the work of other students).

logopedics (lahg-oh-peed'-iks)   The study and treatment of *speech defects.*

long cane   See *Hoover cane.*

longitudinal study   Research that follows a case or situation over a considerable time, usually a number of years.

long-range goals   An element specified in the *individualized education program* as the ultimate learning aim for the term or school year, based on first specifying *short-term objectives*.

long-term goals   See *annual goals*.

long-term memory   A term to denote learning that is relatively lengthy in duration and that the individual can recall over time, in contrast to *short-term memory,* which is brief in duration. Telephone numbers, for example, usually go into short-term memory instead of long-term memory.

lordosis   Irregular curvature in the lumbar and cervical regions of the spine when viewed from the side. Other terms used are "hollowback" and "swayback."

"low grade" mental retardate   A term of *institutional* origin, classifying individuals with *severe retardation* as "low grade," in contrast to those with less severe retardation as "high grade." Terminology not used at this time.

low-incidence handicap   A classification of *impairments* that are few in number in relation to other handicaps of the general population (e.g., those involving vision, hearing, or *orthopedic* impairments).

low-vision aid   Equipment designed to improve an individual's sight, usually through magnification. Used with individuals who may be classed as *blind* but have enough *residual* (remaining) *vision* to be able to see better by using these devices.

LSS   Acronym for local school system; same as *LEA*.

lupus erythematosis (lew'-pus air-ih-them-ah-toe'-sis)   A destructive, *chronic inflammation* of the skin.

macrocephalic (mack-roe-seh-fal'-ik)   A term used to describe an abnormally large head. (see also *hydrocephalus*)

macula (mack'-yuh-luh)   The portion of the *retina* of the eye that provides the clearest vision.

macular degeneration   Deterioration of the center of the *retina* responsible for detailed vision; results in progressive loss of central vision; the individual retains *peripheral vision*.

macular pathology   Diseases or *degeneration* of the *macula* of the eye.

Madison Plan   A *noncategorical* approach to educating the *mildly handicapped*, employing a specialized *resource room* with three activity centers— Preacademic Area I, emphasizing appropriate behavior; Academic Area II, emphasizing intense academic *remediation* in small groups; and Academic Area III, emphasizing larger group instruction and partial *integration* with regular students. The Madison Plan refers specifically to a school within the Santa Monica, California, school system, from which the program is an extension of an earlier *engineered classroom*. (Same as *Santa Monica Project*.)

mainstreaming (mainstreamed)   The concept of serving students with *handicaps* within the regular school program, with *support services* and personnel, rather than placing children in *self-contained special classes*. This practice relates to the concept of *least restrictive environment*. It has been most successful when using appropriate personnel such as *resource teachers*, and with students who have *mild handicaps*.

major work classes   A term originating in Cleveland to designate classes for *gifted* students that have operated since the 1920s.

mal–   A prefix designating abnormal, inadequate, or bad.

maladaptive behavior   A person's actions that are considered outside the bounds of socially accepted standards of the society.

maladjustment   A condition of being out of harmony with one's environment and failure to reach satisfactory compatibility between self desires and behavior; this has a harmful effect on the person, the surrounding society, or both.

malformed (malformation)   Irregular in structure or possessing characteristics of being ill-formed when compared to a standard acceptable configuration.

malignant   Tending or threatening to produce death (often used to denote a cancerous condition).

malinger (v.)   To consciously, willfully, and deliberately feign or exaggerate for personal gain or advantage. **Malingering** is a behavior in which an individual pretends to be ill or unable to do something, in order to gain advantages; e.g., pretending a *hearing loss* to acquire *disability* payments. An individual who displays the above behaviors is called a **malingerer.**

malleus (mal´-ee-us)   The largest of a chain of three small bones in the middle ear that conduct vibrations from the *tympanic membrane* to the inner ear. Also called the hammer. The other two bones are the *incus* and *stapes.*

malocclusion (mal-oh-kloo´-zhun)   Faulty positioning of the teeth that results in an abnormal overbite or underbite.

mandates (mandatory legislation)   Previously referred to state laws requiring school districts to provide services to children with *handicaps.* Since *PL 94-142,* these laws have become moot because that law requires all states to serve handicapped children regardless of severity or other considerations.

mania (may´-nee-uh)   A mental disorder characterized by extreme *hyperactivity,* disorganized behavior, and restlessness.

manic-depressive psychosis   A serious mental disorder characterized by behavior alternating between excessive activity *(mania)* and *depression.*

manneristic behaviors   Rhythmic actions often seen in *blind* persons and those with *emotional disturbance* and *mental retardation.* (see also *automatism; blindism; stereotypic behavior*)

manual alphabet (finger alphabet)   A communication system used by *deaf* persons in which letters are indicated through a variety of positions of the fingers. One type requires both hands to form the letters, but the single-hand alphabet is most common. (see also *fingerspelling*)

manual method (manualism)   A system of communication for *deaf* persons in which *fingerspelling* and/or *sign language* are used in place of speech.

Manually Coded English (MCE)   A communication system for *deaf* people in which signing is done on a syllable-by-syllable basis. It differs from *fingerspelling* but is similar in terms of the time required.

marasmus (mah-raz´-muss)   A form of *malnutrition* usually occurring during infancy and early childhood. It results in growth retardation and progressive wasting away of fatty tissues and muscles. Also called *infantile atrophy.*

masking   1. The use of white noise (sounds of average amplitude across all audible frequencies) in one ear while the other ear is being tested; used to prevent the stronger ear from interfering with results when that ear may be receiving sound vibrations through *bone conduction.* 2. In *amblyopia,* one eye controls the sight, resulting in the other being a *lazy eye.*

mastoid bone   A portion of the temporal bone that extends down the skull behind the ear. *Bone conduction hearing aids* are shaped to fit behind the ear against the mastoid bone. Removal of this bone is termed a **mastoidectomy.**

mastoiditis (mass-toy-die'-tiss)   *Inflammation* of the mastoid process of the temporal bone. This condition is painful and may interfere with hearing.

maturational lag   A slowness of development that may affect growth, *intelligence,* or emotional independence.

mean   The arithmetic average; the sum of all the scores divided by the number of scores.

mediated learning experience (MLE)   A theory from Feuerstein that seeks to explain how children learn *cognitively.* In addition to the ordinary direct learning, Feuerstein postulates that mediating agents such as parents, siblings, and teachers frame, filter, or select the material, sequence, and other factors to promote learning. This is especially pertinent to individuals with *retardation* and *learning disabilities.*

mediation   1. The process through which parents and school districts attempt to mutually agree on solutions to their differences in regard to *identification, evaluation,* placement, and provision of *free appropriate public education* for *exceptional children.* 2. A strategy of attaching a verbal label to information to be learned to facilitate memory. Even the use of music can serve as a *mediator* to assist learning and memory.

medically fragile (adj.)   Describes individuals who have chronic or recurrent physical or psychiatric disorders that require medical services to be closely available or constantly present.

megalomania (meg-ah-loe-may'-nee-ah)   A *psychotic* or serious emotional condition characterized by *delusions of grandeur* (feelings of great value or worth).

megavitamin therapy   A term coined by Linus Pauling in 1968 for the treatment of *behavior* and *learning disorders* with large doses of water-soluble vitamins.

melancholia (mel-an-koe'-lee-uh)   A *mental illness* in which the patient feels *depressed,* sad, and without hope.

melodic intonation therapy (MIT)   A technique applied to *aphasic* individuals; requires the use of vocal sounds at different *pitches* organized into simple melodies, in an effort to improve the *language* of the aphasic person.

memory   One of Guilford's five thinking operations (see *structure of the intellect*) having to do with remembering, mastering facts, and acquiring distinct knowledge.

meninges   The three membranes (dura mater, arachnoid, and pia mater) that surround the brain and spinal cord.

meningitis (men-in-jite'-iss)   *Inflammation* of the membranes that surround the brain and spinal cord.

meningocele (meh-nin'-juh-seel)   A sac-like membranous pouch that protrudes through an opening in the skull or spinal column. The sac contains *cerebrospinal fluid* but no spinal nerves. (see also *spina bifida* and *neural tube defect*)

106

meningomyelocele (meh-nin-juh-my'-loe-seel)   A *meningocele* pouch, as in craniobifida and *spina bifida,* that contains spinal nerves. (see also *meningocele*)

mental age (MA)   The level of an individual's mental ability expressed in terms of the average *chronological age* of others answering the same number of items correctly on a test of mental ability. As an example, a child who has a mental ability equal to that of the average 10-year-old would have a mental age of 10 years, regardless of his/her actual chronological age.

mental deficiency   A term that has been replaced by *mental retardation.* Traditionally, the term was more related to lower levels of functioning and for individuals with demonstrable *organic* involvement.

mental health   A state of mind representing wholesomeness or adequacy of adjustment.

mental hygiene   The fostering of healthy emotional attitudes, habits of thinking, and environmental conditions that help individuals resist personality *maladjustment* or *mental illness.*

mental illness   A condition that results in *deviant* thinking, feeling, and behavior to a degree that causes difficulty in adjusting to life.

mental retardation   A broadly used term that refers to significantly subaverage general *intellectual* functioning manifested during the *developmental period* and existing concurrently with *impairment* in *adaptive behavior.* At present, definitions indicate a person having an *IQ* of 70 or less and showing impairment in adaptation or social ability is mentally retarded.

mental retardation service centers   Terminology that has largely replaced the term "training centers for the retarded."

mentor   May refer to an experienced teacher who serves as a model or consultant for a beginning teacher, or someone who serves as a professional role model for a *gifted* student.

mentorship   An instructional approach of assigning a *gifted* student to a community member to serve as a trusted guide, educator, or counselor.

mesomorphic (mess-oh-more'-fik)   One of the three classifications in Sheldon's description of body types *(somatotypes)*; a body of medium stature with predominance of muscle and bones—usually considered an athletic body build.

metabolic (meh-tuh-bah'-lik) **disorder**   Any condition or disease related to *dysfunction* in the chemical processes and activities of the body.

metabolism (meh-tab'-oh-lizm)   The total of all continuous physical and chemical processes by which living cells and tissues undergo changes necessary for the maintenance of life.

metacognition (adj., **metacognitive**)   Refers to a person's own knowledge of how he/she learns. The term is closely related to *metamemory.*

metamemory   A term that relates to one's own knowledge of how he/she remembers things best. Used in the 1980s with children who have *mental retardation* or *learning disabilities,* emphasizing having them think about when and how they are able to remember information they are trying to learn.

107

MI An abbreviation for *mild handicaps* or *mild retardation*, commonly used in local school systems. Another similar term is MIMH, for *mildly mentally handicapped.*

microcephalus (microcephaly) (my-crow-sef'-uh-lus) (lee) A condition in which the head size is small because of an inherited defect that causes reduced brain size and *severe mental retardation.*

micturate (mik'-chew-rate) To urinate.

midline The middle of the body, or center of gravity. Individuals with neurological problems or *brain injury* may have difficulty crossing a side over the midline in their activities.

migraine A type of headache characterized by periodic attacks of severe intensity, often accompanied by irritability, nausea, and vomiting.

migrant children Youngsters in families that move periodically seeking seasonal employment; as a result, the family doesn't establish a permanent residence where the children remain in school for a complete term. The lack of a consistent school program may inhibit development of these children to the extent that they function below their ability levels.

mild handicap Term applied to individuals with the least severe learning and behavior problems and who generally are educated in regular school programs. Usually, those with *learning disabilities, behavior disorders,* and/or slight *mental retardation* are included in this terminology. (see also *learning handicapped, interrelated*)

mild hearing loss An *impairment* demonstrated by difficulty in hearing faint sounds. Individuals with mild hearing loss need favorable seating arrangements and may benefit from *speechreading,* vocabulary and *language* instruction.

mild mental retardation (mildly retarded) A term introduced by the American Association on Mental Retardation that refers to a level of *intellectual* functioning comparable to the educational classification of *educable mental retardation.* The intellectual level, *assessed* with an individual *intelligence* test, involves *IQ* scores ranging from 55 to 70.

milieu (meel-you') A social setting or environment, including the effects of this environment on one's behavior. Synonymous with *ecosystem.* **Milieu therapy** is a treatment approach based on consideration of the total environment in which the person lives; has many commonalities with ecosystem approaches.

Mills v. Board of Education A *class action* court case brought on behalf of seven *multihandicapped* students against the Washington, DC, Board of Education, resulting in a judgment that children cannot be denied a publicly supported education merely because of their handicapping conditions.

minimal brain dysfunction (MBD) A term referring to children of near average, average, or above average *intelligence* who show learning or *behavior disorders* as a result of *diagnosed* or suspected deviations in functions of the *central nervous system.* The preferred term is *learning disability.*

minimum competency testing (MCT) A movement, which started in the late 1970s and carried into the 1980s, in which school systems set expectancies or test score requirements for promotion to the next grade or graduation. The testing program itself is often simply called MCT. The intent was to ensure that students have attained a certain skill level upon graduation rather than merely being "passed upward." The *concept* has been particularly controversial in its implications for students with *handicaps*.

minority group   A subgroup of the population whose characteristics differ considerably from the *norm* and because of the smaller number of members, lacks authority or power to decree action as a group.

mirror reading   A deviancy in which images of words are thought to be seen in reverse, as in a mirror, and are read from right to left, which may create substantial reading problems.

mirror writing   A distorted *perception* that causes one to write from right to left so that what is written becomes legible when read from the reflection in a mirror. This is not uncommon among young children, who tend to "outgrow" it.

misting   A mild form of aversive stimuli, using a hand-held sprayer to spray water into the face of children who are hand biting, head banging, rocking, etc.

mixed cerebral palsy   Combined forms (e.g., spastic-athetoid cerebral palsy), which represent a large portion of the cases.

mixed dominance   A condition in which neither side of the body is consistently used (e.g., a person may favor use of the left hand and of the right foot). This condition is slightly more evident among the *learning disabled*.

mixed hearing loss   A type of *hearing impairment* in which *conductive* and *sensorineural* loss are both present.

mixed laterality   Confusion of sidedness of the body.

mneumonic (new-mahn'-ik)   A strategy or technique to aid memory. The individual makes up a jingle or the like to facilitate recall. In medical school, for example, students use the mneumonic OOOTTAFAJUSH ("on old Olympus towering top a Fin...") to help them remember the 12 *cranial* nerves. Mneumonic techniques can help children with learning problems study for tests, enabling them to remember larger amounts of information than they normally would.

MO   An abbreviation used by many local school systems to refer to *moderate mental retardation*. Some teachers use MOMH as an equivalent term.

mobility   The process of moving about safely and effectively within the environment. An especially important ability for *blind* persons, who must coordinate mental *orientation* and physical locomotion to achieve safe, effective movement. They may use **mobility aids** such as canes, guide dogs, *sighted guides,* or electronic devices to help move about.

mobility specialist   An instructor in the art of *orientation* and *mobility* skills. (see also **peripatology**)

mobility training   Special instruction of *blind* individuals in the ability to move about safely and effectively from one place to another. Mobility training involves a wide variety of specific techniques according to the needs of the students, including *orien-*

109

tation, foot travel, moving in traffic, crossing streets, accepting human assistance, using a cane, making use of the senses in getting about, and may include use of guide dogs.

modality 1. The form or application of a treatment. 2. A channel of learning (e.g., *visual* modality). 3. Specific treatment used in *physical therapy.*

modeling A teaching technique in which the teacher performs a desired behavior and encourages the pupil to try the same behavior, using the teacher's demonstrated behavior as an example.

modem Computer terminology indicating the telephone connection or connection equipment that allows one type of computer to be connected with another or with auxiliary equipment.

moderate hearing loss A deficiency to the extent of understanding conversational speech at 3–5 feet but probably needing a *hearing aid, auditory training, speech reading,* favorable seating, and/or *speech therapy.* Described generally as 40–55 *db* loss.

moderate mental retardation (moderately retarded) A term introduced by the American Association on Mental Retardation to refer to a level of *intelligence* comparable to the educational classification of *trainable mental retardation.* The *intellectual* level, *assessed* with an individual intelligence test, involves *IQ* scores ranging from 40 to 55.

moderate training residence Terminology that has emerged to replace the term *group home.* It represents the same concepts but removes the negative association attached to the other label.

mon–, mono– Prefix denoting one, single.

monaural amplification Magnification of sound in one ear through the use of a *hearing aid.*

mongolism See *Down syndrome,* the preferred term.

monitoring 1. A requirement of *PL 94-142* that all school systems receiving federal funds under that Act must undergo a thorough external *evaluation.* 2. In general, the function that involves checking a program in process to determine its effectiveness.

mononucleosis (mah-noe-new-klee-oh´-sis) See *infectious mononucleosis.*

monoplegia (mon-oh-plee´-juh) *Paralysis* of one limb only.

monozygotic (mah-noe-zie-gah´-tik) A description of the origin of identical twins, occurring from the splitting of a single fertilized egg, and therefore identical in *genetic* composition.

Montessori (mahnt-eh-soar´-ee) **method** An instructional format developed by Dr. Maria Montessori, an Italian *psychiatrist,* which emphasizes individual instruction using extensive *sensory* and *motor* training, early development of reading and writing skills, and much free physical activity. The method originally was intended for preschool and primary levels but in some situations has been used at other levels.

Moro reflex The response of an infant to loud, sharp noise or to being dropped gently on his/her back; characterized by fanning out the arms and crying. The Moro reflex is commonly referred to as the *startle response* because the behavior is characteristic of what happens when a person is startled.

morpheme (more'-feem) Any sound or group of sounds that has *linguistic* meaning and cannot be further reduced and still retain meaning. The smallest unit of meaningful *language*.

morphology (more-fahl'-oh-jee) 1. In *language development*, the structural level at which meaningful units are created from sounds. 2. The study of word formation.

mosaicism (moe-zay'-ih-siz-im) A form of *Down syndrome* named for its unusual *chromosome* pattern, in which not all cells have an abnormal chromosomal composition.

motivation The *incentive*, force, or thought that makes one act to satisfy needs or achieve goals.

motokenesthetic method A technique used in speech pathology where the speech clinician directs the movement of the production of speech sounds by placing hands on the articulatory mechanism of the client and also employing the client's sense of feeling on the speech mechanism.

motor Refers to movement of body muscles. In education the motor function is often differentiated by *fine motor* and *gross motor* skills.

motor aphasia (ah-fay'-zee-ah) Inability to speak because of a lack of physical coordination to form words. In many cases, the individual may know the words and can communicate by pointing and by gestures. (see also *expressive aphasia* and *apraxia*)

motor disinhibition A form of *distractibility* in which one is unable to resist responding to any *stimulus* that produces a physical activity. Thus, any object that can be pushed, pulled, twisted, poked, traced, bent, folded, or mutilated likely will elicit a response.

motor skills Any acts requiring the ability to control and direct the voluntary muscles of the body. Usually classified by the two types of *fine motor* and *gross motor* skills.

mouthstick A device that *physically handicapped* individuals hold in the mouth to activate electric typewriters, microcomputer keyboards, and *autotelic* devices.

movement therapy A technique often applied in *special education* whereby body actions within space are used to improve body knowledge and *orientation*.

movigenics An approach to the learning process and *curriculum* based on theories proposed by Raymond H. Barsch in 1967 and 1968; involves much *perceptual-motor* activity and considers *perception*, movement, and *language* as a dynamic triad for curriculum implementation.

multi– Prefix denoting many.

multidisciplinary An approach wherein several professions are involved in or contribute to a common objective, such as a *screening committee* consisting of a special educator, a medical doctor, a *psychologist*, a *social worker*, and a school administrator. Similar to *interdisciplinary.*

multifactored testing A term popularized by *PL 94-142* meaning *assessment* using a variety of instruments, to avoid arriving at a *diagnosis* of *mental retardation* or other *handicap* based on only one score.

multihandicapped Having a physical or *sensory handicap* plus one or more additional handicaps that inhibit response to education in the regular classroom. Special services usually are required.

multiple sclerosis (skler-oh'-sis) **(MS)** A disease of progressive deterioration in which the protective *myelin* sheath surrounding the nerves *degenerates* and causes failure in the body's neurological system. MS occurs most often between ages 20 and 40.

multiply handicapped See *multihandicapped.*

multisensory A term generally applied to training procedures that simultaneously utilize more than one sense *modality.* Multisensory learning results from two or more modalities being employed as the means for instruction.

muscular dystrophy (MD) A *hereditary* disorder that causes a loss of vitality and progressive *deterioration* of the body as a result of *atrophy,* or the replacement of muscle tissue with fatty tissue.

music therapy The scientific application of music to accomplish treatment aims; the use of music by a *therapist* to influence changes in behavior.

mutation (mew-tay'-shun) An unexpected difference in a characteristic of certain offspring, resulting from a modification in the determining *genetic* structure. An offspring that has undergone mutation is called a **mutant.**

mute (or **mutism**) One who cannot speak (the inability to speak; sometimes, refusal to speak).

myasthenia gravis (my-uhs-thee'-nee-uh grav'-iss) A defect of nutrition that causes a *syndrome* of fatigue and exhaustion of the muscular system marked by progressive *paralysis* of muscles without *sensory* disturbance or *atrophy.*

myelin A soft, white, fatty-like substance that forms a protective sheath around certain nerve fibers. *Degeneration* of this myelin sheath is associated with *multiple sclerosis.*

myelomeningocele (my-eh-loe-meh-ning'-goe-seel) See *meningomyelocele.*

myoclonic seizure An *epileptic* activity characterized by jerking of the arms and bending of the trunk of the body, which may result in falling.

myopathy (my-op'-ah-thee) Any disease of a muscle characterized by weakness and deterioration without neurological *impairment.*

myopia (my-oh'-pea-ah) **(nearsightedness)** A condition in which one's distance vision is poor, usually because of a lengthened diameter of the eyeball from front to back, causing the image to come in *focus* at a point in front of the *retina.* Myopia usually is corrected by eyeglasses having a *concave lens.* In contrast, see *hyperopia.*

myositis (mie-oh-sigh'-tiss) A *chronic* crippling condition resulting from *inflammation* of the muscles.

myotonic dystrophy (mie-oh-tahn'-ik dis'-troe-fee) A type of *muscular dystrophy* characterized by weakness of fingers, hands, forearms, feet, and lower limbs; does not affect the facial muscles. Also known as *Steinut's disease,* it usually appears in early adulthood.

myxedema (mik-seh-dee'-muh) A condition of the skin caused by a deficiency in *thyroid* function, resulting in dryness and swelling of the affected surfaces.

N

narcolepsy (nar'-coe-lep-see)   A condition in which an individual involuntarily has brief episodes of deep sleep at irregular times; the person has an uncontrollable desire to sleep.

narcotic   Any drug or agent that produces insensitivity or *stupor* in humans.

nasal (nasality)   Refers to a voice quality of excessive, unique *resonance* described as "speaking through the nose," as in *cleft palate* speech.

nasopharynx (nay-zoe-fair'-inks)   The part of the throat above the level of the base of the *uvula,* or the place at which the nose and throat connect.

natal (nate'-uhl)   Pertaining to birth, at the time of birth. A frame of reference, as in *prenatal, postnatal, perinatal.*

near-point vision   Ability to see at close range (usually, normal reading distance).

nearsighted(ness)   See *myopia.*

necrosis (neh-crow'-sis)   The death of body tissues, as from loss of blood supply, burns, or cessation of breathing.

need achievement   A concept advanced to explain the variance in levels of need to achieve or the *motivation* to achieve among individuals.

negative eugenics (you-jen'-iks)   Any program designed to improve the quality of the human race by limiting reproduction of inferior members of society. Sterilization of persons with *severe retardation* would be one example.

negative reinforcement   A *stimulus* that, when removed as a consequence of a response, results in an increase or maintenance of that response.

negligence   The legal *tort* for which teachers are most often charged. To prove negligence, the plaintiff must have suffered actual harm and a sequential connection must be shown between the teacher's conduct and the harm.

Nemeth code   Originated as a *braille*-based system for teaching and doing mathematical computations. Used by *blind* persons and applied in areas such as science, calculus, and physics.

neo–   A prefix meaning new.

neonatal (nee-oh-nate'-uhl)   Pertaining to the first month after birth.

neonatologist (nee-oh-nah-tahl'-oh-jist)   A specialist in *pediatrics* especially trained to care for the newborn.

nephritis (nef-rye'-tiss) *Acute* or *chronic inflammation* of the kidneys. Same as *Bright's disease.*

nephrosis (nef-roe'-siss) A noninflammatory disease of the kidneys marked by protein from the blood escaping into the urine, bringing about a reduction of proteins in the body, accompanied by an increase of fatty substances in the blood. The resulting imbalance in body functions may result in serious illness and, if not treated, severe deterioration of the kidneys.

nerve deafness (neural loss) A form of *hearing impairment* resulting from a defect in the nerve structure of the inner ear or the *auditory nerve.* High-frequency sounds are the most likely to be affected, and the condition rarely can be improved by medical treatment.

neura– or **neuro–** Prefix meaning pertaining to the nerves.

neural tube defect A term that refers to a series of birth defects in which the spine or *cranium* is abnormally open (e.g., *spina bifida*). Detected in utero through *alpha-fetoprotein screening* and *ultrasonography.* (see also *spina bifida*)

neurasthenia (nur-ass-thee'-nee-uh) The term applied to a *syndrome* including complaints of tiredness, headache, dizziness, upset stomach, loss of appetite, and pains in the chest or stomach. Although no *organic* cause has been *diagnosed* for the above *symptoms,* they are real to the person, producing mental and physical fatigue and disrupting normal living and adjustment. A form of *psychoneurosis.*

neurological impress method An approach to teaching reading in which the teacher reads the selection and the student "shadows" the selection by repeating what the teacher has read. The selection is read and re-read until the student assumes a more dominant role. At this point the teacher begins to soften his/her voice.

neurological "soft" signs *Diagnostic* characteristics that are not as readily linked to *brain injury* as are *symptoms* such as *seizures,* for example, but are more subtle, and may be reflected in psychological and *perceptual* tests (coordination problems, awkward gait, etc.)

neurologically impaired or **handicapped** Pertaining to any of a number of conditions resulting from injury or *malformation* of the *central nervous system.* Conditions such as *cerebral palsy, epilepsy,* and the *Strauss syndrome* are examples.

neurologist A medical doctor who has special training in *diagnosis* and treatment of diseases of the nervous system. This doctor practices **neurology.**

neurophrenia (nur-oh-free'-nee-uh) A term first used in 1951 by Edgar Doll in referring to conditions now called *learning disorders.*

neurosis (adj., **neurotic**) A term applied to mental/*emotional disorders* with a variety of characteristics including *anxiety, hysterical* behavior, unusual mannerisms, *phobias,* and obsessions, usually not serious enough to require hospitalization. No *organic* basis is found in most cases.

neurotogenic (nur-ah-toe-jen'-ik) Contributing to the onset of development of a *neurosis.*

Nieman-Pick disease A *metabolic disorder* characterized by enlargement of the liver and spleen; often results in *retardation, deafness,* and *visual* problems.

114

night blindness See *nyctolopia*.

non– A prefix denoting not, absence of, reverse of.

nonambulatory Unable to walk or move about independently; may be bedridden or in a wheelchair.

noncategorical Refers to programs or philosophies that do not *label* or differentiate among the various *handicaps* or *exceptionalities* in providing services. (see *interrelated* and *mildly handicapped*)

nondevelopmental approach (language) A *concept* holding that individuals with *retardation* do not learn *language* as normal children do. Because their language is assumed to be *deviant*, not merely delayed, little emphasis is placed on developmental sequences. The nondevelopmental approach emphasizes training language forms and skills that are perceived to be most useful to the child for interaction and control of the environment. This approach is used with those who have *severe handicaps* and emphasizes imitation and *reinforcement* techniques to establish the desired responses. For comparison, see *developmental approach*.

nondirective therapy (approach) A counseling method that is *client-centered* and emphasizes client selection of solutions. The *therapist* serves as a catalyst but refrains from directing or evaluating the therapy.

nondiscriminatory testing Administering of measures that are not prejudicial against *minority groups* or individuals. This is a provision of certain court cases brought because higher percentages of minority children had been placed in *special classes*, in which the court also ruled that children must be tested in the child's primary *language* and that *psychologists* must develop *assessment* procedures that do not discriminate against minorities; the *evaluation* must be comprehensive, using instruments that accommodate culture, language, and adaptive factors as much as possible.

nondisjunction The incomplete splitting of *chromosome* pairs, resulting in a cell with more than normal chromosome material; often identified with certain forms of *mental retardation* (e.g., *Down syndrome*).

nonfluency *Deviations* in the normal rhythmical patterns of speech.

nongraded class A group of students in which each pupil is functioning at his/her individual performance level without regard to grade level, and each is allowed to progress at his/her own rate of individual achievement.

nonjudgmental Describes an attitude and resulting behavior on the part of personnel who show neutrality toward pupils or clients and indicate neither approval nor disapproval of others' behaviors or attitudes. This is considered an essential quality, especially among counselors.

nonoral communication Specifically denotes the use of a system of pictorial symbols rather than *vocalizations* as a form of *language* interaction, particularly with *nonverbal severely handicapped* persons.

nonverbal Not speaking, as in a child who for a number of reasons has failed to develop verbal *language*. A nonverbal child may have some other language abilities.

115

nonverbal test A measure that does not require the use of words in *stimulus* items or responses to them; e.g., tests that require only pointing or *motor* responses.

norm 1. An average or typical group score against which individual scores can be compared. 2. An acceptable pattern or standard in society.

norm-referenced A term describing tests that compare an individual's performance to that of a group, in contrast to *criterion-referenced* tests, designed to measure an individual's mastery of specific content.

normalization A *concept* derived from Scandinavia and introduced in the U.S. in the 1960s whereby *handicapped* persons are treated and placed in situations that are as nearly like those of normal people as possible. Thus, rather than living in a large *institution,* individuals with *mental retardation* may live in a *group home,* work in the community during the day, and participate in community recreation at night.

numeration *Arithmetic concepts* including *rote* counting, one-to-one correspondence, sets, symbol identification, cardinal numbers, and place value.

nyctolopia (nik-toe-loe´-pea-ah) A condition in which a person sees poorly in the dark but can see well in the light. Commonly called *night blindness.*

nystagmus (nis-tag´-muhs) Continuous, involuntary movement of the eyeballs that usually affects both eyes and is associated with *visual impairment.*

O

objective   Statement of a specific learning goal for a student. These goals should be developed from *assessed* student needs and be the basis for the learning activities carried out in attempting to meet them.

objective test   An instrument designed so that the correct responses are agreed upon and set in advance by the test developer(s); the scores, therefore, are unaffected by opinion or judgment of the scorer. (see also *norm referenced*)

observational training   Essentially the same as *behavior modeling.*

obsessive-compulsive   Describes a *neurosis* in which an individual seems compelled to repeat certain acts or *verbalizations* over and over.

obstacle perception   An ability developed by *blind* persons in which they can sense when they are approaching an object. Certain research conducted with adult blind people has indicated that hearing high-frequency sound waves and their echoes is responsible for obstacle perception.

obstetrician (ahb-steh-trish´-un)   A medical doctor specializing in treatment during pregnancy and childbirth.

obstetrics (ahb-steh´-tricks)   The branch of medicine dealing with treatment during pregnancy and childbirth.

obturator (ahb´-tyew-ray-tore)   A device, usually of plastic or dacron, used to close an opening at the top of the mouth (as in *cleft palate*) to improve *articulation* of speech and/or reduce *nasality.*

occipital (ahk-sip´-ih-tuhl)   Referring to the bone that forms the back part of the skull.

occipital alpha training   A *biofeedback* technique used for improving *visual attention* in some individuals with *handicaps.* Because alpha waves appear to measure visual attention, this technique can reveal whether individuals are really paying attention and teach them an awareness of what attending is.

occluder (uh-klood´-er)   An opaque or translucent device placed in front of an eye to block vision from that eye, as in *visually* testing each eye separately or as prescribed to correct specific visual defects.

occlusion   Obstruction of a passage: (a) in controlling the breath stream during the process of speaking, (b) in referring to the fit of the teeth when the jaws are closed. (see also *malocclusion*)

occupational therapist A graduate of an *occupational therapy* program and approved by the Council on Medical Education of the American Medical Association, or an individual who has the equivalent of such education and training. Utilizes *creative*, educational, and recreational activities.

occupational therapy A *rehabilitative* process directed by *occupational therapists* in which purposeful activities are employed as a basis for improving muscular control of clients; sometimes referred to as "curing by doing." Physical and mental recovery is the main objective, with other emphasis on helping the individual acquire job or *self-help skills*.

ocular (ock'-you-lar) Pertaining to the eyes.

ocular control training Exercises of the eye muscles directed at improving eye coordination and vision. (see also *orthoptist*)

ocular dominance The consistent use of one eye in preference to the other in situations such as sighting, in which fixation is involved.

ocular pursuit Movement of the eyes to *visually* follow a moving target. (see also *visual tracking*)

ocularist A medical doctor who specializes in treatment and replacement of the eye with artificial parts.

oculist A medical doctor whose practice deals with *diagnosis* and treatment of *visual* conditions. The oculist may perform surgery, prescribe drugs, measure refraction, and prescribe glasses.

offender rehabilitation The preferred terminology for the area of government charged with housing and supervision of criminals. This term reflects the change from *custodial* care to training and rehabilitation for persons with prison sentences. (see also *probation*)

Office of Special Education Programs The federal office involved with the education of the *handicapped*. Formerly known as the *Bureau of Education for the Handicapped (BEH)*. One division of the *Office of Special Education and Rehabilitative Services (OSERS)*.

Office of Special Education and Rehabilitative Services (OSERS) See *Office of Special Education Programs. (OSEP)*

OJT See *on-the-job-training*.

olfactory (ahl-fack'-tor-ee) Pertaining to the sense of smell.

oligophrenia (ah-lig-oh-fre'-nee-ah) A term meaning *mental retardation* or deficiency; used primarily in Europe, usually in a medical context.

ombudsman (om'-budz-man) One who investigates complaints for the purpose of achieving more equal treatment or settlements for disabled individuals.

omission (in speech) An *articulatory* defect in which a sound is left out. Often characteristic of *delayed speech* or speech of individuals who have *severe retardation*. Examples are: *cu* for *cup; kni* for *knife; acuum* for *vacuum*.

118

on-the-job training (OJT) A method of teaching high school level students who have *educable mental retardation* or other *handicaps* specific work skills by assigning them to employment on competitive jobs for part of a day or sometimes a full day. If part of a day, the remainder of the day is spent in school; when pupils are in on-the-job training for a full day, this is followed by a period of full-time school attendance. Also referred to as a *work study program.*

open campus A school or program usually conducted at night in which individuals not usually enrolled or who work can attain their high school degree or prepare for an occupation. (a newer term is *alternative schools*)

open court method A *basal* reading program that encompasses a strong *phonetic* element and *kinesthetic/tactile* elements. This program is different enough from most basal texts to provide an alternative method.

operant behaviors A series of actions that are voluntary (as opposed to *respondent behaviors,* which are involuntary or reflexive).

operant conditioning An instructional method in which rewards are controlled so that a pupil has a *reinforcing* experience for performing acts that the teacher desires and does not receive rewards for undesired acts. The behaviors that are rewarded tend to be repeated, and the behaviors that are not rewarded tend to disappear. (see also *behavior modification*)

operant level Refers to an individual's behavior pattern that occurs naturally, prior to training or modification. One must know the operant level to establish a *baseline.*

operations (of thinking) The category of thinking abilities in Guilford's model (see *structure of the intellect*) that includes *cognition, memory, convergent thinking, divergent thinking,* and *evaluation.*

ophthalmia (ahf-thal′-mee-uh) An *inflammation* of the *conjunctiva* of the eye, occurring during the first few weeks of a baby's life and caused by infection contracted during birth or from contamination after birth.

ophthalmologist (ahf-thal-mahl′-oh-jist) A medical doctor with specialized training (beyond the medical degree) in working with the eyes. The ophthalmologist may conduct *diagnosis,* prescribe medications, perform surgery, measure refraction, and prescribe eyeglasses.

ophthalmoscope (ahf-thal′-moe-skope) An instrument used by a physician to observe and examine the interior of the eye.

optacon (ahp′-tuh-kahn) A device for converting print into *tactual* images, for the *visually impaired.* Employs 144 pins that are activated to produce vibratory images that can be "read" by the reader's index finger. An optacon that reads print *aurally* is now available.

optic nerve The *cranial* nerve that carries nerve impulses of sight to the brain.

optician A technician who, upon prescription from a physician or *optometrist,* grinds lenses, fits them into frames, and adjusts the eyeglasses to the wearer.

119

optometrist A licensed, nonmedical person trained to work with the function of the eyes but not the *pathology* of the eyes. The optometrist measures refraction, prescribes eyeglasses, and carries out vision training.

optometry The science of *visual* care and measurement of visual defects caused by errors of refraction that may be corrected by lenses without use of prescribed medication.

oral (adv., **orally**) Pertaining to or surrounding the mouth; especially, done by the mouth, as speech.

oral interpretation Translation for another person without use of the hands, essentially employing the upper part of the body (face, neck, eyes, etc.)

oral method (oralism) A system of teaching children with *hearing impairments* in which communication is carried on through spoken *language, speech reading (lip reading)*, listening, and writing, without the use of *sign language* or *fingerspelling*.

order center A skill area in the *engineered classroom* designed to include materials appropriate for the child to learn and obtain practice in *attention*, sequencing, and similar activities.

organic Describes a condition resulting from disease, damage, or *dysfunction* of a body part (as opposed to a *functional* condition).

organic brain damage Destruction that results from actual injury or abnormal development of the brain.

organic hearing loss An *impairment* caused by damage to or abnormal development of the *auditory* pathway of the ear.

organic therapy A term referring to practices of psychosurgery, aversive, classical, or *operant conditioning,* the use of any drugs, electrical shock, or electrical stimulation of the brain in which unpleasant physical sensations are induced for treatment purposes.

organicity (ore-gan-ih′-sih-tee) Refers to any condition resulting from an *impairment* of the *central nervous system*.

orientation (v., **orient**) With reference to *blind* persons, an individual's sense of determining position with relation to the environment or to a particular person, place, or thing by utilizing the remaining senses. Orientation of a blind person depends upon retaining a "mental map" of his/her environment.

orifice A natural external opening of the body, such as the mouth, nose, and ears.

originality A trait, usually evidenced in *gifted* or *creative* individuals, characterized by inventiveness and ability to develop new, novel plans and actions. One of the factors in creative thinking.

orphan drugs Medications needed for the control of rare diseases, but considered nonprofitable by pharmaceutical firms because of the low patient populations.

ortho– A prefix, whose meanings is corrective.

orthocarintology (ore-thoe-care-in-tahl'-oh-jee) The practice of repeated fitting of the eyes with contact lenses to try to change the shape of the eye and thus improve vision. This practice is done primarily by *optometrists* rather than *ophthalmologists.*

orthodontia (ore-thoe-dahn'-chuh) A dentistry practice dealing with straightening the teeth and jaws, thus correcting problems such as *malocclusion* and faulty alignment; includes fitting of appliances (braces). An **orthodontist** is the person trained to conduct this practice.

orthogenic (ore-thoe jen'-ik) Pertaining to educational, medical, or surgical treatment directed toward stimulating mental growth, developing desirable personality traits, or correcting mental or nervous defects.

orthomolecular psychiatry The practice of treating *learning* and *behavior disorders* through administration of massive doses of water-soluble vitamins *(megavitamin therapy).* Linus Pauling coined the term in 1968 to describe the optimum molecular environment of the mind.

orthopedic (ore-thoe-peed'-ik) Pertaining basically to the bones, joints, and muscles. Orthopedic surgery is performed for the purpose of straightening, restoring, or preserving muscles, bones, or joints, thus correcting body *deformities.* A medical doctor who performs this function is termed an **orthopedist.**

orthopedic handicap A disabling condition caused by physical *impairments,* especially those related to the bones, joints, and muscles.

orthopedist see *orthopedic.*

orthopsychiatry The study and treatment of mental disorders based on combined contributions of *disciplines* such as psychiatry, medicine, psychology, and sociology.

orthoptist (ore-thahp'-tist) A nonmedical technician who directs and supervises *visual* training involving the exercise of eye muscles to develop eye coordination and to correct vision. This is termed *occular control training.*

orthosis (ore-thoe'-sis) A device that gives function to a part of the body; e.g., a brace causes the limbs to have increased *rigidity* so the individual can stand upright. (see also *prosthesis*)

orthoticist (ore-thah'-tih-sist) A skilled technician who works with an *orthopedist* in designing and fitting braces. The orthoticist must have a working knowledge of metals, materials, fabrics, and shoes to be able to interpret the prescription into functional structures.

orthotics (ore-thah'-tiks) The specialty field involved in making limb braces and other *orthopedic* appliances.

OSEP One of the divisions of the *Office of Special Education and Rehabilitation* that deals with specific programs.

OSERS See *Office of Special Education and Rehabilitative Services, Office of Special Education Programs, Office of Rehabilitative Services.*

121

ossicles (ahs'-ih-kulz) The three small bones *(malleus, incus,* and *stapes)* of the middle ear that transfer sound waves from the *ear drum* to the oval window connecting to the inner ear.

ossification (v., **ossify, ossified**) The process of *cartilaginous* substances hardening to form bone.

osteogenesis imperfecta (ahs-tee-oh-jen'-ih-sis im-per-fek'-tuh) An inherited rare bone disease resulting in fragile bones.

osteomyelitis (ahs-tee-oh-my-lite'-iss) An infectious condition of the long bones resulting in *inflammation* of the bone marrow.

osteopathy (oss'-tee-oh-path-ee) A treatment system of healing that emphasizes normal body mechanics and environmental conditions. Generally accepted physical, medicinal, and surgical methods are used if necessary, along with bone and muscle manipulation. A doctor trained in and practicing osteopathy is called an **osteopath.**

ostomy (ahs'-toe-mee) An operation in which a conduit *(stoma)* is made in the abdominal wall to carry urinary or *fecal* matter out of the body.

ostosclerosis (ahs-toe-skluh-roe'-sis) An inherited condition in which the *stapes* bone in the ear is abnormally attached to the oval window and thus does not properly transform mechanical energy into hearing. Surgery may correct the problem.

other health impaired (OHI) A term encompassing health conditions typified by *chronic* ill health, low vitality, and progressive *deterioration,* all of which interfere with a child's educational progress.

otitis media (oh-tight'-iss mee'-dee-ah) One of the most common diseases of early childhood, characterized by fluid and infection in the middle ear. Often results in reduced hearing in children, but is one of the more treatable conditions.

otolaryngology (oat-oh-lair-uhn-gahl'-oh-jee) The branch of medicine dealing with *diagnosis* and treatment of diseases and conditions of the ear and *larynx.* A physician specializing in this area is called an **otolaryngologist.**

otological Pertaining to the ear.

otology The medical specialty that deals with diseases and problems of the ear. A physician who specializes in this area is called an **otologist.**

–otomy (ah'-toe-mee) A suffix that designates cutting or removing (e.g., lobotomy: a surgical operation involving an incision in the *cerebral* lobe).

otoplasty (oat'-oh-plas-tee) The rebuilding and correction of the ear by plastic surgery.

otosclerosis (oat-oh-skler-roe'-sis) A *hereditary* disease affecting the bony capsule that surrounds the inner ear; causes *chronic* and progressive *hearing loss.*

otoscope (oat'-oh-skope) An instrument with a light, designed specifically for examining the ear.

ototoxic (oat-oh-tock'-sick) Poisonous to the ear.

122

outdoor education A term that encompasses all learning activities involving performance in the natural environment "laboratory"; current terminology has shifted to *leisure life skills.*

outreach worker An individual who has special training in locating, identifying, and collecting information on human problems and in referring them within neighborhood settings.

over-age A pupil who is older chronologically than is usual for his/her functional level or educational placement.

overachiever A pupil who achieves at a level above that predicted from prior performance and testing.

overattention A characteristic of some individuals who fix their attention on a particular object and seem unable to break the focus. Often noticed in *autistic* children.

overcompensation A reaction pattern in those who feel a deep-seated sense of inferiority and inadequacy in certain areas. They tend to overinvest energy in an endeavor at which they can achieve. For example, a short, overweight boy who cannot successfully compete in baseball may learn the names and playing records of every major league player.

overcorrection Procedures used to help a student correct misbehavior, through practicing more appropriate behavior or improving the environment in which the student misbehaves.

overgeneralization Application of a *language* rule without regard for exceptions, such as "goed" for "went."

overlearning Learning that results from additional practice after something has been learned, to the level necessary for immediate recall. Overlearning helps many individuals with *handicaps* overcome *short-term memory* deficits and learn academic and other materials to the level that facilitates long-term memory.

overloading An inability to handle all the information coming in through all the senses. Learning may be improved if one or more *sensory modalities* is eliminated or *masked.*

overprotection The sheltering of an individual by another to the extent that the sheltered individual is denied experiences necessary for normal development; a behavior sometimes shown by parents of *handicapped* children.

overt An action that can be objectively observed. Opposite of *covert.*

oxycephaly (ok-sih-seh-fah'-lee) A *congenital* condition in which the top of the head is pointed, eyes are large and widely set, hands and feet are webbed, and *mental retardation* is typical. Same as *acrocephaly.*

P

pacing A teaching procedure in which a pupil's activities are directed by giving an example or indication of the speed at which the activities are to be achieved; often used in teaching reading. Also applied to the *gifted*, who benefit from rapid pacing.

paired-associate learning A teaching technique wherein a *stimulus* and a desired response are presented simultaneously and the learner is conditioned to give the desired response when the stimulus is presented by itself.

palate The roof of the mouth, consisting of a hard part in the forward portion of the mouth and a soft part in the back of the mouth (hence, *hard palate* and *soft palate*).

palsy A neurological condition that causes an individual to be unable to hold affected body parts steady without support and, as a result, is accompanied by a shaking or reciprocating action.

pancreas The gland located behind the stomach that produces digestive *enzymes* and *insulin*. *Inflammation* of the pancreas is termed **pancreatitis** (pan-kree-ah-tie'-tiss).

paperless braille A term applied to the Versabrailler and other equipment that electronically records *braille* on an audiotape, which can be read *tactually* with the fingertips on the machine, or in more advanced forms will produce paper braille tapes.

papilloma A virus that affects the vocal folds, resulting in hoarseness and difficulty in breathing. The excess folds are surgically removed. The condition usually does not occur past age 12.

paradoxical reaction A condition that results when a drug or treatment has an effect opposite to the one expected; e.g., a medication given as a *sedative* produces stimulation and overactivity in an individual.

parageusia (pair-ah-gyew'-see-ah) *Impairment* of the sense of taste, which leaves a bad taste in the mouth.

paragraphia (pair-ah-graf'-ee-ah) A *language disorder* in which the student misspells words and writes one word in place of another.

paralalia (pair-ah-lay'-lee-ah) A disturbance in the production of speech, especially in which the vocal sound produced is different from the desired sound.

paralysis (adj., **paralytic**; v., **paralyze(d)**) Partial or complete loss of the power of voluntary motion or sensation.

paranoia (pair-ah-noy'-ah) A *chronic* mental disorder in which the affected individual has *delusions of persecution,* and is said to be **paranoid**.

124

paraplegia (pair-ah-plee'-juh) (**paraplegic**) *Paralysis* of the lower half of the body, including both legs.

parapro Shortening of the term *paraprofessional,* or *teacher aide.*

paraprofessional An individual such as a *teacher aide* who performs some of the functions of a professional under the general supervision of a professional but who, because of insufficient training or experience, is not allowed total responsibility.

PARC case A landmark lawsuit brought in 1971 by the Pennsylvania Association for Retarded Children against the Commonwealth of Pennsylvania in which the court ruled in favor of PARC and ordered extensive *due process* procedures that provided, in essence, that a student with *mental retardation* could not be expelled, transferred, or excluded from a public education program.

parent education Educational programs designed to improve knowledge about child care, handicapping conditions, program content and goals, family living, and similar topics. (see also *parent training*)

parent involvement A term used to describe a wide range of programs (e.g., parent counseling, volunteer service, *parent education, advocacy* training) in which parents are active participants.

parent-teacher conference A planned meeting, usually held at the school at a specified time, in which the objective is to discuss the student, the school program, the child's achievement in the program, *reinforcement* that might be carried out at home, any problems, and to encourage parental questions, suggestions, and general communication.

parent training A term used in the 1980s that is equivalent to *parent education.* It seeks to train the parent in skills that will augment and extend that which is taught at school.

parental rejection A reaction in which a child is openly repudiated, with undisguised hostility and neglect. Parental rejection is more common among parents of children with *handicaps* than among the general population.

paresis (pair-ee'-siss) Mild *paralysis* that inhibits movement but not sensation.

Parkinson's disease A progressive condition, generally found in older adults, characterized by *tremor,* slow voluntary movements, weakening of muscles, and poor coordination, especially when walking.

partial participation A practice in education of students with *severe/profound retardation* who voluntarily engage in an activity or task to the greatest extent currently possible. The performance may be interim to independent performance or anticipation of the activity to come.

partially sighted A condition in which one's vision is seriously impaired, defined usually as having between 20/200 and 20/70 central *visual acuity* in the better eye, with correction. Various aids and educational techniques allow most partially sighted children to be educated as sighted rather than *blind* children. Preferred terminology has changed to *visually handicapped* or *impaired.*

125

passive aggression   Hostility or antagonism expressed as uncooperative, inefficient, obstructive behavior.

passive-dependent children   Those who present or promote themselves as helpless.

passive learner   A student (usually considered to have a learning disability or mental retardation) whose learning problems result more from a lack of *cognitive* attention or vigilance than from a deficit; if passive learners are taught *metacognitive* and *active listening* skills, they may learn better.

passive motion   A *modality* of *physical therapy* in which the *therapist* moves a bodily joint back and forth through its full range of movement. Stretching and contracting the muscles improves circulation and nutrition to the joints and muscles. Passive motion implies that the child or adult is not an active participant in the exercise.

passive responding   A term used in effective instruction indicating the child is not actively responding to instruction but may be benefiting from it, as in listening to other students involved in instruction.

pathogenic (path-oh-jen´-ik)   Causing a disease, or marked *symptoms* of a disease.

pathological   Describes a *diagnosed* condition of the body that is indicative of disease or physical damage.

pathologist   A medical doctor who specializes in studying the structural and *functional* changes caused by disease, conducts post-mortem examinations, and studies changes in tissues removed during operations for positive or negative indications of disease.

pathology   The science or branch of medicine concerned with studying diseases, their nature, causes, and treatment.

Pathsounder   An electronic device, worn around the neck, which emits a noise when approaching an object. The device aids *blind* persons in *mobility*.

patterning   See *Doman-Delcato method.*

pedagogy (ped´-ah-goj-ee) (adj., **pedagogical**)   The science or profession of teaching.

pediatric(s)   Pertaining to the medical specialty involved in the treatment of children.

pediatric neurologist   A physician trained in the neurological disorders of children.

pediatric psychiatry   The branch of medicine that deals specifically with mental disorders in children.

pediatrician   A physician who specializes in treating children.

pediculosis (peh-dik-you-loe´-siss)   Infestation of the body with head, body, or crab lice.

pedometer (peh-dah´-meh-turr)   A mechanical device for measuring movement of the lower *extremities*. Gives a measure of walking distance and has been used in research to determine the activity of children with various *disabilities*.

peer accounting   A system in which students set up and monitor the consequences of inappropriate and appropriate classroom behaviors. Usually more effective at or above fourth-grade level.

peer group People who are of equal standing with one another in society, as defined by age, grade, or status.

peer tutoring Academic assistance given to a student by another student of approximately the same age or grade except in *cross-age tutoring,* in which case an older student may teach a younger student or a younger *gifted* student may instruct an older student who has learning problems.

pellagra (peh-lah'-grah) A condition characterized by *dermatitis,* gastrointestinal problems, diarrhea, and *central nervous system* disorders; caused by a lack of niacin and protein in the diet.

Pennsylvania Association for Retarded Citizens v. Commonwealth of Pennsylvania See *PARC case.*

permanency planning A requirement of PL 96-272, the Adoption Assistance and Child Welfare Act, which requires planning and implementation of programs at the state level for more stable living arrangements for students with developmental disabilities.

per-pupil cost The amount of money required (usually figured on an annual basis) to educate a student in a given situation, computed by dividing the total expenditure for that situation by the stated pupil figure (e.g., pupils enrolled, pupils in *average daily membership,* pupils in *average daily attendance,* or other defined term).

percentile A rank in a distribution at or below which falls the percent of cases indicated by the percentile. Thus, the 35th percentile means that 35% of the cases are at or below the specified score.

perception Awareness of one's environment through *sensory* stimulation. Perception is an important part of *cognition* and understanding. A child who has faulty perception may have difficulty in learning.

perceptual Refers to any combination of sensations automatically retained and integrated by the brain which give an organism the ability to be aware of the unity of things.

perceptual disorders Difficulties or deficiencies in using the sense of sight, touch, smell, taste, or hearing to correctly recognize the various objects or situations within the environment. This type of disorder may become apparent in a student's poor performance in activities such as drawing, writing, and recognizing forms, sizes, or shapes.

perceptual-motor A term used to refer to interaction of the various aspects of *perception* with *motor* activity. Perceptual areas that commonly affect motor activities are *visual, auditory, tactual,* and *kinesthetic.*

perceptual-motor match A concept advanced by Newell C. Kephart in which motor development is said to occur prior to *sensory* development and learning is based on the match of sensations and motor responses; hence, Kephart's heavy reliance on motor training.

performance test A measure involving some *motor* or manual response on the examinee's part, generally the manipulation of *concrete* materials.

peridontia (pair-ih-dahn'-tshuh)   The area of dentistry specializing in treatment of tissue that surrounds the teeth (gums).

perinatal (pair-ih-nay'-tul)   Refers to the general time period of birth.

perinatologist   A specialist in *obstetrics* and *gynecology* trained to care for *high-risk* maternal and *fetal* patients.

periosteum (pair-ee-ahs'-tee-um)   Thick, vascular connective tissue covering all bones and possessing bone-forming potential. *Inflammation* of this tissue is termed **periostitis** (pair-ee-ahs'-tih-tiss).

peripatology (pair-ih-pah-tahl'-oh-jee)   The art of teaching *orientation* and *mobility* to *blind* persons. An instructor in these skills is termed a **peripatologist** or *mobility specialist* (preferred).

peripheral (purr-if'-er-ul) **vision**   *Perception* of objects, color, or motion by portions of the eye other than the *macula*. The images perceived are not in the center of vision but are seen by the outside parts of the retina.

peritoneum (pair-ih-tone'-ee-uhm)   A membranous tissue lining the abdominal wall and covering most of the internal organs of the abdominal cavity. *Inflammation* of this lining is termed **peritonitis** (pair-ih-toe-nye'-tiss).

Perkins brailler   The most commonly used typing machine for producing *braille*. Has 6 keys and spacer bar for production of letters and numerals.

permanency planning   A requirement of PL 96-272, the Adoption Assistance and Child Welfare Act, which requires planning and implementation of programs at the state level for more stable living arrangements for students with developmental disabilities.

permissive legislation   Laws enabling changes or programs to be started but not requiring them; this type of legislation is obsolete because of *PL 94-142*.

Perry Project   Perhaps the most famous early intervention project, in which disadvantaged high-risk children were given earlier schooling than their age peers. Students who attended the program grew up to have fewer handicaps and fewer encounters with the law, and they demonstrated a highly cost-effective benefit for the program. Also called *Ypsilanti project.*

perseverate (n., **perseveration**)   To persistently repeat an action, word, idea, or sensation, even though the result may not be goal-directed and the response has lost its initial meaning or usefulness. Perseveration may interfere with learning because it tends to inhibit goal-directed activities.

personal adequacy   One's ability to function in society. This is considered one of the goals for persons with *handicaps.*

personality problem   Any trait that reduces *rapport* with people or interferes with adjustment in society but is not serious enough to be considered a severe mental problem.

Perthes disease   See *Legg-Calve-Perthes.*

petit mal (pet'-ee-mahl)   A mild form of *seizure* occurring in *epileptic* conditions, characterized by momentary lapse of consciousness. These seizures can vary in fre-

128

quency from 1 to 200 times a day, lasting from 5 to 20 seconds each. Sometimes referred to as *absence seizures.*

phantom pain   An experience of *amputees* in which sharply felt sensations seem to come from the amputated *extremity.*

pharmacology (far-mah-kahl'-oh-jee)   The science of the uses of drugs and their relationships.

pharynx (fair'-inks)   The passage in the alimentary canal that connects the mouth and *nasal* cavities with the *larynx* and *esophagus;* the throat.

phenocopy (fee'-noe-kah-pea)   The term for a trait (usually ascribed to a particular *genetic* arrangement) that develops in some special instance through environmental factors that are different from those normally operating. The same *intellectual* condition may be attributed in one instance to distinct genetic characteristics and in another to a unique environment.

phenotype (fee'-noe-tipe)   The outward, visible expression of the *hereditary constitution* of an organism, which is measurable. This may vary considerably from the *genetic* structure. A dog that appears phenotypically to be pure bred may actually not be.

phenylketonuria (fen-uhl-kee-toe-new'-ree-ah) **(PKU)**   A *hereditary* condition in which the absence of an *enzyme* essential for digesting protein affects the *metabolism* of the body and results in a gradual buildup of *toxic* substances in the blood and urine of infants having this condition. Interferes with normal development and function of the brain and is possibly the most widely known abnormality of metabolism that causes *mental retardation.*

phobia   A persistent and unreasonable fear, as in fear of fire, heights, or animals.

phocomelia (foe-koe-mee'-lee-ah)   A developmental *deformity* at birth characterized by the absence of a portion of a limb or limbs, so that the hands or feet are attached to the torso by a single small bone, creating a flipper-like appearance. Mothers who took the drug thalidomide often produced children with this condition.

phonation (foe-nay'-shun)   The functioning of the *larynx* to produce vocal sounds and voice.

phoneme (foe'-neem)   One of the 36 sound families recognized in the modern English *language.* Spoken English contains 24 *consonant* phonemes and 12 *vowel* phonemes. The minimal *linguistic* unit of sound.

phonetic   Pertaining to speech sounds.

phonetic alphabet   A means of representing speech sounds, in which each sound is represented by a single written character. Examples of this system are the *initial teaching alphabet (ITA)* and the *international phonetic alphabet (IPA).*

phonetic elements   Parts of words that represent sounds, which may be syllables, letter combinations, or single letters. Blended together, they form words.

phonetics   The science of speech sounds involving analysis of words into separate sound elements.

phonetype   A communication device for persons with *hearing impairment* that incorporates a telephone and teletype; messages are typed, using this equipment, and transmitted to an individual having the same device; a flashing light rather than a sound indicates that a message is being sent. Terminology has changed most recently to *TDD (telecommunication device for the deaf)*.

phonics   The area of *linguistics* dealing with speech sounds and their relationship to symbols. As applied to teaching reading—syllables, letter combinations, and letters that consistently represent sounds are taught, to enable the reader to be more independent in sounding out and recognizing words.

phonological disorder   Deficiency in production and *articulation* of speech sounds, traditionally known as *articulatory defects (omissions, substitutions,* and *distortions)*. This terminology is preferred because the disorder involves more than just articulation.

phonology (foe-nahl´-oh-jee)   The science or study of *language* structures related to the sound system of *oral* language.

photophobia   An extreme sensitivity to and dislike of light. This condition is most often observed in *albino* individuals. (see also *albinism*)

physical disability   A bodily defect that interferes with education, development, adjustment, or rehabilitation; generally refers to crippling conditions and *chronic* health problems but usually does not include single *sensory handicaps* such as *blindness* or *deafness*.

physical reinforcer   A reward utilizing body contact or sensations that are pleasant to a pupil. This may consist of hugging, shoulder pats, etc.

physical therapy   The treatment of *disabilities* by using massage, exercise, water, light, heat, and certain forms of electricity, all of which are mechanical rather than medical in nature. Physical therapy is practiced by a professionally trained **physical therapist** under the referral of a physician.

physiological method   An approach to educating children with *mental retardation* first advocated by Edward Seguin in the mid-19th century, emphasizing the development and training of neuromotor and *sensory* skills, followed by coordinated academic and occupational training.

Piagetian   (pea-ah-gee´-tyan)   A term applied to any concept that incorporates Jean Piaget's sequential development theories.

Pidgin Signed English   A communication system for the deaf employing a combination of Signed Exact English and American Sign Language, in which verbs are conveyed with the eyes or facial expressions.

piece work   Often refers to tasks done in a *sheltered workshop* by individuals without the benefit of assembly line techniques. **Piece rate** refers to the amount paid per unit produced, or the number of units produced or serviced in a specific time period.

pinna   The outer, external portion of the ear.

PIP (Prescriptive Instructional Plan)   Usage in some states as the equivalent of an *individualized education program (IEP)*.

130

pitch   The subjective impression of highness or lowness of a sound; the psychological equivalent of *frequency.* Pitch is a consideration in *voice disorders* in which speech is too high, too low, monotonous, stereotyped, inflectuous, or has pitch breaks.

pituitary (pih-too'-ih-tare-eee) **gland**   An *endocrine* gland that produces secretions contributing to regulation of most basic body functions.

PKU   See *phenylketonuria.*

PL 94-103   Developmental Disabilities Act of 1975.

PL 94-142   See *Education for All Handicapped Children Act of 1975.*

PL 98-199   Education of the Handicapped Amendments, the 1984 amendments to *PL 94-142.*

PL 99-457   The extension of *PL 94-142,* the *Education for All Handicapped Children Act.* In addition to reauthorization, this act will be known as the Early Childhood and Infant Act.

placebo (plah-see'-boe)   A substance that has no effect, given to satisfy a person's perceived need for medication. In research, placebos are sometimes used for comparison to the drug under study.

placement team   A new term for the same type of group formerly called a *screening committee. PL 94-142* calls for a group or team to review *diagnostic* and instructional data with the parents to plan an *individualized education program.* The regular classroom teacher, *resource teacher, diagnostician,* counselor, and other professionals may be involved. This group is also variously called a study team, pupil evaluation team, staffing committee, or eligibility committee.

placenta previa (plah-sen'-tah) (pree'-vee-ah)   Separation of the *placenta* from the *uterine* wall, which results in the loss of oxygen and food for the *fetus.*

plasma   The fluid part of the blood in which corpuscles and other components are suspended. Plasma transfusions are sometimes needed in medical treatment.

plateau   In the context of *special education,* refers to a level of learning or physical growth at which the pupil no longer is showing improvement or advancement.

platelets   Tiny plate-like disks in the blood that control coagulation for clotting.

play audiometry   An approach to testing young children's hearing in which the child being tested responds to spoken signals in a game situation.

play therapy   A technique, used with children who have emotional problems, that allows them to express fear, hate, *aggression, anxiety,* and other emotions through activities with toys and games.

pleoptics (plee-ahp'-tiks)   A Swiss-developed procedure that works toward improving the function of suppressed vision through stimulation by a blinking light.

plosive (ploe'-siv)   Any one of the six *consonant* sounds /p, b, t, d, k, g/ that are formed by a blocking of the breath followed by a sudden release of air.

plumbism   See *lead poisoning.*

pneumoencephalography (new-moe-en-sef-ah-lah´-grah-fee) A medical *diagnostic* procedure in which air or gas is injected into the ventricular spaces of the brain and *x-ray* techniques are used to obtain a picture of the ventricles of the brain. (see also *encephalography*)

pocket brailler A device for electronic production and storage of braille. This device, produced by the American Printing House for the Blind, can store up to 200 pages of braille, provide oral feedback and, through a separate printer, provide a braille hard copy.

poliomyelitis (polio) An *acute* disease that inflames nerve cells of the spinal cord or brain stem and leaves a residual *paralysis* or muscular *atrophy*. Formerly resulted in many individuals with *physical handicaps*.

poly– Prefix denoting excessive or many.

polydactylism (pahl-ih-dak´-tih-lizm) A condition in which a child is born with more than the normal number of fingers or toes.

polygenic inheritance The *genetic hypothesis* that best describes the biological phenomena that occur when a characteristic is determined by the combined action of a large number of randomly assorted genetic influences working together.

Portage model A specific type of *preschool education* program that uses parents of children with *handicaps* as the teachers, with once-a-week *monitoring* and *modeling* by a traveling teacher instructor.

positioning Moving an individual's body and limbs in ways that are helpful or *therapeutic* to the person. Usually applies to individuals with *physical handicaps* or *severe multiple handicaps*.

positive reinforcement Rewards given for a specific desired behavior. (see also *reinforcement*)

possum device An *autotelic* system developed in England for teaching *nonverbal* language to persons with *severe handicaps*.

posterior Toward the rear or back side, as of the body. Opposite of *anterior*.

postictal (poe-stik´-tahl) **state** One's condition after having a *stroke* or a *seizure*.

postlingual deafness Loss of hearing that occurs after an individual has developed speech and *language*.

postnatal Pertaining to a time period after birth.

postpartum Refers to a time period following childbirth. Most often used in reference to the mother, as in "postpartum depression."

Prader-Willi syndrome A genetic disorder resulting in *mental retardation*, obesity, and life expectancy generally not beyond age 30; usually characterized by uncontrollable appetite.

pragmatics The rules governing the use of *language* in *context*, including the speaker's communicative intent—e.g., to inform, persuade, entertain, describe, control. Also includes a child's knowledge of how to use language in social settings and the use of language to communicate.

pragmatism A practical approach with the premise that truth is tested by consequences believed to be true.

pre– A prefix that means coming before or prior to.

preassessment See *prereferral system.*

precision teaching A systematic procedure of continuous and direct recording of behavior, espoused by Ogden Lindsley and others. Precision teaching employs the techniques of *behavior modification* and *task analysis* for management of instruction and behavior. Now more likely referred to as *direct instruction* or *curriculum-based instruction.*

precocious(ness) (prih-koe'-shus) Development that is advanced beyond the usual, mentally and physically. Frequently used in reference to young *gifted* children.

predictive validity A measure of the ability of a test to forecast something. If a test were to be given to predict good teachers, we would be interested in how successfully the test predicts people who are good teachers.

predisposition An inherited potential for development of certain characteristics.

prelingual deafness An absence of hearing at birth or *hearing loss* that develops early in life before acquisition of speech and *language.*

prelinguistic Refers to skills that are *prerequisite* to *language* learning. These include various *sensorimotor* and *cognitive* skills that lead to acquisition of the symbolic function of language.

Premack principle A *concept* effective in reinforcing the classroom environment, whereby pupils are motivated to do low-frequency or less desirable activities by being assured that upon completion of the activities, they have permission to do high frequency or highly desired activities. The principle operates regardless of students' awareness of the *contingencies;* simply following a low-probability behavior with a high-probability behavior increases the probability of the low-probability behavior in the future.

premature baby Any infant weighing less than 5 pounds at birth. Research has indicated that the lower the birth weight in premature babies, the greater is the potential for handicapping conditions.

prenatal Pertaining to a time period prior to birth.

prereferral system A program that functions before referral to *special education,* in which regular educators attempt alternative programs before actual referral. (see also *teacher assistance team* and *student support teams*)

prerequisite skills Abilities that must be developed before proceeding to a given task or objective. *Early childhood education,* for example, focuses on skills prerequisite to academic learning.

presbycusis (prez-bih-cue'-sis) Deterioration in hearing as a result of aging factors.

presbyopia (prez-bee-oh'-pea-ah) A gradual lessening of the ability of the eyes to *accommodate,* because of physiological changes occurring after age 40.

preschool education A training program, usually in the development of social behavior and *language,* that is given a child prior to enrollment in kindergarten or a formal school program. Preschool education is important to children with *handicaps* in that they need early stimulation, experiences, and direction to aid necessary development that might not occur *incidentally.* (see also *early childhood education*)

prescriptive education See *prescriptive teaching.*

prescriptive teaching Educational terminology referring to the process of planning individual educational activities as a result of needs concluded from *diagnostic* test information.

President's Committee on Employment of People with Disabilities A panel appointed by the President to promote and encourage a positive action program of jobs for persons with *disabilities;* includes promotional activities and recognition of outstanding people with handicaps.

President's Committee on Mental Retardation (PCMR) A panel first appointed by President John F. Kennedy to study the problems of *mental retardation* and to make recommendations on how to deal with mental retardation on a national basis.

presumptive disability A term used in conjunction with an administrative provision that allows the Social Security Agency to make an immediate determination of *disabilities* based on the nature of certain *handicaps.* Under this provision, more severe cases of *developmental disability* can obtain *supplemental security income (SSI)* almost immediately rather than waiting.

prevalence How common a condition is in the population (e.g., about 3% of the population is *mentally retarded*).

preventive physical education A program that involves specific activities or exercises selected to promote proper body use as a protection against injury or to prevent the occurrence of predictable *anomalies.*

prevocational level Pertains to programs for students with *handicaps* emphasizing skills necessary for employment.

prevocational teacher (PVT) An instructor trained in coordinating the school activities and job placements of students with *mild handicaps* at the *prevocational level.*

prevocationally deaf The loss of hearing prior to age 19. Persons deafened after that age are not expected to have as severe vocational problems or the same need for special *vocational education.*

primary disability The handicap considered the more overriding disability as far as education, medicine, rehabilitation, or employment is concerned. In some cases the primary disability may change. In cerebral palsy, medicine may consider the physical handicap the primary handicap, whereas in education the same child's retardation may be viewed as the primary handicap.

private speech A person's speech, vocal or subvocal, that is directed to the self. Before age 6 or 7 it is usually *overt;* after 8–10 years of age, most is *covert.*

PRN   A term in medicine meaning "to use as needed or required."

proactive inhibition   Greater difficulty in learning or recalling knowledge as a result of prior learning (e.g., hesitating to cross the street on a green light after learning that cars can run over you). For comparison, see *retroactive inhibition.*

probation   A provision applied to a convicted law offender *(delinquent)* whereby the person is released on a suspended sentence under supervision and with an agreement to report regularly to the court or to a representative of the court, such as a *probation officer.* (see also *offender rehabilitation,* the preferred term)

probation officer   A person appointed by the court to supervise and receive regular reports from a law offender *(delinquent)* whose sentence has been suspended or who has been released from a penal *institution* but is required to serve out the term on *probation.* Same as *correctional counselor.*

procedural due process   A right to a hearing, to be notified of the hearing, to be represented by counsel, and to be given the opportunity to present evidence and confront witnesses. This is one of the *concepts* inherent in *PL 94-142.*

procedural noncompliance   Any situation in which a *local education agency* or *state education agency* does not establish the required procedures of *due process, nondiscriminatory testing, least restrictive environment,* native *language* considerations, or confidentiality.

procedural safeguards   Specific procedures designed by law to protect the rights of children and parents, which include *due process, nondiscriminatory testing, least restrictive environment,* native *language* consideration, and confidentiality.

processing   Internal thinking skills such as generalizing, abstracting, classifying, and integrating, by which thought is carried out.

prodigy   A person whose abilities are expressed at an early age and whose *precociousness* indicates *giftedness* or special *talent,* expressed in *intellect* or performing arts or *creativity.*

products (of thinking)   In Guilford's model (see *structure of the intellect*), the elements of thinking that are cognized, memorized, or evaluated.

professional judgment   A *concept* involving a reasonable collection of data to use in arriving at a decision.

profile   A graphic representation of results of several measures for either a group or individual, with the results expressed in terms of uniform or comparable scores.

profound mental retardation   A term originated by the American Association on Mental Retardation referring to a level of *intellectual* functioning comparable to the educational classification of *severe retardation.* The individual requires supervision throughout life. The intellectual level, when *assessed* with an individual *intelligence* test, is estimated at *IQ* scores below 20.

progeria (pro-jare'-ee-ah)   A rare form of *dwarfism* accompanied by premature *symptoms* of aging including wrinkled skin and gray, thinning hair. Children with this condition have a shortened life span, and no cure has been found.

prognosis A projection of outcome for the future; a prediction of probable result of an illness or disease, or probable status of behavior in terms of achievement or adjustment, e.g., a child's educational and independence level as an adult or the expectancy for a rehabilitation client to become employed sucessfully.

programmed instruction Learning materials designed to present knowledge and skills to pupils so they can learn independently.

programmed reading An instructional approach that uses materials designed for students' self-instruction and self-correction of errors.

Project Re-Ed A program for educating and helping children with emotional problems; originated at George Peabody College; emphasizes *ecological* and *psychoeducational* elements and depends heavily upon teacher-counselors to serve in a limited way as teachers, *social workers, psychologists,* and recreation workers combined.

projective technique A relatively unstructured method used to study and *diagnose* certain problems of personality. A product or response (such as a drawing, interpretation of a picture, or completion of a sentence) is secured from an individual and analyzed in an effort to gain an understanding of the total personality.

proleptic Describes a concept in Vygotsky's theory that instruction should contain enough of the message or meaning so that the students can construct their own extended meaning.

pronation (proe-nay'-shun) A physical condition in which inadequate muscle strength or improper bony structure allows the ankle to roll inward, placing the body weight on the inner side of the foot.

prone A position of lying on one's stomach with the face downward. Opposite of *supine.*

prophylaxis (proe-fih-lack'-siss) Any preventive treatment of disease.

proprioceptors (proe-pree-oh-sep'-tores) *Sensory* nerve endings that give information concerning movements and positions of the body. These endings occur in muscles, tendons, and canals of the inner ear.

prosody The rhythm of speech, its patterns of stress and rate, which help give meaning to speech.

prosthetic (prahs-thet'-ik) **device (prosthesis)** An artifical part attached to one's body following the loss of the natural part, such as an arm or leg. It may return part of the original function, as in the most common artificial hand.

prosthetics (prahs-thet'-iks) The branch of medicine that deals with application of artificial body parts to *amputee* cases, including *evaluation,* treatment, and prescription.

protective services Assuming of temporary or partial guardianship to assure the safety and well-being of a minor person with a *handicap,* or other individual deemed in need of such changes from an existing environment.

protege (proe'-teh-zhay) In *advocacy* circles, refers to the person for whom the advocate intercedes

proximal Near to something. Opposite of *distal* or *lateral*

136

pseudo-mental retardation A condition in which a child appears to have functional *mental retardation,* but *diagnosis* and an eductional program give evidence that the performance results from factors other than mental retardation, such as environmental deprivation or low vitality.

pseudohypertrophy A name applied to *Duchenne disease* (a form of *muscular dystrophy*), but really refers to the enlargement of cell muscles caused by fat deposits.

psyche (sigh'-key) The sum of the psychological processes of the human mind and soul.

psychiatric outpatient services Alternative treatment programs that enable individuals to obtain psychiatric help for emotional, mental, or behavioral problems without disrupting the pattern of their daily lives. The usual procedure involves periodic visits of a relatively short duration.

psychiatrist A medical doctor who specializes in *diagnosis* and treatment of mental/*emotional disorders.*

psychic energizers Drugs (e.g., Ritalin, Dexedrine) used to treat *behavior* and *learning disorders.*

psychoanalytic (adj.) Refers to an approach to psychiatry based on the method of psychoanalysis originally developed by Sigmund Freud. Psychoanalytic methods (e.g., free-association and dream-interpretation) are used to investigate and understand a patient's *psychodynamics.*

psychodrama A *group therapy* method of counseling in which patients dramatize their individual problems.

psychodynamic (adj.) Describes an approach that grew out of the *psychoanalytic* theory of Freud; views the cause of behavior to be ideas and impulse, either conscious or unconscious, that are emotionally charged (psychic energy). Therapeutic methods based on this conceptualization vary according to the school of psychodynamic thought.

psychoeducational (adj.) Refers to a *service delivery* model that has a *psychodynamic* orientation with an emphasis on the reality demands of the school and everyday functioning.

psychoeducational approach One of the theories that has been applied to the treatment of children with *behavior disorders;* utilizes ideas from the *psychoanalytic approach* and the *therapeutic* process of education.

psychoeducational diagnostician A specialist who assesses the educational status of the learner, provides meaningful, educationally relevant *evaluations,* and outlines specific and long-range educational goals.

psychogalvanic (sie-koe-gal-vahn'-ik) **skin response** Measurement of *dermal* response to a *stimulus,* which is used in *audiometry* to detect *hearing loss.*

psychogenic (sie-koe-jen'-ik) Describes conditions resulting from psychological or *psychosomatic* causes; e.g., a person with psychogenic *deafness* has no physical or physiological basis for the *hearing loss.*

137

psycholinguistics Commonly used in reference to programs, services, or *assessment* involving a combination of psychological aspects and the study of *language* or speech.

psychologist A professional person who has had specialized training in **psychology,** and in practice does research or evaluates and treats individuals in any of the areas of mental functioning.

psychometry (sie-kah'-meh-tree) (adj., **psychometric**) The field of *evaluation* or measurement of psychological functioning by means of mental tests. A person qualified to do this work is called a **psychometrist;** he/she usually is a college graduate but is not professionally trained as or certified as a *psychologist.*

psychomotor Pertaining to psychological effects on physical skills, especially *sensory* and *perceptual* effects on *motor* coordination.

psychomotor seizure An *epileptic* activity in which the individual appears to be conscious during the attack but behaves in an unusual or bizarre way, after which he/she does not remember what happened during the episode. Some indications of psychomotor seizure may be chewing, lip smacking, ringing in ears, abdominal pains, dizziness.

psychoneurosis (adj., **psychoneurotic**) A minor mental disorder in which physical manifestations are displayed. (see also *neurosis*)

psychopath (adj., **psychopathic**) An individual having an instability of character represented by traits such as undue conceit, suspiciousness, and perversity of conduct, or lack of emotional stability, self-control, social feeling, honesty, and persistence but, in many cases, no *impairment* of *intellectual* functions.

psychopathology The scientific study of the more serious mental disturbances from a psychological viewpoint.

psychopharmacology (sie-koe-far-mah-kahl'-oh-jee) The science of the use of drugs to influence behavior. Drugs prescribed to influence behavior are broadly classified as *stimulants, tranquilizers,* and *antidepressants.*

psychophysiologic (sie-koe-fiz-ee-oh-lah'-jik) **disorders** Conditions in which emotional and physical elements combine to produce physical *symptoms,* without the individual being aware of the emotional relationship. *Eczema* and *asthma* may be examples of such disorders. The preferred descriptive term at present is *psychosomatic.*

psychosis A broad classification covering severe mental/emotional/behavioral disorders, characterized by persistent ignoring of reality, lack of order in behavior, and inability to function adequately in daily living.

psychosomatic Describes physiological disorders induced by mental or emotional pressures or disturbances.

psychotherapy An approach to treating mental disorders by psychological methods using the influence of suggestion, *nondirective* methods, *psychoanalysis,* and reeducation of the mind.

psychotic (adj.) Describes any of the *psychoses; schizophrenia* is one example.

138

psychotropic drugs Medications used primarily for their behavioral effects; may be used with children to control attention and activity level.

ptosis (toe'-siss) A condition characterized by drooping of the upper eyelid; caused by faulty development or *paralysis* of a muscle. The condition sometimes can be corrected by surgery but if not corrected, the eyelid may grow to the eye.

puberty (pyew'-burr-tee) The period in a person's development at which time secondary sex characteristics appear and the reproductive organs *mature* to the capability of bearing offspring; the period marking the beginning of adolescence.

Public Law 94-142 See *Education for All Handicapped Children Act.*

pulmonary Associated with or pertaining to the lungs.

punctographic symbol An element in a raised, *tactile,* graphic system used by *blind* persons; e.g., *braille.*

pupil (of eye) The contractible opening in the center of the *iris* of the eye, through which light enters.

pure tone audiometer An instrument for measuring the *acuity* of hearing by testing at selected *frequencies,* at a number of different loudness levels, usually graduated in 5-*decibel* steps. The sound is produced in a receiver or an earphone held snug against the subject's ears, and the subject gives a signal for the sounds that he/she can hear.

pyorrhea (pie-ore-ee'-ah) *Inflammation* of the gum tissues surrounding the teeth. If not treated, this condition results in *degeneration* of the gum tissues.

Q

QID A Latin term used in medicine to denote four times daily. Frequently seen on prescriptions for medications.

quadriplegia (kwad-rih-plee'-jah) (adj., **quadriplegic**) *Paralysis* involving all four of the body *extremities* (arms and legs).

quality control The random sampling of product or services to ensure that the production meets or is better than minimum requirements set by those for whom the work is being done. This term is applied in *sheltered workshops,* among other working environments.

quality disorder A voice defect that may be described as *nasal,* strident, falsetto, *breathy, hoarse,* or similar terms.

quartile One of three points that separate the four equal parts of a whole. If a person is said to be in the upper quartile, he/she is in the top 25%.

R

radio reading   A procedure used in teaching reading in which the teacher encourages a child to read the passage like a radio announcer, telling the child that he/she does not have to read each word as it is written but instead the child can paraphrase or give the gist of the text.

radius   The smaller of the two bones in the forearm, located on the thumb side of the arm. The other is the *ulna.*

RAID   A *behavior management* system employing the use of rules, approval, ignoring, and disapproval to improve behavior.

ramp   A sloping passageway built to connect varying levels of buildings or terrain. Ramps are built to allow greater *mobility* for individuals in wheelchairs or on crutches who have difficulty climbing or cannot climb stairs. Ramps are becoming increasingly used because of various codes to reduce *architectural barriers.*

random sample   A selection of a certain percentage of individuals in a defined group in which each member of that group has an equal chance of being drawn for study; application of this procedure in research is based on the selection's being representative and, therefore, generalizable to a larger population.

range   The lowest and highest scores for a specified group, showing the extent of variation within those extremes.

rapport (rah-pore´)   A relationship between two individuals that is harmonious, understanding, and involves mutual confidence. This is a desirable relationship between teacher and student in creating a good learning climate.

rationalization   A psychological *defense mechanism* in which one justifies illogical behavior by thinking of motives that seem plausible; this is done to hide the true motives or desires that might be causing *anxiety* or distress.

raw score   The number of items answered correctly on a test.

readability level   A measure of the difficulty of specific material expressed in terms of the grade level at which it can be read best and most appropriately. This is one consideration in selecting materials for individuals or classes.

reader services   Includes *rehabilitation* teaching services such as readers, note-taking services, and *orientation/mobility* services for blind persons.

readiness   The point in a child's *maturation* at which he/she has developed the necessary *sensory* and *intellectual* skills to be able to learn the task or skill involved.

reading comprehension The ability to understand the meaning of what one has read.

reading disability Inability to read at the achievement level for one's *chronological age*. Usually considered as being a significant disability if reading is more than one level below grade-level placement. Children with *mental retardation* read below chronological age, but reading achievement usually is compared to their *mental age*.

reading readiness The stage in a pupil's development at which he/she is ready for learning to read. Reading readiness requires a combination of physical, emotional, *sensory*, and mental maturation.

reality therapy A treatment method emphasizing behavior in the real world and the client's responsibility for his/her behavior. The therapy teaches *coping behavior* in the client's environment without removal to another setting for treatment. Originated by William Glasser.

reauditorization The ability to retrieve *auditory* images; the capability of experiencing or recreating auditory experiences simply by thinking about them. In some children with *learning disorders,* this ability is impaired or lacking, so they are not able to recall auditory images that could be of great value to them.

rebus (ree'-bus) Representation of a word or a phrase by pictures that suggest the syllables or words. The Peabody Rebus Reading Program is an example of a *programmed* approach to *reading readiness* and beginning reading utilizing a vocabulary of rebuses.

receptive aphasia See *sensory aphasia.*

receptive language The aspect of communication that involves an individual's receival and *comprehension* of information from others.

recessive genes See *autosomal recessive inheritance.*

recidivism (reh-sid'-ih-viz-uhm) The return to lawlessness by an individual who had been released or paroled from institutional confinement and, as a result, is returned to an *institution.*

reciprocal inhibition Wolpe's *conceptualization* involving *counter-conditioning,* in which an *anxiety* response is eliminated by training an individual to make a different response.

reciprocal teaching A method of teaching based on the Russian psychologist Vygotsky's theory of social context in learning; teacher uses considerable structure, which is gradually reduced as students are able to monitor their own work. The four main activities are summarizing, question generating, clarifying, and predicting.

reciprocation (adj., **reciprocal**) In *physical therapy,* an approach in which joints or limbs are *flexed* backward and forward; also, both arms and/or both legs are moved at the same time but in opposite directions.

recreational therapy (RT) The use of games and other activities of a pleasant nature as a form of treatment.

red measles See *rubeola.*

142

redundancy A teaching technique in which the same information is presented over and over with a different format each time. Thus, math facts could be taught by counting blocks, ditto masters, counting to music, etc.

reeducation Presenting learned material for the purpose of establishing new understandings and relationships that are necessary because of *inhibition* of use of the original learning resulting from physical, mental, or emotional *handicaps* or improper application of the original learning.

referral The process of informing a *clinic,* school, medical doctor, or other appropriate specialist about an individual for the purpose of *evaluation* or treatment.

reflex A consistent, involuntary muscular or neurological response resulting from *sensory* stimulation. A commonly referred-to reflex is the *knee-jerk.*

reflex audiometry Testing one's responses to sounds by observing *reflex* actions such as the *Moro reflex.*

refraction The bending or deflection of light rays through the eye as used by an eye specialist to assess and correct vision.

regression A behavioral reaction to frustration in which the individual returns to an earlier, more immature form of behavior.

regression effect The tendency for scores on a test to move toward the true *mean.* The implication for *special education* is that disproportionately high or low scores will tend to move more toward the *norm* on future tests.

regression/recoupment syndrome Refers to loss of learned *cognitive,* social, and *motor* skills during the summer months and the resultant time required to relearn the same skills when the child returns to school. The term came into use in the 1980s in relation to extended-school litigation for individuals with *severe retardation.*

regular education initiative (REI) An effort starting in about 1985 to combine regular education and *special education* into one system. REI would provide maximum *mainstreaming* for students with *handicaps.*

rehabilitation The process of helping a nonproductive or *deviant* person toward restoration or the desired standard, through education or retraining. **Rehabilitative** services are often vocational or physical in nature.

Rehabilitation Act of 1973 (PL 93-112) A comprehensive piece of federal legislation that expanded federally funded *rehabilitation* services to persons with severe disabilities. This law contains *Section 504,* which prohibits discrimination on the basis of *handicap* in all federally assisted programs and mandates accessibility of programs to people with disabilities. Originally, Section 504 was restricted primarily to employment, but Public Law 93-516, passed in 1974, amended Section 504 to cover broader services for handicapped people.

rehabilitative services More recent term for *vocational rehabilitation.*

reinforcement, (reinforcer) (v., reinforce) Any consequence of behavior that increases the probability of the behavior it follows. A reinforcer is any event or reward that, when given following a behavior, increases the probability of that behavior being repeated in the future.

rejection   Attitudes and behavior toward another person that lead that person to believe he/she is not accepted, loved, or appreciated. These attitudes may be conscious or unconscious.

related services   Described by *PL 94-142* as services that are supportive of and may or may not be part of classroom instruction, including transportation, *occupational therapy,* etc. Also called *support services.*

related vocational instructor (RVI)   An educator authorized in some states through vocational education funds to assist students with regular vocational and technical education curriculum. Usually not associated with or funded as part of special education.

relatively profoundly handicapped   A term coming into use in the late 1980s to denote that group of *profoundly handicapped* students for whom instructional methodology can produce a measurable difference, as opposed to those labeled *absolutely profoundly handicapped.*

reliability   The consistency with which a test or method measures. In behavior observation, the degree to which independent observers agree on what they have observed during the same observation session.

religious interpreter   A slang term referring to an interpreter for the deaf who tells the deaf person what the interpreter wants him/her to hear rather than translates literally.

remedial reading   Corrective instruction specially offered to students who are achieving in reading at a level below the achievement expected for their *chronological age.*

remediation (adj., **remedial**)   The process of correcting inappropriate behaviors or skills; any methods or exercises designed to correct deficiencies and help a student perform nearer the level expected of his/her *chronological age.*

remission   Reduction in the intensity of a disease; or the period during which the intensity of a disease abates, or lessens.

renal   Pertaining to the kidneys or kidney function.

repression   An unconscious or conscious rejection or blocking out, in order to prevent natural expression, activity, or development of something having disagreeable content.

residential   Refers to a living arrangement in which individuals are housed 24 hours a day.

residential alternatives   See *alternative living.*

residential institution   A facility, either private or state-supported, designed to provide designated care and other services on a 24-hour basis to those housed there. People with *mental retardation* and *mental illness* constitute the largest groups of *handicap* categories in residential institutions.

residential services   Amenities and functions necessary to maintain persons with *handicaps* in residential facilities. These services may extend to institutions, group homes, and other community living arrangements.

144

residual hearing The remaining hearing that can be measured or is usable by a *hearing impaired* person.

residual vision The remaining *acuity* of *visually impaired* persons; usually refers to individuals' using or learning to use their remaining vision.

resistive motion A mode of *physical therapy* wherein the patient moves a bodily part against something, which may be weights or pressure by the *therapist*.

resonance The quality of the sound imparted by the size, shape, and texture of the organs in the vocal tract.

resonator Any of the bodily cavities—*oral, nasal, pharynx*—that affect voice quality and *pitch.*

resource center See *instructional materials center.*

resource room A specially equipped and managed setting where a teacher with special training instructs students who are assigned to go at designated times for assistance in some aspect of learning or guidance. One of the *service delivery system* options in *special education.*

resource teacher A specialist who works with students who are having difficulty learning in the regular classroom setting. This teacher serves as a *consultant* to the regular classroom teachers and searches to secure appropriate materials to use in teaching these children. The resource teacher also may function in a *resource room* where students come for specialized instruction. (see also *consultant*)

respiratory Pertaining to breathing.

respite (res'-pit) **care** Temporary measures to relieve parents of a child with a *handicap* from having to care for him/her continuously with no breaks. Respite care may be in the home, in a special home outside the child's home, or in available beds in a residential facility.

respondent behavior Actions produced by classical *conditioning.*

responsive environment approach See *autotelic responsive environment.*

retardation (retarded) See *mental retardation.*

retention Holding or being able to recall knowledge acquired previously.

retina (adj., **retinal**) The innermost component of the eye, which contains sensitive nerve fibers that connect to the *optic nerve* to produce sight. **Retinal detachment** is the loosening or pulling away of the retina from its normal position in the eye. In children, this condition usually is caused by accidents and may start with a slight loss of vision that might progress to almost complete *blindness.*

retinitis pigmentosa (ret-ih-ny'-tiss pig-men-toe'-suh) A condition of reduced *peripheral vision,* leaving the ability to see in the central visual area but with tunnel-like vision.

retinoblastoma (ret-ih-noe-blast-oh'-mah) A *malignant* tumor originating from the *retina.* The condition occurs in childhood, and surgical removal of the eye usually is successful.

145

retinopathy of prematurity   The new term, replacing *retrolental fibroplasia,* for a condition of the eyes resulting from too much oxygen administered to infants after birth (in an incubator).

retroactive inhibition   Greater difficulty in recalling knowledge or activities because of learning that takes place after that which is being recalled (e.g., difficulty recalling a word learned on Monday because of being taught a similar word on Tuesday). For comparison, see *proactive inhibition.*

retrolental fibroplasia (ret-roe-lent'-uhl fie-broe-play'-zee-ah) **(RLF)**   See *retinopathy of prematurity,* now the preferred term.

reversal   In reading, an irregularity in which a reader misperceives the order of letters, resulting in a tendency to read from right to left, to confuse letters with each other, or to mix the order of letters in words.

reverse chaining   See *backward chaining.*

reverse mainstreaming   A procedure whereby children without handicaps are placed in *special education* for a limited time. May involve regular education children visiting a special class or a residential school.

revisualization (v., **revisualize**)   The ability to retain a mental picture in the mind's eye; an extremely important characteristic that often is impaired in *mental retardation* and *learning disabilities.*

Rh factor   An element in the blood that determines compatibility of the mother's blood and the developing *fetus'* blood during the *prenatal* period. An incompatibility causes an *allergic* reaction resulting in a breakdown of red blood cells and the release of large amounts of *bilirubin* (the red pigment in the red blood cells); at birth, *degenerative* changes cause the infant to show *jaundice,* drowsiness, listlessness, muscle twitching, and possibly *flaccidity,* which later result in severe *handicaps.* (see also *erythroblastosis*)

rheumatic (roo-mat'-ik) **fever**   A disease, usually following a *streptococcus* infection, that is characterized by *acute inflammation* of the joints, fever, *chorea,* skin rash, nosebleeds, and abdominal pains. The disease is considered serious because it often damages the heart by scarring its tissues and valves. **Rheumatic heart** is a general term referring to heart murmurs or irregular heartbeat as a residual effect of rheumatic fever.

rheumatism (roo'-mah-tiz-uhm)   *Inflammation* of the muscles, joints, or nerves causing stiffness of joints and muscle pain during motion.

rheumatoid arthritis   One of the most *chronic* of all diseases and the form of *arthritis* most often contracted by children. In severe cases, the pain and stiffness become so debilitating as to cause periods of *paralysis.*

rhythm disorder   A speech problem characterized by a breakdown or interruption in the normal outflow of speech sounds affecting or affected by breathing rate, tension, and emotional set.

ribonucleic (rye-boe-new-klee'-ik) **acid (RNA)**   An element of the body cell that is the means by which chromosomal *DNA* exerts control of protein *synthesis.*

146

rickets A childhood condition caused by a deficiency in vitamin D or sunlight, which results in softness of the bones and, consequently, bending and distortion under muscular action.

right to education A principle supporting the obligation to provide an *appropriate education* to all children; defined by the Pennsylvania Association for Retarded Children *(PARC)* court decision and spelled out with specific reference to persons with *mental retardation.*

right to treatment A principle set forth by Alabama case *Wyatt* v. *Stickney,* in which the judge ruled that if an individual is placed in an *institution,* the State has the moral responsibility to provide adequate educational treatment.

rigidity 1. A manifestation of *cerebral palsy* in which hypertension of muscles creates stiffness; both the contracting muscles and their paired relaxing muscles are affected. 2. An inability or inflexibility in shifting from one task, activity, or behavior to another, particularly observable in some persons with *mental retardation* and *brain injury.*

RLF See *retrolental fibroplasia.*

Rochester method A communication system for *deaf* people based on *fingerspelling;* term originated at Rochester School for the Deaf. *Total communication* is now the preferred term.

role play A technique of teaching and counseling wherein individuals act out or walk through the desired role for the purpose of learning it or better understanding any problems they have had with it.

role tutor A student with a *handicap* who teaches a younger regular class student in an attempt to improve self-image, especially of students with behavior disorders; also gives the tutor added practice in basic skills.

Rood therapy A form of physical treatment applied to those with *cerebral palsy* that emphasizes use of pressure to activate hard muscles and light brushing to activate light working muscles.

rote drill Numerous repetitions of a specific activity without applying the skills to problem-solving situations.

rote learning Knowledge acquired by memorization with little attention to meaning.

rubella (German measles) A *communicable disease* transmitted by *virus.* Infection of a woman during early stages of pregnancy produces a high probability of severe *handicaps* in the offspring, including *mental retardation, cardiac* abnormalities, *cerebral palsy,* and *sensory* (hearing and vision) handicaps. It is a highly preventable disease that can be eradicated by vaccinating children under age 12. Generally runs its course in about 3 days without serious complications, except for an unborn child. For comparison, see *rubeola.*

rubeola The "old-fashioned" 10-day measles, or *red measles,* which is accompanied by a red rash and fever. The disease can be prevented with vaccine, but is far less threatening to the unborn *fetus* than is *rubella.*

RVI See *related vocational instructor.*

S

Santa Monica Project A program in Santa Monica, California, that served *educationally handicapped* students in a highly structured and individualized learning environment. Terminal goals were to be achieved through use of *behavior modification* principles. Also termed *Madison Plan.*

satiation Satisfaction to the point of excess. One specific situation would be in offering unlimited amounts of a *reinforcer* that has been maintaining a behavior to a point at which it no longer stimulates the behavior.

savant syndrome An individual with generally low *intelligence* but with a specialized area of extraordinary ability. This might be a person with *severe retardation* who can add numbers in his/her mind or who paints or plays a musical instrument with great proficiency. The term *savant syndrome* is now more acceptable.

schedule of reinforcement The ratio or interval at which responses are rewarded.

schizophrenia (skit-so-freh′-nee-ah) (adj., **schizophrenic, schizoid**) A severe mental disorder *(psychosis)* characterized by a fragmented personality involving *fantasies,* illusions, *delusions,* and, in general, being out of touch with reality.

school phobia A general fear of school or fear of some specific aspect of school, which causes a child to resist attending school. Current theories suggest that the young child really fears separation from parents rather than school.

school-to-home telephone A learning arrangement that enables a mature student with a *physical handicap* to work daily in complete contact with the regular classroom while homebound (or hospitalized). The school-to-home telephone program usually is supplemented by visits from someone from the hospital or through *homebound instruction.* Most recently called Teleschool.

scissor gait In walking, one foot passes in front of the other because of *spasticity* of the thigh muscles. Common in *ataxic cerebral palsy.*

sclera (skler′-uh) The tough protective covering of the eye.

sclerosis (skler-oh′-sis) Thickening and hardening of body tissue or part of an organ.

scoliosis (skoe-lee-oh′-sis) Characterized by lateral curvature of the spine. Bracing and surgery are both methods of treatment. The condition is most commonly first noted in girls age 10–13.

screening Abbreviated testing procedures by a variety of *disciplines* conducted on a large scale to locate children requiring more detailed testing or specialized teaching. The procedures have become quite elaborate to protect the rights of children and for making proper decisions on placement in the *least restrictive environment.*

screening committee   See *placement team.*

scurvy (skur'-vee)   A disease caused by a deficiency of ascorbic acid (vitamin C) in the diet and characterized by *anemia,* low vitality, spongy gums, and bleeding into the skin and mucous membranes.

SEA   See *state education(al) agency.*

second injury clause   A provision that allows worker with *handicaps* to be protected by *workmen's compensation* while not requiring the employer to assume all the responsibility. This clause helps persons with *handicaps* to get jobs, because a special fund assumes much of the risk. Also called *subsequent injury clause.*

secondary drives   Forces present in most humans but with little or no influence on lower animals or humans who function at a *profound mental retardation* level; for example, desires for wealth, social prestige, beauty.

secondary handicap   Additional condition(s) of lesser severity than the major or primary *handicap,* but which contributes to the total condition.

secondary reinforcer   A *stimulus* which, when paired with a primary reinforcer, takes on the reinforcing properties of the first. (see also *reinforcement*)

Section 504   Under the *Rehabilitation Act of 1973,* the last section, which prohibits discrimination against persons with *handicaps* in employment and other fields. A set of regulations (*Federal Register,* May 4, 1977) was established in an effort to assure their civil rights.

SEE   See *Signing Exact English.*

seeing eye dog   An animal that is especially trained to aid *blind* persons in *mobility* and to protect them. The terms "lead dog" or *guide dog* are preferred.

segregation   In this context, the placement of *exceptional children* in programs in which they relate only to other exceptional children and do not have an opportunity to interact with regular class pupils. This term represents the opposite of *mainstreaming* and *integration.*

seizure   An outward expression of abnormal brain discharges that may be expressed in several forms of behavior, from mild to severe in intensity; associated with *epilepsy.* (see also *grand mal, petit mal, akinetic, myoclonic seizure*)

self-contained class (program)   One in which pupils with similar needs and skills are assigned and taught by the same teacher throughout the school day.

self-control curriculum   A program taught to students with *behavior disorders* that emphasizes *metacognition* and the use of conscious and unconscious thought to help the student control his/her own behavior.

self-help (self-care) skills   Knowledge that allows one to carry out daily living tasks without assistance or with a minimum of assistance. These skills are included in *curricula* for people with *handicaps.*

self-injurious behavior (SIB)   Actions that may result in tissue damage or may be even life-threatening (e.g., face slapping, eye gouging, head banging, scratching).

149

self-instructional training   A procedure developed by Meichenbaum in which the individual uses his/her thought processes to control behavior. The procedure is now known as *cognitive behavior modification.*

self-mutilation   A characteristic of some forms of *pathology* in which the individual does harm to his/her own body. (see also *self-injurious behavior*)

self-stimulatory behavior   Mannerisms frequently encountered in *autistic* and *severely retarded* individuals consisting of repeated rocking, flapping of the arms, and other movements. (see also *blindism* and *stereotypic behavior*)

semantics (seh-man'-tix)   The study of the significance or meaning of words.

semantography (seh-man-tog'-ruh-fee)   An international system of symbols developed by Charles Bliss, born in Old Austria in 1877, where 20 different *languages* were spoken. Currently being used with individuals with *severe retardation.* (see *Bliss method*)

semicircular canals   The loop-shaped tubular parts of the labyrinth of the inner ear that function in determining one's position in space, equilibrium, and balance.

semi-independent living arrangement (SLA)   A group home for adults with *handicaps* who require assistance with some minimal needs in order to live nearly independently.

semiskilled   Describes a job or worker that requires some specialized training and usually doesn't require close supervision.

sensorimotor (sensory-motor) training   The use of activities involving a transition from gross *stimuli* to refined ones, for the purpose of eliciting specific *motor* responses useful in problem solving.

sensorineural (sensory-neural) hearing loss   A condition involving *impairment* in the inner ear or the *central nervous system.* Also referred to as *neural* or *nerve deafness.*

sensory   Pertaining to any of the senses (sight, hearing, taste, smell, touch), or to sensations.

sensory aphasia (ah-faze'-yuh)   Inability to understand the meaning of written, spoken, or *tactile* speech symbols because of disease or injury to the *auditory* and *visual* brain centers.

sensory disability   An impairment in one of the main senses—vision and hearing—or both such that the individual's input is restricted through that channel.

sensory vocabulary   Words, such as "cold" and "loud," which relate to any of the five senses.

SEPs   See *Office of Special Education Programs.*

Separation Anxiety Disorder (309.21)   One of the classifications of the *DSM* III System. Individuals who have the condition express excessive distress, withdrawal, *apathy,* or sadness when separated from a person to whom they feel an attachment.

sequenced instruction   The logical, step-like succession of educational activities that form a continuum of educational experiences based on the learning potential and needs of students at various *chronological ages.*

seriously emotionally disturbed   A term used in *PL 94-142* referring to children with *behavior disorders* or disturbances. "Seriously" was added in the hope of limiting programs to those who are more severely disturbed.

service delivery system   The range of possible types of programs offered in *special education,* involving a gradient from full-time placement in regular classes to the most restrictive environment of a *special day school* or *institutionalization.*

severe discrepancy   A concept closely tied to *learning disabilities,* in which school systems must establish a significant difference in potential and measured achievement in order to determine *eligibility* for service.

severe mental retardation (severely retarded)   1. A term of educational origin that refers to an *intellectual* level of functioning lower than *trainable mentally retarded.* These individuals usually have an *IQ* 4 *standard deviations* below the *mean.* Severely retarded individuals may be able to live in a group or *alternative living* system but require supervision throughout life. 2. One of the levels of *retardation* in the American Association on Mental Retardation's (AAMR) classification system. It is the next to lowest category, characterized by *IQs* in the 25 to 39 range.

severely handicapped   A term applied to individuals having physical, mental, or emotional problems to a degree requiring educational, social, psychological, and/or medical services beyond those traditionally offered by regular and *special education.* Current preferences are against using this term as a noun ("the severely handicapped").

shape vocabulary   An educational term referring to words identified with physical attributes of *configurations*—e.g., square, circle.

shaping   A procedure of reinforcing specific behavior, requiring ever closer approximations to the desired terminal behavior. Shaping involves the *reinforcement* of desired behavior and *extinction* of undesirable behavior.

shared services   An arrangement whereby a number of districts too small to provide *special education* to serve *low-incidence* handicapping conditions pool their resources and develop a service across district boundaries to reach all those in the cooperating districts who are in need of a specific service. Sometimes referred to as *cooperative plans* or *intermediate districts.*

sheltered employment   A structured program of activities involving work *evaluation,* work adjustment, occupational skill training, and remunerative employment designed to prepare individuals either for competitive employment or for continued work in a protective environment.

sheltered workshop   A facility that offers individuals who are not able to work in competitive employment an opportunity to work in a controlled environment at their level of functioning. The two basic purposes of a sheltered workshop are: to help a person develop an acceptable self-image through productive work, and to increase the individual's potential for becoming competitively employed.

151

shoreline Any continuous physical element that functions as a guide for *blind* persons in *mobility*—e.g., edge of sidewalk

short-term memory A memory state that is very short. In research it usually refers to memory of less than a minute. When a student forgets assignments or directions just given by the teacher, this might be attributed to a short-term memory problem.

short-term objectives An element of the *individualized education program* that involves a written listing of specific tasks targeted for a child to accomplish toward achieving *long-range goals* for the school term or year.

shunt (shunting) A technique involving implantation of a tube to drain or provide a bypass for excess *cerebrospinal fluid,* as in *hydrocephalus.*

sibilant (sih′-bill-ant) One of the high-frequency sounds produced in making /ch, s, z, j/.

sibling rivalry Competition, resentment, and jealousy that occur to varying degrees between children of the same parents. A certain amount of this is considered "normal."

sickle cell anemia A condition of the blood in which the red cells assume a crescent shape and do not function properly in carrying oxygen. The condition is *genetic* and largely limited to the black race. It results in low vitality, pain, sloughing of blood cells, interference with *cerebral* nutrition and, if severe enough, may cause *mental retardation* or death.

sight vocabulary Words basic to formal reading consisting of those that are memorized or recognized as a whole, rather than by a blending of parts.

sighted guide technique A form of assisted travel for *blind* persons in which a seeing person allows a blind person to lightly hold the inside of the arm. This is the most common form of *mobility* for blind children under 11 years of age.

sign language Any form of communication based on the systematic use of physical gestures, that can be differentiated by *deaf* individuals. Current educational practice uses the term *total communication* to refer to combined use of sign language, *fingerspelling,* speech, *speech reading,* and *residual hearing* for communication purposes.

Signing Exact English (SEE) A *manual method* of communications for *deaf* people that follows the English order for basic words. SEE is much more likely to be used in school instruction than *Ameslan,* which is a language in itself and structurally different from English.

simultagnosis (sie-mull-tag-noe′-sis) The ability to recognize when two different parts of the body are touched simultaneously. One's not being able to recognize this may be considered a *"soft"* sign of *minimal brain dysfunction.*

sip and puff chair A type of electric wheelchair with a control device that is activated by the mouth. A short inhaling turns the wheelchair to the left; a long inhaling causes the chair to go in reverse; a short puff or exhaling turn the chair to the right; a continous puff carries the wheelchair forward.

six-hour retarded A term used in the 1970s to describe disadvantaged and minority children who were *labeled* as *retarded* while at school but functioned and coped normally in their environment the remainder of the time.

152

slate and stylus An instrument for writing *braille*. The slate consists of two hinged metal plates, the lower one having rows of indented braille cells and the top one having rows of windows corresponding to the indented braille cells. The braille paper is inserted between the two plates, and the braille dots are impressed with an awl-like stylus into the paper.

slow learner A term used to describe children who have educational *retardation* and whose *IQ* range is 70–89. These children have some of the same problems in learning as students who have *mild retardation,* but to a lesser degree.

smooth muscles The muscles of internal body organs that contract and relax involuntarily and do not fatigue as easily as the voluntary muscles. Reactions to tense, unpleasant emotional situations may have an unfavorable effect on these muscles, and children living under environmental pressures who chronically complain of stomach pain may be suffering this effect.

Snellen chart A white background with black letters or symbols of graded size, used to test distant field *visual acuity.* This chart, combined with teacher observation, is one method used for *screening* for visual problems.

social competence The ability to function adequately in society; more specifically, includes grooming, eating, etiquette, and social graces. Also called *social maturity.*

social learning The process of developing *social competence* in interaction with other individuals.

Social Learning Curriculum A program for *educable mentally retarded* children originated by Herbert Goldstein in 1969; developed on a theoretical base for social training and through a continuous sequence of experiences that considers the learning characteristics of pupils with *retardation.*

social maturity The ability to behave appropriately in various situations and to accept the obligations of good citizenship. Equivalent in meaning to *social competence.*

social mobility Movement of individuals or groups from one socioeconomic level to another, either upward or downward; greatly influenced by family goals, educational potential, level of education, earning power, and sometimes by the birth of a child with a *handicap* into the family.

social perception The ability to interpret the social environment, as in being aware of people's moods and realizing the causes and effects of one's own behavior. Persons with *mental retardation* and some individuals with *learning disabilities* have problems in this area.

social promotion Advancement of a pupil to the next higher grade level at the time the peer group advances, even if the student has not completely mastered the content. Research supports this practice, which is now being questioned by educational reformers.

social quotient An expression of development derived from a measurement device such as the Vineland Social Maturity Scale; computed in a manner similar to *IQ*—i.e., social age divided by *chronological age* multiplied by 100. A term in greater use at this time is *adaptive behavior.*

social reinforcement The use of personal attention, friendly remarks, a smile, positive comments, etc. to motivate desired responses.

social worker A professionally trained person who serves *handicapped* and disadvantaged persons by collecting home and environmental information and coordinating and dispensing services.

socialized-aggressive Describes a child who exhibits his/her aggression as a member of a group (gang). (see also *socially maladjusted*)

socialized delinquency A *syndrome* of *behavior disorders*, including truancy, gang membership, theft, and *norm* violation.

socially maladjusted Describes a state of persistent refusal to behave within the minimum standards of conduct required in society. Socially maladjusted children tend to destroy school property, abuse privileges, ignore responsibility, and ridicule teachers, peers, and others with whom they come in contact. (see also *socialized-aggressive*)

sociodrama A technique involving simulation of social or vocational situations in which the pupils play the roles of individuals as they might be in real life. This technique offers an opportunity to explore and have experiences prior to actually being involved in similiar situations in real life, thus preparing individuals to select behaviors for life adjustment.

sociogram A graphic product that utilizes answers to questions concerning, for example, choices of classmates as partners, to indicate members of the group who are causing friction, who are isolates, who are looked upon as leaders, etc.; i.e., the structure of a group or class.

sociopath An individual who has a morbid attitude toward society and lacks conscience in accepting responsibility for unacceptable behavior; e.g., criminals often reveal **sociopathic** behavior.

soft palate See *palate.*

"soft" sign Refers to mild abnormalities that are more difficult to detect than the obvious or gross problems but indicate the possibility of a handicapping condition. Soft signs usually are measured by *psychometric* means and are suggestive of neurological disorders.

somatopsychology (soe-mat-oh-sigh-kahl'-oh-jee) The science that relates to knowledge of both body and mind, specifically of the effect of body deviation on behavior.

somatotype (soe-mat'-oh-tipe) A bodily *configuration* of one of three types as classified by Sheldon. (see *ectomorphic, endomorphic, mesomorphic*)

SOMPA See *System of Multicultural Pluristic Assessment.*

sonic glasses A set of eyeglasses equipped with small disc elements that emit different *pitch* sounds depending on the closeness of objects. These glasses help *visually handicapped* persons locate objects by discriminating differences in echoes, similar to the skill used by bats. Also employed in a cane, in which case is it called a "sonic cane."

sonogram An *x-ray* type of examination of a pregnant woman in which the *fetus* is outlined by sonar waves; used to identify certain deviations in size, position, and physical defects of the fetus. Another term is *ultrasound.*

Spalding Unified Phonics A system of teaching reading and spelling that emphasizes the 70 phonograms representing the 44 sounds of English. The sounds, rather than the names of the alphabet letters, and their various combinations are taught.

spastic 1. **Spasticity** generally refers to muscular incoordination resulting from muscle spasms, opposing contractions of muscles, and *paralytic* effects. 2. The name for one form of *cerebral palsy* having the above characteristics.

spatial (spay'-shul) Anything related to or involving the interpretation of space. Spatial concepts are often difficult for those with mental *handicaps;* children with *learning disabilities* sometimes have this problem and, as a result, encounter rather severe learning problems.

special class A *self-contained program* in which students spend all or most of their day with others who have similar problems. Special classes were the primary *service delivery* option for *handicapped* students prior to 1972.

special day school Any institution for learning that serves *exceptional* children during daytime hours. This type of school has no *residential* services.

special education A broad term covering programs and services for children who *deviate* physically, mentally, or emotionally from the normal to an extent that they require unique learning experiences, techniques, or materials in order to be maintained in the regular classroom, and specialized classes and programs if the problems are more severe. As defined by *PL 94-142,* specifically designed instruction, at no cost to the parent, to meet the unique needs of a *handicapped* child, including classroom instruction, physical education, home instruction, and instruction in hospitals and *institutions.*

special education diploma Graduation certification now given in many states in place of the regular diploma; awarded to *handicapped* students who have met the objective of their *individualized education program.*

Special Education Programs (SEP) See *Office of Special Education Programs.*

special health problem Any condition that interferes with well-being and educational potential but is not classified under *orthopedic, sensory,* or mental handicaps. Progressive deterioration and low vitality conditions such as *muscular dystrophy, cystic fibrosis, myasthenia gravis, cardiovascular* disorders, *diabetes,* and *arthritis* are examples of special health problems.

Special Olympics An athletic organization for youngsters with *handicaps* that functions at local, state, and international levels for enhancement of the skills of participants in a way similar to the regular Olympics.

specialized health care needs A term that has come into use with reference to children who require technological health care procedures for life support. Examples are ventilation dependence and kidney dialysis.

specific language disability Lack of achievement in any prescribed *language* area.

specific learning disability. See *learning disability.*

spectogram A visual "voice print" analogous to a finger print. An electronic instrument, a **spectograph,** plots frequencies of overtones in a sine wave against time and allows playback of speech and sound patterns for special analysis.

155

speech and language pathologist (SLP)   A person approved by the American Speech–Language–Hearing Association to work with children who have *speech* and *language disorders.* Also known as *speech clinician.*

speech audiometer   An instrument for measuring hearing, used to determine when the testee can identify words being said, rather than just tones, at controlled levels of *intensity.* (see also *audiometer*)

speech clinician (pathologist) (therapist)   A professional person who has special training in speech improvement and correction; works with individuals who have some problem with speech, *language,* or spoken communication and are not expected to improve through normal *maturation* alone.

speech correction   A treatment program or service with the objective of improving the abilities of learners who have a deficiency or difficulty in spoken *language* production.

speech defect (disorder)   Any imperfection in the production of the sounds of *language,* caused by problems such as inadequate muscle coordination, faulty *articulation,* poor voice quality, or *organic* defects. The most accepted definition emphasizes that the condition, to be so identified, must interfere with communication, call attention to the speaker, or cause the person *anxiety* or *maladjustment.*

speech pathology   The field of *diagnosing* and treating speech problems and lack of speech development; involves individual testing and instruction, as well as work with small groups.

speech reading (lip reading)   A skill taught to *deaf* and *hard of hearing* persons through which they can understand what is said by another person by observing the *context* of the situation and the *visual* cues of speech production, such as movements of lips and facial features.

speech reception threshold (SRT)   The *decibel* (loudness) level at which an individual can understand speech.

speech therapy   A planned program of speech improvement and correction for individuals who are *handicapped* in *language* communication and speech adjustment and are not expected to improve solely through normal *maturation.*

sphincter (sfingk′-ter)   A ring-like muscle that constricts a passage or closes a natural *orifice* (body opening).

spina bifida   A *congenital malformation* of the spine characterized by lack of closure of the vertebral column, which often allows protrusion of the spinal cord into a sac at the base of the spine. The degree of severity may vary, but this condition often causes *paralysis* of the lower *extremities,* changes in *tactile* and thermal sensations, and a lack of bowel and bladder control. Whenever possible, surgery is performed at an early age to reduce the handicapping effects. Spina bifida frequently is associated with *hydrocephalus* and a reduction of *intelligence,* unless *shunting* is done.

spina bifida occulta   A form of *spina bifida* in which the spinal cord is not injured or exposed, and these children do not have the usual *paralysis* and other characteristics associated with spina bifida.

spinal meningitis   See *meningitis*

156

splinter skills Selected activities or abilities that develop in a child with *handicaps* to an excessive level while other skills are at a much lower level; most often observed in children with *retardation* or *autism.*

SQ3R A method associated with the *learning strategies approach;* emphasizes *s*urvey (rapid preview of material), *q*uestion (convert each section or subtitle to a question), (1) *r*ead (rapidly read sections, (2) *r*ecite (answer questions), (3) *r*eview (make a written or an oral statement of what has been learned).

SSI See *Supplemental Security Income.*

staff development See *inservice training.*

staffing A meeting of teachers, *therapists,* administrators, and others involved in the planning or *evaluation* of an educational or a *therapeutic* program. The term may vary from state to state; in some states it may mean an *IEP* meeting, etc. Also termed *case conference.*

stammer A speech problem in which the speaker makes involuntary stops and repetitions with the effect of jerky, halting speech. (see also *dysfluency, stuttering*)

standard deviation A measure of expressing the variability of a set of scores or attributes. Small standard deviations mean the scores are distributed close to the *mean;* large standard deviations mean the scores are spread over a wider range.

standard practice The professional "method of choice" that can reasonably be expected to be replicated from one area to another.

standard score A general term referring to transformed or normalized scores; used to compare an individual's performance to that of a *norm* group.

standardized test A measure that is administered and scored by uniform objective procedures and for which *norms* have been established so the scores of anyone completing the test can be compared to the norms.

standing table A special piece of equipment with a half-circle cut out of it and having a gate in the back that allows a person with *physical handicaps* who is otherwise bedridden or in a wheelchair to stand erect for physical relief or strength and, at times, for social interaction.

Stanford-Binet A widely used, individually administered test for measuring *intelligence;* consists of a number of different types of items arranged in ascending order of difficulty.

stapes The innermost of the three small bones in the middle ear that conduct vibrations from the *tympanic membrane* to the inner ear. Often called "stirrup" because of its shape. The other two bones are the *incus* and the *malleus.*

staphylococcus (staf-luh-kahk'-uhs) Ball-shaped bacteria occurring in clusters and giving rise to infections such as boils, abcesses, and carbuncles; sometimes called "staph" infections.

startle response 1. The reaction of an individual to loud shouts of "No!" or bangs on a table, which interrupts behavior. 2. An innate *reflex* when confronted with frightening *stimuli (Moro reflex).*

157

state education(al) agency (SEA) Terminology used in federal and state legislation to refer to the department in state government with primary responsibility for public school education.

state plan The stated organization and description of implementation to adhere to federal legislation. *PL 94-142* and other laws have required state plans.

status offenders A term applied to young people who run away from home, create *discipline* problems, and generally exhibit behaviors that, because of their age, are against the law (if these persons were adults, these acts would not be against the law).

status seizure (status epilepticus) A *grand mal* seizure that starts, stops, and repeats itself after 5 minutes, or may last longer than 10 minutes. Status seizures, unlike certain other seizures, are viewed as serious enough to warrant calling an ambulance or physician.

Steinut's disease See *myotonic dystrophy.*

stenosis (steh-noe'-sis) Narrowing of any canal or passage, especially one of the *cardiac* valves.

stereognosis (stair-ee-og-noe'-sis) The ability to recognize objects by touch. Inability to do this may be a *"soft"* sign of *minimal brain dysfunction.*

stereotoner An electronic instrument that converts printed images to audible tones; useful with *blind* individuals.

stereotype 1. A fixed or standardized response to specific *stimuli* or situations; a characteristic often displayed by children with *handicaps* that tends to make certain responses and behaviors predictable. 2. A *label* applied to a person who has characteristics common to and identified with members of a given group.

stereotypic behavior or **stereotypics** Repetitive, nonfunctional behavior sometimes observed in *retarded, emotionally disturbed,* and *blind* populations. These actions, possibly resulting from *brain injury* or a lack of *overt* stimulation, include rocking, rubbing eyes, and flipping objects in front of the eyes. With blind persons, the term *blindism* has been used but is giving way to this term.

stereotypies The rhythmic actions of normal infants, seen in the arms, legs, and trunk.

stigmata Physical features or markings that are used in *diagnosis.* In *Down syndrome,* the *epicanthal fold* of skin around the eyes, short stubby fingers, and palm crease are identifying stigmata.

Still's disease A chronic form of *arthritis* that affects most of the joints of the body and is accompanied by irregular fever and enlargement of the spleen and lymph nodes.

stimulant Anything that temporarily arouses or heightens physiological or *organic* activity.

stimulus (pl., **stimuli**) Any object or happening that excites a response from an organism.

stoma An external opening on the body created by surgery—in the abdomen by an *ileostomy* or *colostomy;* on the throat by *laryngectomy.*

158

strabismus (strah-bis'-mus)   A condition in which a person's eyes do not see on the same plane. The eyes can assume any pattern of convergence or divergence. Such a condition may result in a lack of *fusion*, or *binocular vision*. The basic problem is with balance of the muscles of the eyes.

Strauss syndrome   A term describing a *hyperactive*, uncoordinated child with poor concentration and learning problems. A.A. Strauss connected this set of *symptoms* with *brain damage*. More recently the term has been used to designate children demonstrating the symptoms that Strauss described but who may not have a *diagnosed* brain injury.

strephosymbolia (stref-oh-sim-boe'-lee-ah)   A disorder in which *perception* of objects results in *reversal*, as in a mirror. This condition may affect the ability to distinguish between letters such as *b–d* or *q–p*, and it also may cause a tendency to reverse direction in reading. (see also *dyslexia* and *learning disability*)

streptococcus (strep-toe-kah'-kus)   Ball-shaped bacteria that occur in chain-like formations and are found in many *pathological* infections such as the sore throat that precedes *rheumatic fever.* Shortened term is "strep," as in "strep throat."

stress   The condition of being under emotional or physical pressure, usually caused by adverse external influences that may contribute to bodily or mental tension.

stretch reflex   The tendency for a muscle to contract involuntarily when it is extended quickly.

striated (or striped) muscles   The muscles that voluntarily move the body. These are the muscles that are conditioned when an individual learns an action.

stroke   A sudden or severe bodily attack caused by a rupture of a blood vessel in the brain, too much heat, or injury to the brain or spinal cord. Residual effects may include varying degrees of *paralysis*, memory loss, inhibited *language*, and psychological *disorientation.*

structural analysis   *Decoding* skills of reading, stressing understanding of a word by breaking it down into its parts (root, suffix, prefix).

structure of the intellect   A model, developed by Guilford, that postulates certain *contents* of thought that are associated with certain *operations* or thinking functions to produce certain *products* of thinking. This model is one of the most systematic attempts to describe *intellectual* processes.

structured learning   A group technique used to teach social skills, employing four components: modeling, role playing, performance feedback, and transfer of training. All four elements must be incorporated in the order in which they are listed. *Feedback* may be in terms of rewards or knowledge of performance.

structured program   1. A concept advanced by Cruickshank in which learning activities and the environment are carefully designed by the teacher. 2. Any systematic, programmed *curriculum* deemphasizing group or informal instruction.

student support team (SST)   A group of educationally related personnel set up in the school system to receive referrals before children are *screened* by *special education* personnel. The SST determines and documents the severity of the problem and whether alternative approaches might be used before special education is considered. In many cases, other services are offered in lieu of special education. This represents a new practice of the 1980s. (see also *teacher assistance team*)

study booth See *carrel.*

stupor A condition of extreme *apathy* with a lack of sense or feeling, resulting from *stress* or shock.

stuttering Speech characterized by *blocking,* hesitation, or repetition of single sounds, words, and sometimes sentences. (see also *dysfluency*)

subcutaneous A term referring to the area below the skin.

sublimate (sublimation) To direct energy from its natural course to one that is more socially acceptable or more useful to the person. Sublimation is the result of this action.

subsequent injury clause See *second injury clause.*

substance abuse The inappropriate intake of alcohol or other drugs or chemical substances.

substitute consent An agreement made by a person on behalf of someone who is considered incapable of making his/her own decisions.

substitution (in speech) An *articulatory* defect of speech in which an incorrect sound replaces the correct sound, such as saying "wed" instead of "red."

subtest A part of a test; items measuring a particular type of skill arranged together.

successive approximation Emitted behavior that must improve each time in order to receive *reinforcement.* Used by teachers working with children who have *autism* and other *severe handicaps* to guide the child more closely to the desired behavior response.

superego A term first discussed in Sigmund Freud's writings on *psychoanalytic theory* in the 1890s as the aspect of one's being that contains the conscience and serves as a guide for achieving socially acceptable solutions to problems.

superlearning A concept based on the work of Georgi Lazanov, emphasizing the body and mind working in harmony. Techniques involve the use of music *therapy,* relaxation exercises, breathing rhythm, etc. during the learning process.

super phone A form of telephone communication device that translates a message from a *deaf* person into a speech-synthesized message.

supine A position of lying on one's back with the face upward. Opposite of *prone.*

Supplemental Security Income (SSI) A federally financed and administered income maintenance support program based upon need. Mentally and *physically handicapped* persons unable to support themselves can qualify for this program. The funds often are used to maintain a person in a *group home* or nursing home.

support services Programs not of a strictly educational nature but which are essential for the educational development of students with *handicaps* (e.g., *physical therapy,* medical *intervention*). These services must be delineated in an *IEP; PL 94-142* refers to them as *related services.*

supported employment A program of the 1980s emphasizing placement of individuals with handicaps in competitive employment with a job coach who essentially does on-the-job training and supervision; the job coach is usually an employee of the company.

supportive braces Adaptive devices designed to support specific parts of the body. They may be worn temporarily until an injury mends or a muscle strengthens, or they may be needed indefinitely.

suppression Intentionally excluding thoughts or feelings from consciousness. This may be done to avoid or overcome unacceptable thoughts or desires.

surrogate parent(s) As stipulated in *PL 94-142*, a substitute parent who is to be appointed if the real parent cannot be present in *due process* hearings. The surrogate parent is to serve as an *advocate* for the rights of the child.

survival education or **camping** See *wilderness education*.

suspension The removal of a student from school for ten days or less. Suspensions do not require parental notification or a hearing. Suspension of a handicapped student does require an IEP review and development of disciplinary plan that may include suspension.

sweep check A *screening* test, as for hearing, in which *acuity* at certain representative *frequencies* is checked at a predetermined level (e.g., 30 *db*). The sweep check allows for administration of a large number of tests in a relatively short time.

symbiotic psychosis A severe *behavior disorder* of childhood marked by *autistic*-like behavior and excessive clinging to parents.

symbolic function Representing one thing with another; i.e., using words to represent people, objects, and ideas.

symbolic material In Guilford's model (see *structure of the intellect*), elements that have no natural meaning; e.g., numbers, syllables, alphabet.

symbolization Representation of ideas or tangible objects with words, figures, marks, or signs. This is a more *abstract* level than dealing with the tangible objects themselves, and thus may be more difficult for a child to learn.

symptom An outward sign that indicates the possibility of a disease or mental/emotional problem (e.g., a cough may point toward *diagnosis* of a cold, flu, pneumonia, etc.). If symptoms are treated without removing the cause, the condition may be masked or, in the case of *maladaptive behavior,* other symptoms may replace the original ones; this is called **symptom substitution.**

syndactylism (sin-dak´-til-izm) A *congenital syndrome* characterized by webbed fingers or toes.

syndrome A group or complex of signs that comprise a particular condition. More specifically applied—an accumulation of *symptoms* that jointly characterize a disease.

synkinesis (sin-kih-nee´-sis) A *"soft"* sign of *minimal brain dysfunction* described as "mirror movement"; e.g., in testing, the serial touching of the thumb to the fingers may be mirrored by the opposite hand that is not being tested.

161

synovial (sin-oh'-vee-uhl) **membrane**   The sheath that lines the ligmental surfaces of joint capsules and tendons and secretes **synovia,** a lubricating fluid that facilitates articulation between the tendon and bone.

synovitis (sin-oh-vie'-tiss)   A condition in which the *synovial membrane* becomes *inflamed,* resulting in more limited movement of joints.

syntax (or **grammar**)   The *linguistic* rules of word order for meaningful sentences. **Syntactic** is the descriptive term that applies to grammar and rules governing sentence structure and word/phrase sequence.

synthesis (sin'-theh-sis) (v., **synthesize**)   Formation of a whole by combining the various components. Children who have difficulty learning often have trouble recognizing and combining individual observations to perceive a total incident or idea.

synthesized (synthetic) speech   Mechanically produced sounds that are intelligible and carry meaning.

synthetic touch   A concept used with *blind* children in which the person's *tactile* exploration of small objects is used as the basis for the child's *perception.* If a child feels a baseball, we say his/her concept of it is based on the tactile experiences of feeling the whole ball. (see also *analytic touch*)

syphilis (sif'-ih-liss)   A *venereal* disease progressing in three stages—primary, secondary, and tertiary—that if untreated will lead to *chancres, lesions,* general ill health, and eventually death. A pregnant woman with untreated syphilis may deliver a *malformed* baby with active syphilis.

System of Multicultural Pluristic Assessment   An approach to assessment developed by Jane Mercer which included social and ethnic consideration in judging individuals' potential for learning.

162

T

tachistoscope (tak-iss´-toe-skope) A simple device with a "window" or frame to control the number or amount (and sometimes the length of exposure) of words, numbers, pictures, or other *visual stimuli* exposed for reading. The principle behind this concept is to focus on the exact learning desired and to avoid distractors. (see also *typoscope*)

tactile (tactual) Pertaining to the sense of touch. (see also *haptic*)

tactile agnosia (ag-noe´-zee-ah) The inability to recognize *stimuli* through the sense of touch.

tactile discrimination One's ability to determine sameness or difference between two or more *stimuli* through the sense of touch/feel alone.

tactile perception The ability to interpret (attach meaning to) environmental information, including size, shape, and texture, via the sense of touch.

tactilear (tack´-till-ear) Refers to a type of electronic device that changes speech into a *tactile* form that is produced on the arm by a watch-like device.

talent(ed) Showing a natural aptitude or ability in a specific field without the implication of an exceptionally high degree of general *intelligence*. The concept of talent is sometimes used in reference to *gifted and talented.*

talking book A record or tape of a book or periodical recorded for use by *blind* or *visually impaired* people. Listening to a recording is a faster, more efficient means of receiving information than is reading *braille* or print using *low-vision aids.*

tandem gait Walking a line toe to heel in sequential steps. A child who does not do this well or displays loss of control may be exhibiting a *"soft" sign* of *minimal brain dysfunction.*

tantrum A violent fit of bad temper manifested by crying, sudden destructiveness, striking the wall or floor, and the like. Continued tantrums may signal a *behavior disorder* warranting special services.

tardive dyskinesia (tar´-dive dis-kih-nee´-zee-ah) A medical condition resulting as a side effect of long-term use of antipsychotic medications. Some drugs produce involuntary movements of the face, mouth, tongue, trunk, and upper extremities. Grimacing, blinking, and lip smacking are among the expressed behaviors.

target behavior   A specifically selected action or goal to be attained under *behavior modification* principles and techniques.

task analysis   The process of breaking down learning tasks into the smallest elements in the proper sequence. The resulting instruction involves systematic instruction of specific elements in sequence or, in the case of *backward chaining,* using the knowledge to learn "backward" to the just-previous element.

taxonomy   A scheme or system that categorizes or classifies, as for *behavior disorders* or *objectives* in education.

Tay-Sachs disease   A fatal condition resulting from a *metabolic* error in processing fats, which leads to *severe mental retardation* (also called *amaurotic family idiocy*). Often called an "ethnic" disease because it is found mainly in people of Ashkenazi Jewish descent.

TBI   See *traumatic brain injury; closed head injury.*

TDD   See *telecommunication device for the deaf.*

teacher aide   A subprofessional, or *paraprofessional,* person assigned to a classroom to help with certain tasks and details, usually of a noninstructional nature. The aide's duties generally consist of material preparation, supervision of independent study and activities, record keeping, and errand running.

teacher assistance team (TAT)   A term equivalent to *student support team,* which functions as *prereferral* and *intervention* before *special education* services are attempted.

technological aids   Telecommunication, *sensory,* and other devices used by persons with *disabilities* to help reduce the effects of handicapping conditions.

telebinocular   Describes optical instruments used to test an individual's *visual efficiency,* by observing how well the testee combines images, perceives depth, and so on.

telecommunication device for the deaf (TDD)   Terminology of the 1980s to indicate an electronic device through which *hearing impaired* individuals can communicate. A telephone number followed by TDD means that an agency or company (or other deaf person) has a device for communicating electronically with *deaf* individuals.

telescopic lenses   One, two, or three lenses, usually in eyeglasses or clip-on glasses, that improve distance vision, especially for those having severe *visual handicaps.*

telescoping   A programming option for *gifted* students that means teaching the same amount of material in less than the usual amount of time. A form of *acceleration.*

terminal objectives   The *short-term objectives* or *long-range goals* specified by an *individualized education program.*

test item   The smallest unit of a test (e.g., "How are an apple and a peach alike?").

tetanus (tet′-nus)   An *acute* infectious disease commonly called "lockjaw," characterized by *spasms* of voluntary muscles, especially of the jaw. This condition is caused by a bacillus usually introduced through a break in the skin.

164

therapeutic recreation A form of treatment that employs leisure activities of a mildly physical nature as corrective measures.

therapy (adj., **therapeutic**) Any treatment or structuring of the environment to improve one's well-being. A person whose work is specifically intended for therapy may be called a **therapist.**

thinning Gradually presenting *reinforcers* less frequently as a new, desired behavior is acquired.

threshold The smallest amount of *stimulus* energy capable of arousing an impulse in a receptor or nerve cell resulting in a sensation. Below that level, terminology is "below threshold" or "does not elicit sensation."

thyroid An *endocrine gland,* located in the front lower portion of the neck, that secretes *hormones* that regulate the body's rate of *metabolism.*

tibia The larger of the two bones of the lower leg, located to the inside of the smaller bone, the *fibula.*

tic A habitual spasmodic movement or twitching of a muscle or group of muscles, often involving the face.

time and motion study A comparison of the speed at which an individual without a *handicap* can do a task and the speed at which an individual with a handicap can do the same task, to determine a ratio of *efficiency* in productivity; commonly used in *sheltered workshops* to determine wages and set piecemeal job rates.

time-out A *behavior management* technique that eliminates possible reinforcing events for undesirable behaviors for a given time. For example, a child may be moved from classmates to a corner of the room or a *carrel.*

time sampling Recording behaviors at specific intermittent periods, as contrasted with continuous recording for the full time. Time sampling could consist of, for example, recording behaviors during the initial 10 minutes of each 30-minute period during a 3-hour daily program.

tinnitus (tih-nih'-tus) A condition in which one hears an abnormal noise in the ears without external *stimuli.* This noise may be a ringing, buzzing, roaring, clicking, or similar sound.

titmus A test of *visual acuity* administered by use of a viewing instrument that the subject looks into; the examiner obtains a measure of visual acuity at near and far points.

TMR See *trainable mentally retarded.*

token An object, to which a value is assigned, used in *behavior management* as a reward. Accumulated tokens can be exchanged for desired objects or activities corresponding to the values of the tokens attained.

tone deafness A condition in which an individual is unable to hear or distinguish certain sound *frequencies.*

tongue thrust An undesirable pushing of the tongue forward or between the teeth and the lips. Sometimes seen in children with *Down syndrome,* for example.

tonic neck reflex An involuntary movement in which one arm straightens and stiffens and the other bends and stiffens when the head is turned.

tonus Muscle firmness or mild *rigidity* that indicates a muscle is in a state of being ready to respond normally to *stimuli*. A muscle without tonus is said to be *flaccid*.

tool subject An area of learning that presents knowledge and skills that have to be mastered to effectively study other subjects. Reading, writing, and arithmetic are commonly regarded as being tool subjects.

tort A legal term referring to an actionable wrong or injury to another; a civil wrong for which a private citizen may recover money damages.

torticollis (tore-tih-coal'-iss) See *wryneck.*

total communication A system of *expressive/receptive language* in which *manual* signs and *fingerspelling* are simultaneously combined with speech, *speech reading,* and listening in the way deemed most beneficial to a *hearing impaired* individual.

Total Service Plan The part of the *individualized education program (IEP)* that describes *long-term goals* and strategies for both instruction and *related services,* and recommends placement.

Tourette syndrome (too-ret') A rare disease that manifests itself as multiple *tic*-like movements and vocalizations. The condition usually starts between 2 and 14 years of age with rapidly blinking eyes or facial tics, and progresses to other parts of the body. The best control at this time is the use of strong *tranquilizers.*

toxemia (tock-see'-mee-uh) Blood poisoning caused by a specific secretion, chemically related to proteins, in the *metabolism* of a vegetable or animal organism. Toxemia during pregnancy may increase the risk of birth of a child with *handicaps.*

toxic Poisonous, as in having poison or a poisonous substance in the blood.

toxoplasmosis (tock-so-plaz-moe'-sis) A disease caused by an infection of a parasitic microorganism, **toxoplasm.** If contracted *congenitally,* the condition probably is one of the most damaging of all *prenatal* infections; about 75% of the offspring born of mothers having *acute* toxoplasmosis have some involvement, such as *hydrocephalus, seizures, spasticity, anemia, jaundice,* or enlarged liver and spleen.

trachea (tray'-kee-ah) The *cartilaginous* tube leading from the *larynx* to the lungs that serves as the air passage to and from the lungs. Often referred to as the windpipe.

tracheotomy (tray-kee-ah'-toe-me) An incision of the windpipe through the skin and muscles to improve breathing.

trachoma (trah-koe'-mah) A *chronic inflammation* of the mucous membrane that lines the inner surface of the eyelid; believed to be conveyed to the eye through use of common washcloths, towels, handkerchiefs, or by the fingers.

traction A technique used in setting or straightening bones and in treating back problems, in which weights are used to exert a steady pull on the portion of the body being treated.

trailing A technique used by *blind* persons in which they trace lightly over a straight surface with the back of the fingers, as in moving down a wall or hall. This aids *mobility.*

trainable mentally retarded (TMR) A term introduced in state educational codes to define children who are not able to profit suitably from regular classes or classes for *educable mentally retarded* students. Most *criteria* in state codes stipulate that the *intellectual* level, when *assessed* with an individual *intelligence* test, would involve *IQ* scores ranging from 35 to 55, along with other characteristics that indicate the potential for profiting from a program designed to help pupils with social adjustment, *self-help skills,* and controlled work settings. Trainable mentally retarded children score lower than 3 *standard deviations* below the *mean* on individually administered intelligence tests and generally have an intellectual ability of from one third to one half that of an average child of comparable *chronological age.* (see also *moderate mental retardation*)

tranquilizer Any drug that quiets and calms but does not have a *hypnotic* effect.

transcendence One of the concepts in Feuerstein's *mediated learning experience,* which seeks to train *generalization* or the use of principles. The idea is to train students with *mental retardation* so that they are able to learn more than just what they are taught and, rather, acquire certain principles, rules, and functions for application in future situations.

transdisciplinary programming An educational approach that emphasizes communication and shared performance among members of various professional specialists and others on a child's educational planning team.

transduce (n., transduction) To convey information from one *sensory modality* to another. (Transduction: the conversion of received information from one sensory modality to another.) In *learning disabilities,* for example, students may be able to look at an object and recognize it *visually,* but cannot recognize it by touching it, and thus have problems in transduction.

transfer (of learning) Application of already learned knowledge and skills in a variety of new and related situations.

transformation 1. A change in composition or structure of a basic sentence (e.g., You solved those problems. Transformation: You didn't solve those problems.) 2. One of Guilford's *products* of thinking in which existing information is changed to be used in another form. (see *structure of the intellect*)

transition or **transition programming** Services that provide a bridge between school and employment, stemming from a concern in the 1980s about children graduating from high school and not being prepared for employment.

transitional time-limited employment A type of supported work specially designed to meet the needs of persons with chronic *mental illness.*

translocation Attachment of a portion of a *chromosome* of one group to another group, thereby giving an excess of *genetic* material in one cell and a deficiency in another.

167

transposition The interchanging of positions of two words or of two letters or sounds in a word, or the pronunciation of a word out of *context* when reading aloud. May indicate a *language disorder* or *learning disability*.

trauma An undesirable, abrupt physical or emotional change in an organism, caused by violence, shock, or force.

traumatic brain injury Injury to the head that produces severe memory disorder with poor carryover of new learning. These individuals will express some characteristics similar to those of individuals with *learning disabilities* and may be placed in such programs, but this may not be the most appropriate placement.

Treacher-Collins syndrome A *genetic mutation* involving facial bone abnormalities, defects of the *auditory canal, ossicle,* and *palate. Mental retardation* and *deafness* are usually present.

tremor 1. A quivering or vibratory motion of any part of the body. 2. A *symptom* of a form of *cerebral palsy* characterized by trembling or shaking motions or involuntary alternate movements.

triplegia (try-plee´-juh) A form of *paralysis* in which three limbs are affected.

trisomy (try´-suh-mee) The general term describing a *genetic* condition in which three *chromosomes* are present rather than the normal two in a pair. Trisomy 21 is a technical term for the most common form of *Down syndrome*. The 21st chromosome pair is actually a triplet; thus, the individual cell contains 47 chromosomes rather than the normal 46.

TTY An abbreviation for a telecommunication system used by *deaf* persons in which they can use a portable keyboard to communicate with other deaf individuals or agencies that have corresponding equipment. (see also *TDD*)

tubal ligation (lie-gay´-shun) Sterilization of a female by tying, severing, or crushing the *uterine* (fallopian) tubes to prevent passage of eggs that otherwise could be fertilized.

tuberculosis (TB) A *chronic communicable disease* caused by the tubercle bacillus, which destroys tissues of body organs and bones. The lungs are most often affected.

tuberous sclerosis (too´-burr-us skler-oh´-sis) A neurological disorder characterized by one or more of the following: *epileptic seizures, mental retardation,* tumors, skin *lesions.* A common skin manifestation is a reddish/bluish "birthmark" area on the cheeks, nose, and chin.

tuning fork A metal instrument with two prongs that, when caused to vibrate, produces a tone of a certain *pitch.* Tuning forks are used for testing hearing through both *air conduction* and *bone conduction.*

tunnel vision A defect in which the *visual field* is contracted to a degree at which only central *visual acuity* is functioning. The resulting sight is similar to the effect of looking through a tunnel.

168

Turner syndrome   A disorder in females resulting from an absence of one of the sex *chromosomes*. The condition affects secondary sex characteristics and may include *mental retardation* or learning problems.

turtle technique   A behavior approach taught to children in which *cognitive* processes are involved to help a child retard response, delay anger, or neutralize *aggressive* behavior.

tutorial plan   A teaching program sometimes used with *gifted* children in which the pupils remain assigned to their regular classes but are released at specific times during the day to work individually or in small groups with a teacher. The intent is to assist the pupils in exploring their fields of interest more fully and in expanding their opportunities for experiences.

tympanic membrane   The *ear drum,* or thin membranous structure between the outer and middle ear. The ear drum's vibrations, caused by sound waves striking it through the *auditory canal* of the outer ear, are conveyed to the *ossicles,* which transmit the vibratory movement to the fluid in the inner ear.

tympanogram   A recording produced by a **tympanometer.** (see *tympanometry,* below)

tympanometry (tim-pan-ah′-meh-tree)   Audiometric measurement involving a device inserted in the ear to apply air pressure against the *ear drum* so that the internal pressure of the middle ear can be determined. It provides physical measurements in the form of a *tympanogram,* which can point up abnormalities of the ear drum, middle ear cavity, and bones of the middle ear *(ossicles).* (see also *impedance audiometry*)

tympanostomy (tim-pan-oss′-toe-mee) **tubes**   Polyurethane devices inserted in the ear drum to reduce pressure on the middle ear; colloquially called "tubes in the ears."

type-token   The ratio of the total number of different words (types) to the total number of words (tokens). This measure is frequently used in studies of *language development* as an indication of complexity.

typoscope   A simple reading device used to isolate single words or a row of words; used with students who have difficulty seeing words separately and distinctly. Usually made of poster paper, construction paper, or any heavy paper into a which a slit is cut in the size of a word or line of words. (see also *tachistoscope*)

U

UAF See *UAP.*

UAP (University Affiliated Program) Any of the *interdisciplinary* training centers sponsored by the federal government to demonstrate innovative methods of delivering services, to train specialists, and to do research in *developmental disabilities.*

ulna The larger of the two bones in the forearm, located on the little finger side of the arm. The other is the *radius.*

ultrasonography A medical testing procedure through which an unborn *fetus* can be viewed without producing potential danger as in *x-ray* testing. Referred to generally as *ultrasound.* (see also *sonogram*)

ultrasound See *sonogram; ultrasonography.*

unconditioned reflex A natural, innate reaction to an external *stimulus* that is not learned or acquired by *conditioning;* e.g., when air is blown into the face, the eyes will blink.

underachiever An individual who produces at a level below that predicted by general testing; indicates that the individual is functioning significantly below capability.

ungraded class A group of students organized to permit each to work at his/her own rate with the assistance of individual instruction and without assignment to grade level.

unilateral On one side only; used to refer to conditions on only one side of the body.

unit 1. One of a series of learning activities organized around a central topic or problem area; these activities span several subject matter areas, although one area may be emphasized more than another. 2. The simplest *product* of thinking in Guilford's model, represented by *figural* or *symbolic* structures. (see *structure of the intellect*)

uremia (you-ree'-mee-ah) A condition marked by an excess of chemical urea and nitrogenous waste in the blood, causing a *toxic* condition.

urinalysis A chemical study of urine, taken routinely during medical examinations, to determine any abnormal excretion of substances into the urine that are caused by physiological conditions.

Usher's syndrome A condition in which the individual has *retinitis pigmentosa* plus *hearing impairment.*

uterus (adj., **uterine**) The organ of the female body that contains and nurtures a fertilized egg and developing *fetus.*

uvula (you'-vyuh-luh) The flap of connective tissue that extends downward at the back of the soft *palate* in the throat area. The uvula assists the individual in closing the *nasal* cavity; thus, problems with the uvula or its absence produce nasal speech sounds.

170

V

VAKT   A *multisensory* approach to teaching reading developed by Grace Fernald to assist children with severe *reading disabilities.* VAKT stands for *visual, auditory, kinesthetic,* and *tactile.* The approach employs tracing and auditory responses to supplement a weak visual channel. Also called the *Fernald method.*

validity   A term referring to how well an instrument or method measures what it is supposed to measure.

valproic acid   A drug approved for use in the United States during the 1980s for control of seizures. The drug was effectively used in Europe before becoming approved in this country.

variable interval   A term applied to *reinforcement* based on non-set times.

variable ratio   A term applied to *reinforcement* based on a non-set number of performances.

vasectomy   Surgical removal of the tube or a portion of the tube (vas deferens) that carries sperm. This is generally considered a permanent form of sterilization, just as *tubal ligation* in females is considered permanent.

velum   The small structure at the end or back of the soft *palate* that closes the *nasal* cavity during the production of most English. When it is missing or nonfunctional, a person's speech becomes *hypernasal.*

venereal disease (VD)   A group of contagious diseases usually transmitted by genital contact or sexual intercourse. Untreated venereal disease during pregnancy may contribute to the birth of a child with *handicaps.*

verbal test   An *intelligence* test or subtest that requires spoken *language* and the use of words to measure *intellectual* potential.

verbal unreality (or verbalism)   Usually refers to *blind* persons' use of terms of sighted persons that are not within their *sensory* experience, as in describing blood as "red" rather than "sticky and warm."

verbalize (n., verbalization)   To express something in spoken *language.* Verbalization of conscious emotions and thought often is helpful in bringing about psychological adjustment.

verbo-tonal method   An approach to developing the speaking and listening skills of *hearing impaired* persons, developed by Prof. Gubcrina of the University of Zagreb, Yugoslavia. This method emphasizes the training or retraining of *auditory perceptual* areas of the brain to assist an individual in perceiving speech sounds and making the best use of *residual hearing.*

vertex   Refers to the normal presentation of head first during birth. For comparison, see *breech birth.*

vertigo   A disorder of the sense of balance, or equilibrium, which causes dizziness or giddiness.

vestibule (ves'-tih-bule)   A space or cavity at the entrance of a body canal, as in the **vestibular** mechanism of the inner ear.

vicarious (vie-care'-ee-us) **learning**   Knowledge that is attained as an unexpected or unplanned outcome of experiences. This type of learning results from watching others or *modeling* after them. Sometimes this may be done to the extreme that a person "lives through" another.

vigilance   The ability to maintain attention to a task despite challenges or, in the case of some *disabilities,* to marshal attention to pay initial attention.

virus (adj., **viral**)   A group of tiny infectious agents that can replicate only within living host cells.

visual (adj., **visually**)   Pertaining to the sense of sight.

visual acuity   One's ability to see things and to accurately distinguish their characteristics; how well one sees.

visual agnosia   See *agnosia.*

visual closure   Being able to perceive wholes from seeing only parts of the whole, as in recognizing that a picture of part of a face represents a face, or identifying a word after seeing only a part of that word. Training in visual closure is beneficial to children who have difficulty relating parts to the whole.

visual discrimination   One's ability to use the sense of sight to determine whether things he/she sees are the same or different.

visual efficiency   The effectiveness with which an individual uses his/her eyesight. Two persons with equal *visual acuity* may not use their vision equally; the person who makes better use of vision would be said to have greater visual efficiency. Visual efficiency can be trained, according to Natalie Barraga and others.

visual field   See *field of vision.*

visual impairment   Educationally defined as a deficiency in eyesight to the extent that special provisions are necessary in education. (see also *blindness; legal blindness*)

visual memory   The ability to recall images after a lapse of time. Visual memory is important in academic achievement, and *impairment* results in *learning disorders.*

visual-motor coordination   The ability to combine vision with movement of the body or its parts. This is a necessary skill in many academic areas including handwriting, mathematics, and physical education.

visual-motor memory   The ability to accurately remember previously seen experiences involving movement.

visual-motor perception   Formation of an idea or concept through use of vision and physical activity. In *visual perception,* only visual processes are involved; in visual motor perception, the acts of physically creating (e.g., drawing) and perceiving an object are combined.

172

visual perception   The ability to interpret what is seen.

visual reception   The ability to receive information through the seeing channel.

visual screening   1. A *time-out* procedure in which the therapist or teacher screens his/her face or turns the face away as a form of removal without removing the child from the environment. 2. Preliminary assessment of a group of children to determine those who may have problems with eyesight and need further testing.

visual tracking   An early developmental visual ability in which an infant follows a person or object moving across the field of vision. In work with individuals with severe and profound retardation this ability may be an objective for instruction.

visualization   The act of interpreting in visual terms or describing in visible form.

vitreous (vih'-tree-us) **humor**   The fluid in the back chamber of the eye that fills the space between the *retina* and the *lens.*

vocal nodules   Callous-like growths that form on the vocal folds, resulting in harshness or *hoarseness* of the voice.

vocalize (n., **vocalization;** adv., **vocally**)   To make sounds with the voice.

vocational counseling   Discussions with a specially trained person that concentrate on selecting an occupation, including the education or training needed to prepare for the occupation selected, and in seeking, making application, and obtaining employment. This term is similar to, but less formalized than, *vocational guidance.*

vocational education   A formalized program with the goal of preparing individuals to work in a chosen occupation or upgrading employed workers in their existing work situations.

vocational (work) evaluator   An individual skilled in the administration and interpretation of vocational *assessment* tests and other types of vocationally oriented *evaluation* procedures.

vocational guidance   An organized program to assist pupils in choosing, securing training for, and becoming successfully employed in an occupation for which their abilities qualify them. *Vocational counseling* is a less formalized approach having the same general objectives.

vocational rehabilitation   The service of providing *diagnosis,* guidance, training, physical restoration, and placement to persons with *disabilities* for the purpose of preparing them for and involving them in employment that helps them to live with greater independence. The preferred term is now *rehabilitation services.*

vocational workshop program   A specific educational offering that is work-oriented and is carried out in a controlled environment.

vocoder   A device that allows the *deaf* to make fine speech *discriminations* by use of the *tactual* mode.

voice disorder   An abnormal spoken *language* production as exhibited by unusual *pitch,* volume, or quality of sounds.

vowel   An alphabet letter representing the sounds of /a, e, i, o, u/ and sometimes /y/. Spoken English has 12 vowel *phonemes.*

W

walker A type of equipment designed with handgrips or rails to support an individual with *physical handicaps* in an upright position and in walking.

Warkany's syndrome See *intrauterine growth retardation.*

watch-tick test An informal *screening* measure of hearing in which the tester holds a watch or clock with a loud tick near the pupil's ear and asks the pupil to indicate when he/she ceases to hear the ticks as the tester moves away. The tester should use the same watch or clock for each test and should know the approximate distance at which a person with normal hearing ceases to hear the tick in order to recognize *hearing losses* in the population being tested.

weighted designation system A means of determining class sizes in which students having *handicaps* are counted differentially. Thus, a child with *mild mental retardation* who is *mainstreamed* into a regular class may be counted twice, the assumption being that the student requires twice the attention and time from the teacher.

Wild Boy of Aveyron A 12-year-old male found abandoned and living in a forest in France by Jean Itard around 1800. Itard used a *sensory* training program to make Victor more social and knowledgeable.

wilderness education (camping) An approach to treatment of behavior disordered students by immersing them into a wilderness with a counselor(s) in which survival and progress is synonomous with group involvement.

Wilson's disease The *generic* term for a *syndrome* associated with *mental retardation* and characterized by copper deposits in some body organs.

word-finding problem A term used by *speech and language pathologists* to characterize the speech of children who have difficulty in mentally locating a word to use and thus will have difficulty in labeling and will substitute a similar word (e.g., boot for sock).

words in color An innovation by Gattegno to make the 26-letter alphabet more phonetic by designating a color to consistently represent each *phoneme.*

work activity center A sheltered setting for severely disabled persons where they are taught work and daily activities of life. This type of center can involve cooking, cleaning, dressing, caring for clothes, and a variety of activities associated with daily living.

work evaluation Selective analysis of simulated or real job samples for the purpose of *assessing* a client's aptitude and skills for specific application.

work experience   A program having as its purpose the supervised part-time or full-time employment of students by helping them to acquire desirable job skills, attitudes, and habits.

work-study program   A situation providing for high school level students with *mild handicaps* to work on a job part-time and attend class the remainder of the time. The intent is to give the pupil some actual experiences to relate to the class work so it will be more practical. This program may be referred to as "on-the-job training" (OJT).

workmen's compensation   An insurance program carried by an employer and required by all states; covers employees for time lost as a result of injuries or certain occupational diseases. This insurance includes liability coverage to protect the employer against most damage suits brought by employees or their survivors. (see also *second injury clause*)

wryneck   A spasmodic condition in which the neck draws the head to one side; observed in young children and those with certain forms of *cerebral palsy.* Same as *torticollis.*

Wyatt v. Stickney   A significant piece of litigation (1971) affirming the right to treatment of residents with *mental illness* and *mental retardation* in two Alabama state *institutions,* setting a precedent for the right of involuntarily committed residents to adequate treatment within state facilities.

X

x-ray A form of radiation that has wave lengths much shorter than those of light, has the property of penetrating various thicknesses of solids, and acts on photographic plates and fluorescent screens like light. X-rays are used in medical *diagnosis* and for medical treatment of selected conditions.

xerophthalmia (zee-rof-thal′-mee-ah) Dryness of the *cornea* and *conjunctiva* of the eye resulting from a vitamin A deficiency. This condition begins with *night blindness.*

Yerkish   A communication system originally used in the Yerkes Primate Laboratory to teach a chimpanzee to communicate. The system utilizes a large symbol board that is touched to translate into commands. Recently the system has been tried with individuals who have *severe handicaps.*

Ypsilanti project   See *Perry project.*

Z

zero reject   One of the principles upon which *PL 94-142* and numerous court cases have been based. Essentially, it says that no child, regardless of the degree of *handicap*, may be refused a *free appropriate public education* if other children of that age are served.

zone of proximal development   One of the constructs in Vygotsky's theory that is the equivalent of saying a child has a zone of readiness for instruction and teachers must be aware and instruct within the available zone.

Associations and National Centers

AAAC, International Society of Augmentative and Alternative Communication, 428 E. Preston St., Baltimore, MD 21201

AASK (Aid for the Adoption of Special Kids), Box 11212, Oakland, CA 94611

Academy of Dentistry for Handicapped, 611 E. Chicago Ave., Chicago, IL 60611

Accrediting Council for Services for Mentally Retarded and Other Developmentally Disabled Persons, 875 N. Michigan Ave., Chicago, IL 60611

Acoustical Society of America, 500 Sunnyside Blvd., Woodbury NY 11797

Alexander Graham Bell Association for the Deaf, 3417 Volta Pl. NW, Washington, DC 20007

Alternative Living Managers Association (ALMA), 1642 N. Winchester Ave., Chicago, IL 60622

Alzheimers Disease and Related Disorders Association, 70 E. Lake St., Suite 600, Chicago, IL 60601

American Academy for Cerebral Palsy and Developmental Medicine, 1910 Byrd Ave., #118, P.O. Box 11086, Richmond, VA 23230

American Academy of Neurology, 2221 University Ave. S.E., Suite 335, Minneapolis, MN 55414

American Academy of Optometry, P.O. Box 565, Owatonna, MN 55060

American Academy of Orthotists and Prosthetists (AAOP), 717 Pendleton St., Alexandria, VA 22314

American Academy of Otolaryngology, Head and Neck Surgery, 1101 Vermont Ave. NW, Suite 302, Washington, DC 20005

American Academy of Physical Medicine and Rehabilitation, 122 S. Michigan Ave., Suite 1300, Chicago, IL 60603

American Alliance for Health, Physical Education, Recreation, and Dance, 1900 Association Dr., Reston, VA 22091

American Archives of Rehabilitative Therapists and Specialists, P.O. Box 93, North Little Rock, AR 72116

179

American Association for the Blind, 1511 K St. NW, Washington, DC 20005

American Association for Counseling and Development (AACD) 5999 Stevenson Ave., Alexandria, VA 22304 (formerly American Personnel and Guidance Association)

American Association for Gifted Children, 15 Gramercy Park, New York, NY 10033

American Association on Mental Retardation, 1719 Kalorama Rd. NW, Washington, DC 20009 (formerly American Association on Mental Deficiency)

American Association for Rehabilitation Therapy, W. 32 Ferndale Rd., Paramus, NJ 07652

American Association of Special Educators, 29 Bolton Rd., Flanders, NJ 07836

American Association of University Affiliated Programs, 1100–17th St. NW, Washington, DC 20036

American Association for Vocational Instructional Materials, University of Georgia, 120 Engineering Center, Athens, GA 30602

American Association of Workers for the Blind (see Association for Education and Rehabilitation of Blind and Visually Impaired)

American Athletic Association of the Deaf, 1052 Darling St., Ogden, UT 84403

American Bar Association, Commission on the Mentally Disabled, 1800 M St. NW, Washington, DC 20036

American Board of Otolaryngology, 1301 E. Ann St., Ann Arbor, MI 48104

American Brittle Bone Society, 1256 Merrill Dr., West Chester, PA 19380

American Cancer Society, 46 Fifth St. NE, Atlanta, GA 30308

American Cleft Palate Educational Foundation, University of Pittsburgh, 1218 Grandview Ave., Pittsburgh, PA 15211

American Coalition of Citizens with Disabilities (ACCD), 1346 Connecticut Ave. NW, Suite 1124, Washington, DC 20036

American College of Surgeons, Dept. of Otorhinolaryngology, 55 E. Erie St., Chicago, IL 60611

American Congress of Rehabilitation, 130 N. Michigan Ave., Chicago, IL 60602

American Council for the Blind, 1010 Vermont Ave. NW, Suite 1100, Washington, DC 20005

American Council on Rural Special Education, Western Washington University, Miller Hall 359, Bellingham, WA 98225

American Deafness and Rehabilitation Association (ADARA), 814 Thayer Ave., Silver Spring, MD 20910

American Diabetes Association, 2 Park Ave., New York, NY 10016

American Foundation for Autistic Children, 4510 Cumberland St. NW, Chevy Chase, MD 20015

American Foundation for the Blind, 15 W. 16th St., New York, NY 10011

American Heart Association, 7320 Greenville Ave., Dallas TX 75231

180

American Hospital Association, Section for Rehabilitation Hospitals and Programs, 840 North Lake Shore Dr., Chicago, IL 60611

American Laryngological Association, 1300 N. Vermont Ave., Suite 502, Los Angeles, CA 90027

American Laryngological, Rhinological, and Otological Society, Landenau Medical Bldg., Philadelphia, PA 19107

American Lung Association, 1740 Broadway, New York, NY 10019

American Medical Association, 535 N. Dearborn St., Chicago, IL 60610

American Occupational Therapy Association, 1383 Piccard Dr., Rockville, MD 20580

American Optometric Association, 243 N. Lindberg Blvd., St. Louis, MO 63141

American Orthopsychiatric Association, 1775 Broadway, New York, NY 10019

American Orthotic and Prosthetic Association, 717 Pendleton St., Alexandria, VA 22314

American Personnel and Guidance Association (see American Association for Counseling and Development)

American Physical Therapy Association, 111 N. Fairfax St., Alexandria, VA 22314

American Printing House for the Blind, 1839 Frankfort Ave., Louisville, KY 40206

American Psychiatric Association, 1400 K St. NW, Washington, DC 20005

American Psychological Association, 1200–17th St. NW, Washington, DC 20036

American Rehabilitation Counseling Association, 5999 Stevenson Ave., Alexandria, VA 22304

American Rhinologic Society, 4177 Broadway, Kansas City, MO 64111

American Schizophrenia Foundation, Box 160, Ann Arbor, MI 48107

American Society for Deaf Children, 814 Thayer Ave., Silver Spring, MD 20910

American Speech-Language-Hearing Association, 10801 Rockville Pike, Rockville, MD 20852

American Spinal Injury Association, 1333 Moursand Ave., Houston, TX 77030

American Vocational Association, 1410 King St., Alexandria, VA 22314

American Wheelchair Bowling Association, 6718 Pinehurst Dr., Evansville, IN 47711

Amyotropic Lateral Sclerosis Association (ALS), 2102 Ventura Blvd., Suite 321, Woodland Hills, CA 91364

Architectural and Transportation Barriers Compliance Board (ATBCB), 330 C St. SW, Rm. 1010, Washington, DC 20202

Arthritis Foundation, 1314 Spring St. NW, Atlanta, GA 30309

Arthrogryposis Association, 106 Herkimer St., North Bellmore, NY 11710

Association for Advancement of Behavior Therapy, 420 Lexington Ave., Suite 2549, New York, NY 10170

Association for Advancement of the Mentally Handicapped, Leo Prince St., Elizabeth, NJ 07208

Association for Children and Adults with Learning Disabilities, 4156 Library Rd., Pittsburgh, PA 15234

Association for Education and Rehabilitation of the Blind and Visually Impaired, 206 N. Washington St., Suite 320, Alexandria, VA 22314

Association for the Gifted (TAG), 1920 Association Dr., Reston, VA 22091

Association on Handicapped Student Service Programs in Post-Secondary Education, P.O. Box 21192, Columbus, OH 43221

Association of Learning Disabled Adults, P.O. Box 9722, Washington, DC 20016

Association of Mental Health Administrators, 425–13th St. NW, Washington, DC 20004

Association for Mentally Ill Children, 12 W. 12th St., New York, NY 10033

Association for Persons with Severe Handicaps, 7010 Roosevelt Way, Seattle, WA 98115 (formerly The Association for the Severely Handicapped)

Association of Rehabilitation Nurses, 2506 Grosse Point Rd., Evanston, IL 60201

Association of Rehabilitative Facilities, 5530 Wisconsin Ave., Suite 955, Washington, DC 20015

Association for Retarded Citizens of the United States, 2501 Ave. J, Arlington, TX 76005

Association for the Severely Handicapped (see Association for Persons with Severe Handicaps)

Autism Society of America, 1234 Massachusetts Ave. NW, Suite 1017, Washington DC 20005 (formerly National Society for Autism)

Better Hearing Institute, 1430 K St. NW, #800, Washington, DC 20005

Bliss Symbolics Communication Foundation, 862 Eglinton Ave., Toronto, Ontario, Canada M4E 2L1

Canadian Association for the Mentally Retarded, Kinsmen NIMR Bldg., York University Campus, 4700 Keele St., North York, Toronto, Ontario, Canada M3J 1P3

Canadian Association for Research in Rehabilitation, 13325 St. Albert Trail, Edmonton, Alberta, Canada T5L 4R3

Canadian Council for Exceptional Children, 2 Robert Speck Pkwy, Suite 750, Mississauga, Ontario, Canada L4Z 1H8

Canadian Hearing Society, 60 Bedford Rd., Toronto, Ontario, Canada M5R 2K2

Canadian National Institute for the Blind, 1924 Bayview Ave., Toronto, Ontario, Canada M4G 3F8

Canadian Rehabilitation Council for the Disabled, 1 Young St., Suite 2110, Toronto, Ontario, Canada M5E 1A5

Captioned Films for the Deaf, Distribution Center, 5034 Wisconsin Ave. NW, Washington, DC 20016

Center for Sickle Cell Disease, Howard University, College of Medicine, 2121 George Ave. NW, Washington, DC 20059

Center for Special Education Technology, 1920 Association Dr., Reston VA 22091

Center for Studies in Schizophrenia, 5600 Fishers Ln., Rm. 10-95, Rockville, MD 20857

CHAMPUS (see OCHAMPUS)

Child Abuse Source System, Northwestern University, Technological Institute, Rm. 3390, Evanston, IL 60201

Children's Brain Disease Foundation for Research, 350 Parnassus Ave., Suite 900, San Francisco, CA 94117

Clearinghouse on Research in Child Abuse and Neglect, P.O. Box 1182, Washington, DC 20013

Clearinghouse on the Handicapped, Switzer Bldg., Rm. 3132, Washington, DC 20202

Cleft Palate Foundation, University of Pittsburgh, 1218 Grandview Ave., Pittsburgh, PA 15211

Closer Look (see National Information Center for Children and Youth with Handicaps)

Coalition on Sexuality and Disability, 380 Second Ave., 4th Floor, New York, NY 10010

Commission on Accreditation of Rehabilitation Facilities, 101 N. Wilmot Rd., Tucson, AZ 85711

Convention of American Instructors of the Deaf (CAID), 1081 Rockville Pike, Rockville, MD 20852

Council of Administrators for Special Education (CASE), 615-16th St. NW, Albuquerque, NM 87104

Council for Children with Behavioral Disorders (CCBD), 1920 Association Dr., Reston, VA 22091

Council on Education of the Deaf, 800 Florida Ave. NE, Washington, DC 20002

Council for Exceptional Children (CEC), 1920 Association Dr., Reston, VA 22091

Council for Learning Disabilities, P.O. Box 40303, Overland Park, KS 66204

Council of State Administrators of Vocational Rehabilitation, 1055 Thomas Jefferson St. NW, Washington, DC 20007

Cystic Fibrosis Foundation, 6931 Arlington Rd., Bethesda, MD 20814

Disabled American Veterans, 807 Maine Ave. SW, Washington, DC 20024

Disabled Student Services, Southern Connecticut State College, 501 Crescent St., New Haven, CT 06515

Division on Career Development (DCD), 1920 Association Dr., Reston, VA 22091

Division for Early Childhood (DEC), 1920 Association Dr., Reston, VA 22091

Division for Learning Disabilities (DLD), 1920 Association Dr., Reston, VA 22091

Division on Mental Retardation (CEC-MR), 1920 Association Dr., Reston, VA 22091

Dyslexia Institute, 133 Gresham Rd., Staines, England TW18 2AJ

Ear Research Institute, 2130 W. Third St., Los Angeles, CA 90057

Easter Seal Research Foundation, National Easter Seal Society, 70 E. Lake St., Chicago, IL 60601

Educators of Professional Personnel for the Hearing Impaired (EPPHI), Columbia University Teacher's College, Dept. of Special Education, Box 223, New York, NY 10027

Epilepsy Foundation of America, 4351 Garden City Dr., Landover, MD 20785

ERIC Clearinghouse on Handicapped and Gifted, Council for Exceptional Children, 1920 Association Dr., Reston, VA 22091

Federation of the Handicapped, 211 W. 14th St., New York, NY 10011

Foundation for Children with AIDS, 7713 Warren St., Brighton, MA 02135

Foundation for Exceptional Children, 1920 Association Dr , Reston, VA 22091

Friends of the Sensorially Deprived, P.O. Box 186, Belmont, MA 02178

Gallaudet College, 800 Florida Ave. NE, Washington, DC 20002

Gifted Child Society, 190 Rock Rd., Glenrock, NJ 07452

Goodwill Industries of America, 9200 Wisconsin Ave., Bethesda, MD 20814

Handicapped Information Resource Center/Architectural Planning Unit, P.O. Box 413, Milwaukee, WI 53201

Head Injury Foundation, 1629 Columbia Rd., Washington, DC 20009

HEATH (Higher Education and Adult Training for People with Handicaps), One Dupont Circle, Suite 800, Washington, DC 20026

Helen Keller National Center for Deaf-Blind Youth and Adults, 111 Middle Neck Rd., Sandy Point, NY 11050

Human Resources Center, IU Willets Rd., Albertson, NY 11507

Inter-National Association of Business, Industry and Rehabilitation, 12100 Portree Dr., Rockville, MD 20852

International Association of Parents of the Deaf, 814 Thayer Ave., Silver Spring, MD 20910

International Parents Organization, Alexander Graham Bell Association, 3417 Volta Pl. NW, Washington, DC 20007

John Tracy Clinic, 806 W. Adams Blvd., Los Angeles, CA 90007

Joseph P. Kennedy, Jr. Foundation, 1350 New York Ave. NW, Washington, DC 20005

Juvenile Diabetes Foundation International, 432 Park Ave. S., New York, NY 10157-0706

Kempe National Center for the Prevention and Treatment of Child Abuse and Neglect, 1205 Oneida St., Denver, CO 80220

Kids on the Block, Inc., 9385 C Gerwig Lane, Columbia, MD 21046

Louis Braille Foundation for Blind Musicians, 215 Park Ave. S., New York, NY 10033

Lupus Foundation of America, 11921A Olive Blvd., St. Louis, MO 63141

Mainstream Information Center, 1030–15th St. NW, Washington, DC 20005

March of Dimes Birth Defects Foundation, 1275 Mamaroneck Ave., White Plains, NY 10605

Mental Retardation Association of America, 211 E. Third St., Suite 212, Salt Lake City, UT 84111

Muscular Dystrophy Association, 810 Seventh Ave., New York, NY 10019

Myasthenia Gravis Foundation, 15 E. 26th St., New York, NY 10010

National Aid to the Visually Handicapped, 3201 Balboa St., San Francisco, CA 94121

National Alliance for the Mentally Ill, 2101 Wilson Blvd., Suite 302, Arlington, VA 22201

National Amputee Foundation, 1245–150th St., Whitestone, NY 11357

National Association of Activity Therapy and Rehabilitation Program Directors, c/o Glen Eden Hospital, 6902 Chicago Rd., Warren, MI 48902

National Association of Addiction Treatment Providers, 2082 Michelson Dr., Suite 101, Irvine, CA 92715

National Association of Alcoholism and Drug Abuse Counselors, 3717 Columbia Pike, Suite 300, Arlington, VA 22204

National Association of the Deaf, 814 Thayer Ave., Silver Spring, MD 20910

National Association of Developmental Disabilities Councils (NADDC), 1234 Massachusetts Ave. NW, Suite 103, Washington, DC 20005

National Association for Gifted Children, 4175 Lovell Rd., Suite 140, Circle Pines, MN 55014

National Association for Hearing and Speech Action, 10801 Rockville Pike, Rockville, MD 20852

National Association for Ileitis and Colitis, 295 Madison Ave., New York, NY 10017

National Association of Juvenile Correctional Agencies, 36 Locksley Lane, Springfield, IL 62704

National Association for Mental Health, 1800 N. Kent, Arlington, VA 22209

National Association for Music Therapy, 1001 Connecticut Ave. NW, Suite 800, Washington, DC 20036

National Association of the Physically Handicapped, 76 Elm St., London, OH 43140.

National Association to Preserve the Use of Braille (PAPUB), 3618 Dayton Ave., Louisville, KY 40207

National Association of Private Psychiatric Hospitals, 1319 F St. NW, Suite 1000, Washington, DC 20004

National Association of Private Residential Resources, 6400 Seven Corners Pl., Falls Church, VA 22044

National Association of Private Schools for Exceptional Children (NAPSEC), 1625 Eye Street NW, Suite 506, Washington, DC 20006

National Association of Rehabilitation Facilities, P.O. Box 17675, Washington, DC 20041

National Association for Retarded Citizens, See Association for Retarded Citizens of the United States

National Association for Sickle Cell Disease, 4221 Wilshire Blvd., Suite 360, Los Angeles, CA 90010

National Association of State Directors of Special Education (NASDSE), 2021 K St. NW, Suite 315, Washington, DC 20006

National Association of State Mental Health Program Directors, 1101 King St., Suite 160, Alexandria, VA 22314

National Association of State Mental Retardation Program Directors, 113 Oronoco St., Alexandria, VA 22314

National Association for Visually Handicapped, 22 W. 21st St., New York, NY 10010

National Ataxia Foundation, 6681 Country Club Dr., Minneapolis, MN 55427

National Braille Association, 654A Godwin Ave., Midland Park, NJ 07432

National Braille Press, 86 St. Stephens St., Boston, MA 02115

National Center for a Barrier Free Environment, 1015–15th St. NW, Washington, DC 20005

National Center for Children with Learning Disabilities, P.O. Box LD 2929, 99 Park Ave., New York, NY 10016

National Center on Child Abuse, P.O. Box 1319, Denver, CO 80201

National Clearing House for Professions in Special Education, 1920 Association Dr., Reston, VA 22091

National Clearinghouse for Drug Abuse Information (NCDAI), 5600 Fisher Ln., Rm. 10A-43, Rockville, MD 20857

National Clearinghouse for the Gifted and Talented, c/o Council for Exceptional Children, 1920 Association Dr., Reston, VA 22091

National Clearinghouse for Mental Health Information (NCMHI), 11A-33 Parklawn Bldg., 5600 Fisher Ln., Rockville, MD 20857

National Clearinghouse of Rehabilitation Training Materials, Oklahoma State University, 115 Old USDA Bldg., Stillwater, OK 74078

National Committee, Arts for the Handicapped, 1701 K St. NW Washington, DC 20006

National Committee for Prevention of Child Abuse, 111 E. Wacker Dr., Rm. 510, Chicago, IL 60601

National Congress of Organizations of the Physically Handicapped, 16630 Beverly Ave., Tinley Park, IL 60427

National Council on Disability, 800 Independence Ave. SW, Suite 814, Washington, DC 20591

National Council on Intellectual Disability, Action House, Edinburgh Ave., GPO Box 647, Canberra, ACT, Australia 2601

National Council of Juvenile and Family Court Judges, University of Nevada, P.O. Box 8978, Reno, NV 89507

National Council for Special Education, 1 Wood St., Stratford-Upon-Avon, Warwickshire, England CV37 6JE

National Council of State Agencies for the Blind, 206 N. Washington St., Suite 320, Alexandria, VA 22314

National Crisis Center for the Deaf, University of Virginia Medical Center, Charlottesville, VA 22908

National Crisis Prevention Institute, 3315-K N. 124th St., Brookfield, WI 53005

National Down Syndrome Congress, 1800 Dempster St., Park Ridge, IL 60068

National Down Syndrome Society, 666 Broadway, New York, NY 10012

National Easter Seal Society, 70 E. Lake St., Chicago, IL 60601

National Employment Counselors Association, 5203 Leesburg Pike, Falls Church, VA 22041

National Federation of the Blind, 1800 Johnson St., Baltimore, MD 21230

National Federation for Ileitis and Colitis, 295 Madison Ave., New York, NY 10019

National Foundation of Dentistry for the Handicapped, 1121 Broadway, Suite 5, Boulder, CO 80302

National Foundation for Gifted and Creative Children, 395 Diamond Hill Rd., Warwick, RI 02886

National Foundation, March of Dimes (see March of Dimes)

National Handicapped Housing Institute, 12 S. Sixth St., Suite 500, Minneapolis, MN 55402

National Handicapped Sports and Recreation Association, 1341 G St. NW, Washington, DC 20005

National Head Injury Foundation, 333 Turnpike Rd., Southborough, MA 01772

National Hearing Aid Society, 20361 Middlebelt Rd., Livonia, MI 48152

National Hemophilia Foundation, 110 Greene St., New York, NY 10012

National Industries for the Severely Handicapped (NISH), 4350 East-West Hwy., Bethesda, MD 20814

National Information Center for Children and Youth with Handicaps P.O. Box 1492, Washington, DC 20013

National Information Center for Deaf-Blindness, Gallaudet University, 800 Florida Ave. NE, Washington, DC 20002

National Information Center for Educational Media (NICEM), University of Southern California, University Park, Los Angeles, CA 90007

National Information Center for Special Education Materials (NICSEM), University of Southern California, University Park, Los Angeles, CA 90007

National Institute on Alcoholism and Alcohol Abuse (NIAAA), Prevention Branch, 5600 Fisher Ln., Rm. 16C-14, Rockville, MD 20857

National Institute on Disability and Rehabilitation Research (NIDRR), 330 C St. SW, Switzer Bldg., Washington, DC 20202

National Institute on Drug Abuse (NIDA), Prevention Branch, 5600 Fisher Ln., Rm. 11A-33, Rockville, MD 20857

National Institute of Dyslexia, 3200 Woodbine St., Chevy Chase, MD 20815

National Kidney Foundation, 2 Park Ave., Suite 908, New York, NY 10016

National Lekotek Center, 2100 Ridge Ave., Evanston, IL 60204

National Library Service (NLS) for the Blind and Physically Handicapped, Library of Congress, Washington, DC 20542

National Medical Foundation for Eye Care, 1100–17th St. NW, Washington, DC 20036

National Multiple Sclerosis Society, 205 E. 42nd St., New York, NY 10017

National Network of Learning Disabled Adults (NNLDA), P.O. Box Z, ET Station, Commerce, TX 75428

National Neurofibrometosis Foundation, 70 W. 40th St., New York, NY 10018

National Organization on Disabilities, 910–16th St. NW, Washington, DC 20006

National Paraplegic Foundation (see National Spinal Cord Injury Association)

National Parents Resource Institute for Drug Education (PRIDE), 100 Edgewood Ave., Suite 1002, Atlanta, GA 30303

National Rehabilitation Association, 633 S. Washington St., Alexandria, VA 22314

National Rehabilitation Information Center, 8455 Colesville Rd., Suite 935, Silver Spring, MD 20910

National Rural and Small School Consortium, Western Washington University, Miller Hall 359, Bellingham, WA 98225

National Society for Autistic Children and Adults with Autism, 1234 Massachusetts Ave. NW, Suite 1017, Washington, DC 20005

National Society for the Prevention of Blindness (NSPB), 500 Remington, Schaumburg, IL 60173

National Special Education Alliance, 20525 Mariana Ave., Cupertino, CA 95041

National Spinal Cord Injury Association, 149 California St., Newton, MA 02158

National/State Leadership Training Institute on the Gifted and Talented, 316 W. Second St., Suite PH-C, Los Angeles, CA 90012

188

National Stroke Association (NSA), 300 E. Hampden Ave., Englewood, CO 80110

National Tay-Sachs and Allied Diseases Association, 385 Elliot St., Newton, MA 02164

National Technical Institute for the Deaf, Rochester Institute of Technology, One Lomb Memorial Dr., P.O. Box 9887, Rochester, NY 14623

National Theatre of the Deaf, 305 Great Neck Rd., Waterford, CT 06385

National Tourette Syndrome Association, 41-02 Ball Blvd., Bayside, NY 11361

National Tuberous Sclerosis Association (NTSA), 4351 Garden City Dr., Landover, MD 20785

NICEM (see National Information Center for Educational Media)

NICHCY (see National Information Center for Children and Youth with Handicaps)

NICSEM (see National Information Center for Special Education Materials)

North American Riding for the Handicapped Association, P.O. Box 33150, Denver, CO 80233

OCHAMPUS (Office of Civilian Health and Medical Programs of the Uniformed Services), Aurora, CO 80045

Office of Special Education Programs, U.S. Dept. of Education, 400 Maryland Ave. SW, Washington, DC 20202-2570

Orton Dyslexia Society (ODS), 724 York Rd., Baltimore, MD 21204

Osteogenesis Imperfecta Foundation, P.O. Box 428, Van Wert, OH 45891

Parents of Down Syndrome Children, 11507 Yates St., Silver Spring, MD 20922

People-to-People Committee for the Handicapped, P.O. Box 18131, Washington, DC 20036

President's Committee on Employment of People with Disabilities, 1111-20th St. NW, Suite 636, Washington, DC 20210 (formerly President's Committee on Employment of the Handicapped)

President's Committee on Mental Retardation, Wilbur J. Cohen Federal Bldg., 3330 Independence Ave. SW, Washington, DC 20201

Recordings for the Blind, 20 Roszel Rd., Princeton, NJ 08540

Rehabilitation International USA, 1123 Broadway, New York, NY 10010

Resources for Rehabilitation, 33 Bedford St., Suite 11A, Lexington, MA 02173

Royal National Institute for the Deaf, 105 Gower St., London, England WCE 6AH

Science for the Handicapped, SSS 200 University of Wisconsin–Eau Claire, Eau Claire, WI 54701

Seeing Eye Guide, Morristown, NJ 07960

Society for Experimental Analysis of Behavior, Indiana University, Dept. of Psychology, Bloomington, IN 47405

Society for Learning Disabilities and Remedial Education, 5341 Industrial Oaks Blvd., Austin, TX 78735

Society of University Otolaryngologists, Eastern Virginia Medical School, 825 Fairfax Ave., Norfolk, VA 23507

Special Education Programs, 400 Sixth St., Donohue Bldg., Washington, DC 20016

Special Olympics, 1350 New York Ave. NW, Suite 500, Washington, DC 20005

Spina Bifida Association of America, 1700 Rockville Pike, Suite 540, Rockville, MD 20852

TASH (see Association for Persons with Severe Handicaps)

Teacher Education Division (TED), Council for Exceptional Children, 1920 Association Dr., Reston, VA 22091

Telesensory Systems Inc., 455 N. Bernardo Ave., P.O. Box 7455, Mountain View, CA 94043

Teletypewriters for the Deaf, 2301 N. Upton St., Arlington, VA 22207

Tourette Syndrome Association, 42-40 Bell Blvd., Bayside, NY 11361

Tracy Clinic (see John Tracy Clinic)

Tuberous Sclerosis Association of America, P.O. Box 44, Rockland, MA 02320

United Cerebral Palsy Association, 66 E. 34th St., New York, NY 10016

United Ostomy Association, 2001 W. Beverly Blvd., Los Angeles, CA 90057

Vinland National Center (Health Sports Center), 3675 Ihduhapi Rd., Loretto, MN 55357

Periodicals and Journals (English Speaking)

AAC: Augmentative and Alternative Communication, P.O. Box 1496, Baltimore, MD 21203

Academic Therapy, 8700 Shoal Creek Blvd., Austin, TX 78758

ACEHI Journal, Association of the Canadian Educators of the Hearing Impaired, Dept. of Educational Psychology, 6-102 Education N., University of Alberta, Edmonton, Alberta, Canada T6G 2G5

Achievement, 925 N.E. 122nd St., North Miami, FL 33161

Adapted Physical Activity Quarterly, Human Kinetics Publications, Champaign, IL 61820

Advanced Development (A Journal on Adult Giftedness), P.O. Box 3489, Littleton, CO 80122

American Annals of the Deaf, 800 Florida Ave. NE, Washington, DC 20002

American Archives of Rehabilitation Therapy, 36 Pine Valley Rd., Conway, AR 72032

American Journal of Art Therapy, P.O. Box 4918, Washington, DC 20018

American Journal of Diseases of Children, 535 N. Dearborn St., Chicago, IL 60610

American Journal of Mental Retardation, American Association on Mental Retardation, 1719 Kalorama Rd. NW, Washington, DC 20009

American Journal of Occupational Therapy, 1383 Piccard Dr., P.O. Box 1725, Rockville, MD 20850

American Journal of Orthopsychiatry, 1775 Broadway, New York, NY 10019

American Rehabilitation, Superintendent of Documents, P.O. Box 1533, Washington, DC 20402

AMP, National Amputation Foundation, 12-45 150th St., Whitestone, NY 11357

Analysis and Intervention in Developmental Disabilities (AIDD), Pergamon Press/Maxwell House, Fairview Park, Elmsford, NY 10523

Annals of Dyslexia, 724 York Rd., Baltimore, MD 21204 (formerly *Orton Bulletin*)

Applied Linguistics, Cambridge University Press, 32 E. 57th St., New York, NY 10022

Archives of Otolaryngology — Head and Neck Surgery, 535 N. Dearborn St., Chicago, IL 60610

Asha (American Speech-Language-Hearing Association), 10801 Rockville Pike, Rockville, MD 20852

Audecibel, 20361 Middlebelt, Livonia, MI 48152

Australasian Journal of Special Education, Australian Association of Special Education, Box 1998 GPO, Canberra, ACT, Australia 2601 (formerly *Australian Journal of Special Education*)

Australia and New Zealand Journal of Developmental Disabilities, Macquarie University, School of Education, North Ryde, NSW, Australia 2109

Australian Teacher of the Deaf, 25 Marshall Ave., KEW 3101, Victoria, Australia

B.C. Journal of Special Education, University of British Columbia, Dept. of Educational Psychology and Special Education, Vancouver, BC, Canada V6T 1Z5

Behavior Modification, Sage Publications, 275 S. Beverly Dr., Beverly Hills, CA 90212

Behavioral Disorders, Council for Children with Behavior Disorders (CCBD), 1920 Association Dr., Reston, VA 22091

Braille Monitor, National Federation of the Blind, 1800 Johnson St., Baltimore, MD 21230

Breakthrough, National Tay-Sachs and Allied Disease Association, 385 Elliot St., Newton, MA 02164

Bridge, The, Beecher House, P.O. Box 11, Guilford, CT 06437

British Journal of Disorders of Communication, 4345 Annandale St., Edinburgh, Scotland EH7 4AT

British Journal of Mental Subnormality, Monyhull Hospital, Birmingham, 30 B, England

British Journal of Special Education, National Council for Special Education, 1 Wood St., Stratford-Upon-Avon, Warwickshire, England CV37 6JE

Bulletin, American Association for Rehabilitation Therapy, P.O. Box 93, North Little Rock, AR 72116

Canadian Journal for Exceptional Children, Canadian CEC, Mississauga Executive Center, 2 Robert Speck Pkwy, Suite 750, Mississauga, Ontario, Canada L4Z 1H8

Canadian Journal of Rehabilitation, 13325 St. Albert Trail, Edmonton, Alberta, Canada T5L 4R3

Canadian Journal of Special Education, University of British Columbia, Educational Psychology and Special Education, 2125 Main Mall, Vancouver, British Columbia, Canada V6T 125

Career Development for Exceptional Individuals (CDEI), Division on Career Development (DCD), 1920 Association Dr., Reston, VA 22091

CASE, Newsletter, Council of Administrators for Exceptional Children, 615–16th St. NW, Albuquerque, NM 87104

Clearing House Memo, National Clearing House of Rehabilitation Materials, Oklahoma State University, Stillwater, OK 74074

Counseling and Human Development, Love Publishing Co., 1777 S. Bellaire St., Denver, CO 80222

192

Counterpoint, 10860 Hampton Rd., Fairfax Station, VA 22039

Creative Child and Adult Quarterly, National Association of Creative Children and Adults, 8080 Spring Valley Dr., Cincinnati, OH 45236

Deaf American, National Association of the Deaf, 814 Thayer Ave., Silver Spring, MD 20910

Deficience Mentale/Mental Retardation, York University, 4700 Keele St., North York, Ontario, Canada M3J 1P3

Diagnostique, Council on Eductional Diagnostic Services (CEDS), 1920 Association Dr., Reston, VA 22091

Disability, Handicap and Society, Bristol Polytechnic, Dept. of Education, Redland Hill, Bristol, England BS6 6UZ

DPH Journal, Division on the Physically Handicapped, 1920 Association Dr., Reston, VA 22091

Dyslexia Review, Dyslexia Institute, 133 Gresham Rd., Starnes, England TW18 2AJ

Education and Training of the Mentally Retarded, Division on Mental Retardation, CEC, 1920 Association Dr., Reston, VA 22091

Education and Treatment of Children, Pressley Ridge School, 530 Marshall Ave., Pittsburgh, PA 15214

Education of the Handicapped, P.O. Box 1453, Alexandria, VA 22313

Education for the Handicapped Law Report, 421 King St., P.O. Box 1905, Alexandria, VA 22313

Education of the Hearing Impaired Bulletin, 1537–35th St. NW, Washington, DC 20007

Education of the Visually Handicapped (see *Re:View*)

Emotionally Handicapped Children Bulletin, Southern Connecticut State College, New Haven, CT 06515

Exceptional Child (see *International Journal of Disabilities: Development and Education*)

Exceptional Child Education Resources, Council for Exceptional Children, 1920 Association Dr., Reston, VA 22091

Exceptional Children, Council for Exceptional Children, 1920 Association Dr., Reston, VA 22091

Exceptional Education Quarterly (see *Remedial and Special Education*)

Exceptional Parent, Boston University, School of Education, 605 Commonwealth Ave., Boston, MA 02215

Exceptionality: A research journal. Division for Research, 1920 Association Dr., Reston, VA 22091 or Springer-Verlag, 175 Fifth Avenue, New York, NY 10010

Focus, National Technical Institute for the Deaf, One Lomb Memorial Dr., P.O. Box 9887, Rochester, NY 14623

Focus on Autistic Behavior, 8700 Shoal Creek Blvd., Austin, TX 78758

Focus on Exceptional Children, Love Publishing Co., 1777 S. Bellaire St., Denver, CO 80222

Fountainhead, American Association for Education of the Visually Handicapped, 919 Walnut St., Philadelphia, PA 19107

Future Reflections, National Federation of the Blind, 1800 Johnson St., Baltimore, MD 21230

G/C/T, P.O. Box 6448, Mobile, AL 36660

Gifted Child Quarterly, National Association for Gifted Children, 4175 Lovell Rd., Suite 140, Circle Pines, MN 55014

Gifted Children, P.O. Box 115, Sewell, NJ 08080

Gifted Education International, AB Academic Publishers, P.O. Box 97, Berkhamsted, Herts, England HP4 2PX

Hearing Rehabilitation Quarterly, New York League for the Hard of Hearing, 71 W. 23rd St., New York, NY 10010

In the Mainstream, 1200–15th St. NW, Washington, DC 20005

Infants and Young Children, Aspen Publications, 7201 McKinney Cir., Frederick, MD 21701

Innotek Newsletter, National Lekotek Center, 2100 Ridge Ave., Evanston, IL 60201

Interaction, National Council on Intellectual Disability, Action House, Edinburgh Ave., GPO Box 647, Canberra, ACT, Australia 2601

International Journal of Disabilities: Development and Education, University of Queensland, St. Lucia, Queensland, Australia 4067

International Journal of Special Education, University of British Columbia, Educational Psychology and Special Education, 2125 Main Mall, Vancouver, British Columbia, Canada V6T 125

International Journal of Special Education and Disability, Eleanor Schonell Special Education Research Center, University of Queensland, St. Lucia, Queensland, Australia 4067

JCD, Journal of Counseling and Development, American Association for Counseling and Development, 5999 Stevenson Ave., Alexandria, VA 22304

John Tracy Clinic Bulletin, John Tracy Clinic, 806 W. Adams Blvd., Los Angeles, CA 90007

Journal of Abnormal Child Psychology, Plenum Publishing Corp., 233 Spring St., New York, NY 10013

Journal of the Acoustical Society of America, 335 E. 45th St., New York, NY 10017

Journal of the American Optometric Association, 243 N. Lindburgh Blvd., St. Louis, MO 63141

Journal of Applied Behavior Analysis, P.O. Box 1577, Lawrence, KS 66045

Journal of Applied Rehabilitation Counseling, 633 S. Washington St., Alexandria, VA 22314

194

Journal of the Association for Persons with Severe Handicaps, 7010 Roosevelt Way NE, Seattle, WA 98115

Journal of Association for Study of Perception, P.O. Box 744, DeKalb, IL 60115

Journal of Auditory Research, Box N, Groton, CT 06340

Journal of Autism and Developmental Disabilities, 233 Spring St., New York, NY 10013

Journal of Behavior Therapy and Experimental Psychiatry, Pergamon Press/Maxwell House, Fairview Park, Elmsford, NY 10521

Journal of the British Association of Teachers of the Deaf, Royal School for the Deaf, 50 Topsham Rd., Exeter, England EX2 4NF

Journal of Child Language, Cambridge University Press, 32 E. 57th St., New York, NY 10022

Journal of Childhood Communication Disorders, Division for Children with Communication Disorders (DCCD), Council for Exceptional Children, 1920 Association Dr., Reston, VA 22091

Journal of Communication Disorders, American Elsevier Publishing Co., 52 Vanderbilt Ave., New York, NY 10017

Journal of Counseling and Development (see *JCD*)

Journal of Creative Behavior, 1300 Elmwood Ave., Buffalo, NY 14222

Journal of the Division for Early Childhood (see *Journal of Early Intervention*)

Journal of Early Intervention, Division for Early Childhood Special Education, 1920 Association Dr., Reston, VA 22091

Journal for the Education of the Gifted, Association for the Gifted, University of North Carolina Press, P.O. Box 2288, Chapel Hill, NC 27514

Journal of Experimental Analysis of Behavior, Dept. of Psychology, Indiana University, Bloomington, IN 47405

Journal of Experimental Education, Box 1605, Madison, WI 53701

Journal of Head Trauma Rehabilitation, Aspen Publishing Co., 7201 McKinney Cir., Frederick, MD 21701

Journal of Human Behavior and Learning, Western Kentucky University, College of Education, Bowling Green, KY 42101

Journal of Learning Disabilities, 8700 Shoal Creek Blvd., Austin, TX 78758

Journal of Mental Deficiency Research, 86 Newman St., London, England W1P 4AR

Journal of Motor Behavior, Heldref Publications, 4000 Albemarle St. NW, Washington, DC 20016

Journal of Music Therapy, 505–11th St. SE, Washington, DC 20003

Journal of Physical Therapy, American Physical Therapy Association, 1156–15th St. NW, Washington, DC 20005

Journal of Practical Approaches to Developmental Handicaps, 2500 University Dr., University of Calgary, Calgary, Alberta, Canada T2N 1N4

Journal of Prosthetics and Orthotics, American Academy of Orthotists and Prosthetists, 717 Pendleton St., Alexandria, VA 22314

Journal of Reading, Writing and Learning Disabilities International, Hemisphere Publishing Co., 1010 Vermont Ave. NW, Washington, DC 20005

Journal of Rehabilitation of the Deaf, 814 Thayer Ave., Silver Spring, MD 20910

Journal of Special Education, 8700 Shoal Creek Blvd., Austin, TX 78758

Journal of Special Education Technology, Peabody College, Vanderbilt University, Technology and Media Division, Nashville, TN 37203

Journal for Special Educators (see *Remedial and Special Education*)

Journal of Speech and Hearing Disorders (JSHD), 10801 Rockville Pike, Rockville, MD 20852

Journal of Speech and Hearing Research (JSHR), 10801 Rockville Pike, Rockville, MD 20852

Journal of Visual Impairment and Blindness, 15 W. 16th St., New York, NY 10011

Journal for Vocational Special Needs Education, Penn State University, 110 Rackley Bldg., University Park, PA 16802

Juvenile Diabetes Foundation International, 23 E. 26th St., New York, NY 10010

Juvenile Justice, National Council of Juvenile and Family Court Judges, University of Nevada-Reno, Box 8978, Reno, NV 89507

Language, Speech and Hearing Services in Schools, 10801 Rockville Pike, Rockville, MD 20852

Law and Behavior, Research Press, 2612 N. Mattis, Champaign, IL 61820

Learning Disabilities Focus, 1920 Association Dr., Reston, VA 22091

Learning Disability Quarterly, Council for Learning Disabilities (CLD), P.O. Box 40303, Overland Park, KS 66204

Learning Disabilities Research, 1920 Association Dr., Reston, VA 22091

Mental and Physical Disability Law Reporter, Commission on the Mentally Disabled, 1800 M St. NW, Washington, DC 20036

Mental Retardation, American Association on Mental Retardation, 1719 Kalorama Rd. NW, Washington, DC 20009

Mental Retardation Bulletin (see *Mental Retardation and Learning Disability Bulletin*)

Mental Retardation and Learning Disability Bulletin, University of Alberta, Developmental Disabilities Centre, 6-123d Education North, Edmonton, Alberta, Canada T6G 2G5

NARIC Quarterly, National Rehabilitation Information Center, 8455 Colesville Rd., Silver Spring, MD 20910

National Rural Project Newsletter (see *Rural Special Education Quarterly*)

New Outlook for the Blind (see *Journal of Visual Impairment and Blindness*)

NTID Focus, One Lomb Memorial Dr., Rochester, NY 14623

Occupational Therapy Newspaper, 1382 Piccard Dr., Rockville, MD 20850

Orthotics and Prosthetics, 717 Pendleton St., Alexandria, VA 22314

Orton Society Bulletin (see *Annals of Dyslexia*)

Otolaryngology, 1101 Vermont Ave. NW, Suite 302, Washington, DC 20005

Paraplegic News, 5201 N. 19th Ave., Suite 111, Phoenix, AZ 85015

Perceptions: Newsletter for Parents of Children with Learning Disabilities, P.O. Box 142, Milburn, NJ 07041

Personnel and Guidance Journal (see *JCD*)

Perspectives for Teachers of the Hearing Impaired, Gallaudet College, 800 Florida Ave. NE, Washington, DC 20002

Physical Medicine and Rehabilitation, Hanley & Belfus, Inc., 210 S. 13th St., Philadelphia, PA 19107

Physical Therapy, 1111 N. Fairfax St., Alexandria, VA 22314

Pointer, 5341 Industrial Oaks Blvd., Austin, TX 78735

RASE (see *Remedial and Special Education*)

Rehabilitation Gazette, 4502 Maryland Ave., St. Louis, MO 63108

Remedial and Special Education, 8700 Shoal Creek Blvd., Austin, TX 78758

Research in Developmental Disabilities, Fairview Park, Elmsford, NY 10523

Re:View, Heldref Pub., 4000 Albermarle St. NW, Washington, DC 20016 (formerly *Education of the Visually Handicapped*)

Roeper Review: A Journal on Gifted Child Education, P.O. Box 329, Bloomfield Hills, MI 48013

Rural Special Education Quarterly, American Council on Rural Special Education, Miller Hall 359, Western Washington State University, Bellingham, WA 98225

Schizophrenia Bulletin, National Institute of Mental Health, Supt. of Documents, Washington, DC 20402

Seeing Eye Guide, Box 375, Morristown, NJ 07960

Sexuality and Disability, Human Sciences Press, 72 Fifth Ave., New York, NY 10011

Sign Language Studies, Livstock Press, 9306 Mintwood St., Silver Spring, MD 20901

Special Children, American Association of Special Educators, 29 Bolton Rd., Flanders, NJ 07836

Special Educator, CRC Publishing Co., 1035 Camphill Rd., Ft. Washington, PA 19034

Special Services in the Schools, CASE, 615–16th St. NW, Albuquerque, NM 87104

Sports 'n Spokes, 5201 N. 19th Ave., Phoenix, AZ 85015

TAG Up-Date, Association for the Gifted, CEC, 1920 Association Dr., Reston, VA 22091

Talent Tabloid, Talent Identification Program, Duke University, Box 40077, W. Duke Bldg., Durham, NC 27708

Talents and Gifts, Association for the Gifted, Council for Exceptional Children, 1920 Association Dr., Reston, VA 22091

Teacher of the Deaf, 50 Topsham Rd., Exeter, England EX2 4NF

Teacher Education and Special Education, (TESE), Teacher Education Division, CEC, 1920 Association Dr., Reston, VA 22091

Teaching Exceptional Children, Council for Exceptional Children, 1920 Association Dr., Reston, VA 22091

Their World, Foundation for Children with Learning Disabilities, 99 Park Ave., New York, NY 10016

Topics in Early Childhood Special Education, 8700 Shoal Creek Blvd., Austin, TX 78758

Topics in Language Disorders, 8700 Shoal Creek Blvd., Austin, TX 78758

Topics in Learning and Learning Disabilities, 8700 Shoal Creek Blvd., Austin, TX 78758

Understanding Our Gifted, Snowpeak Publishing, P.O. Box 3489, Littleton, CO 80122

Visually Handicapped–International Archives for Research, Rheinstrasse 5, 7512 Rheinstetten 3, West Germany

Volta Review, 3417 Volta Pl. NW, Washington, DC 20007

Worklife, President's Committee on Employment of People with Disabilities, 1111–20th St. NW, Suite 636, Washington, DC 20036

Sources of Legal Assistance

American Bar Association, 1800 M St. NW, Washington, DC 20036

American Civil Liberties Union, 132 W. 43rd St., New York, NY 10036

American Coalition of Citizens with Disabilities, 1346 Connecticut Ave. NW, Washington, DC 20036

Architectural and Transportation Barriers Compliance Board, 330 C St. SW, Washington, DC 20202

Association for Retarded Citizens, 2709 Ave. E East, Arlington, TX 76011

Center on Human Policy, 724 Comstock Ave., Syracuse, NY 13244

Center for Law and Education, Harvard University, Larson Hall, 14 Appian Way, Cambridge, MA 02138

Children's Defense Fund, 1520 New Hampshire Ave. NW, Washington, DC 20036

Closer Look (see Special Education Information Center)

Commission on the Mentally Disabled, 1800 M St. NW, Washington, DC 20036

Council for Exceptional Children, Governmental Relations Unit, 1920 Association Dr., Reston, VA 22091

Disability Rights Center, 1346 Connecticut Ave. NW, Suite 1124, Washington, DC 20036

Disability Rights Education and Defense Fund Inc. (DREDF), 2032 San Pablo Ave., Berkeley, CA 94702

Education Law Center Inc., 155 Washington St., Newark, NJ 07103

Mainstream, Inc., 1200–15th St. NW, Suite 403, Washington, DC 20005

Mental Disability Legal Resource Center, 1800 M St. NW, Washington, DC 20036

Mental Health Law Project, 2021 L St. NW, Suite 800, Washington, DC 20036

National Association of Coordinators of State Programs for the Mentally Retarded, 2001 Jefferson Davis Hwy., Suite 802, Arlington, VA 22202

National Association on Legal Problems of Education, 3601 Southwest 29th, Suite 223, Topeka, KS 66614

National Center for Law and the Deaf, Seventh and Florida Ave. NE, Washington, DC 20002

National Network of Learning Disabled Adults, P.O. Box 2, ET Station, Commerce, TX 75428

Office of Special Education Programs, Litigation Services, Washington, DC 20202

Public Interest Law Center, 1315 Walnut St., Philadelphia, PA 19107

Special Education Information Center, Box 1492, Washington, DC 20013

U.S. Dept. of Justice, Office of Special Litigation, Washington, DC 20530

Washington Legal Foundation, Court-watch, 1705 N Street NW, Washington, DC 20006